The Domestic Abroad

The Domestic Abroad

Diasporas in International Relations

Latha Varadarajan

UNIVERSITY PRESS

2010

OXFORD
UNIVERSITY PRESS

Oxford University Press, Inc., publishes works that further
Oxford University's objective of excellence
in research, scholarship, and education.

Oxford   New York
Auckland   Cape Town   Dar es Salaam   Hong Kong   Karachi
Kuala Lumpur   Madrid   Melbourne   Mexico City   Nairobi
New Delhi   Shanghai   Taipei   Toronto

With offices in
Argentina   Austria   Brazil   Chile   Czech Republic   France   Greece
Guatemala   Hungary   Italy   Japan   Poland   Portugal   Singapore
South Korea   Switzerland   Thailand   Turkey   Ukraine   Vietnam

Copyright © 2010 by Oxford University Press, Inc.

Published by Oxford University Press, Inc.
198 Madison Avenue, New York, New York 10016

www.oup.com

Library of Congress Cataloging-in-Publication Data
Varadarajan, Latha.
The domestic abroad: diasporas in international relations / Latha Varadarajan.
   p.   cm.
Includes bibliographical references and index.
ISBN 978-0-19-973391-0
1. Transnationalism—Social aspects—Developing countries.   2. Dual nationality—
Developing countries.   3. Developing countries—Emigration and immigration.
4. Developing countries—Foreign relations.   I. Title.
JV9480.V37 2010
305.9'06912—dc22   2009046214

9   8   7   6   5   4   3   2   1
Printed in the United States of America
on acid-free paper

Acknowledgments

This book has been in the works for a good decade. During this period, I have met, studied with, and learned from a large number of people, all of whom contributed in myriad ways to its making. While they may not all agree with the paths taken and the arguments made, I am truly grateful for their support and encouragement through the process.

I first met Bud Duvall as a student at the University of Minnesota. As a scholar, teacher, mentor, and critical interlocutor, Bud has few equals. His intellectual curiosity, generosity of spirit, and constant willingness to engage with ideas have always been and continue to be a source of inspiration. Mary Dietz taught me to find the "theorist in myself," and challenged me to go beyond taking the easy route. Though I flinch when I think about how I must have sounded in my early verbal and written conversations with her, I take consolation in the fact that over the years, I might have at least started learning the lessons she hoped to teach me. In her fair mindedness and consistently generous support through the years, Kathryn Sikkink has been a true role model. For that, I thank her. The University of Minnesota was, for me, a wonderful and intellectually stimulating place. It was made so by the presence of a group of people, some of whom remain close friends. For conversations about this project that challenged me, frustrated me, forced me to learn, and stayed with me over the years, I would like to thank Shampa Biswas, Bruce Braun, Arjun Chowdhury, Jigna Desai, Deepali Dewan, Lisa Disch, Boğaç Erozan, Giunia Gatta, Jim Glassman, Guang Lei, Ayten Gündoğdu, Leila Harris, Premesh Lalu, Humaira Mahi, Monika Mehta, Kristin

Mercer, Himadeep Muppidi, Richa Nagar, Govind Nayak, Meghana Nayak, Kartik Raj, Amit Ron, Bahar Rumelili, Ajay Skaria, Mary Thomas, Ann Towns, Uygar Özesmi, and Joel Wainwright.

The research and writing of this book would not have been possible but for the institutional support I received through the years at the University of Minnesota and San Diego State University. At Minnesota, the MacArthur Program and Ames Library were in many ways a home away from home, in large measure due to the generosity of David Faust, Allen Isaacman, Don Johnson, Jim Johnson, Claudia Shores Skue, and Karen Brown Thompson. Fellowships from the political science department and the Humanities Institute helped at critical junctures. At San Diego State, course releases made possible through the RSCA and Critical Thinking grants provided the much needed time to make final revisions. In addition, the Junior Fellowship grant from the American Institute of Indian Studies enabled me to spend a year in India, conducting interviews and archival research. I thank all the people in Delhi, Madras, and Hyderabad who generously shared their knowledge with me, making the whole process far easier than I expected. I also wish to acknowledge the helpful assistance of the staff at FICCI, the Ministry of External Affairs Library, and the Nehru Memorial Library.

My colleagues in the political science department at San Diego State have been remarkably supportive and helpful during the process of turning out a publishable manuscript. I would like to thank in particular Farid Abdel Nour, Jonathan Graubart, Kristen Hill Maher, and Ronnee Schreiber for their invaluable input as well as for proving that it is possible to be friends with your colleagues. As the manuscript made its way toward its final form, it benefited tremendously from the generous critique of Laurie Brand and two other anonymous reviewers. At Oxford University Press, Angela Chnapko and her wonderful team, particularly Liz Smith, have worked tirelessly to make the production process as smooth as possible. I am grateful to have had the opportunity to work with them.

The writing of a book can be an arduous journey, especially for those who are forced to hear about every twist and turn in the path, time and time again. For always listening and never giving in to what must have been a very real urge to either fall asleep or slam the phone down, I wish to express my thanks and promises for eventual repayment to Anna Maria Addari, Madhavi Bokil, Prachi Deshpande, Sujatha Korappath, Bakirathi Mani, Gowri Ramesh, Aniruddh Ramesh, Ramesh Santhanam, Anjana Tandon, Anand Varadarajan, Gianni Verrucci, and Kim Zabora. To my parents, who watched the process with increasing bemusement and unwavering belief in its eventual completion, I can never fully express my gratitude. The fact that I could count on their support in this, as in every other journey, is something that I am profoundly grateful for.

To find a person who embodies a peculiar combination of intellectual rigor, scathing wit, mule-headedness, and generosity is, perhaps, a matter of luck. I am fortunate to have found that person in Emanuele, who has been a true partner every step of the way. Appearances notwithstanding, his passionate and heartfelt belief in a better future has inspired me and challenged me in ways I had not even imagined and made this book a far better one than it would have been. I dedicate this book to him and to Amma and Appa who never stopped asking when it would be completed.

Contents

The Domestic Abroad

1

Introducing the Domestic Abroad

In July 2000, Vicente Fox Quesada, the leader of the opposition PAN (Party for National Action) won a historic presidential election in Mexico. While numerous commentators hailed his victory as a triumph of democracy in Mexico and the beginning of a new political chapter, only a few took notice of Fox's preelection claims that he intended to "govern on behalf of 118 million Mexicans."[1] Declarations by political candidates regarding their intent to govern "for the people" are, of course, hardly noteworthy. What made Fox's declaration striking was that the population of Mexico during his election was around 100 million. The other 18 million people on whose behalf Fox intended to govern were actually those of Mexican origin living outside the territories of Mexico, primarily in the United States.[2]

Fox's declaration that "our beloved migrants, our heroic immigrants" were an intrinsic part of the Mexican nation marked a distinct change from the rhetoric of the past, wherein Mexican migrants had been denigrated as *pochos* (overly anglicized or denationalized Mexicans) who had forsaken their language and culture for the "illusory blandishment of life in the US."[3] Soon after the inauguration, in a symbolically potent first act as the president of Mexico, Fox honored 200 Mexican immigrants and U.S.-born Mexican Americans, hailing them as shining examples of what Mexicans are capable of achieving when provided with the right opportunity.[4] Far from being denationalized, Mexicans living abroad were presented as embodying a spirit of entrepreneurship and success that needed to be emulated by the rest of Mexico.

In December 2000, echoing themes that had been popularized by two earlier administrations, Fox declared that the Mexican nation and *mexicanidad* ("Mexicanness") extended "beyond the territories contained by [Mexico's] borders."[5] Consequently, to be truly representative, the Mexican state would have to look beyond its borders and strengthen its policies toward its citizens abroad. As part of this program, his administration would push for institutional changes within Mexico[6] and ensure that Mexican consulates around the world (and especially in the United States) would become not just the representatives of the Mexican state, but the "best allies for immigrants' rights."[7] These reiterations of the notion of a transnational Mexican nation fit very well with Fox's preelection claims that the people he would govern, the people he would serve—his *domestic* constituency—lived not just in territories within the boundaries of the Mexican nation-state, but *abroad* as well. To put it differently, the Mexican state in the new millennium was willing to acknowledge its "domestic abroad" and to empower this constituency through what it framed as "transnationally informed policy-making."[8]

In January 2003, two years after Fox's victory in Mexico, the Indian capital of New Delhi was the site of an event touted as the "largest gathering of the global Indian family."[9] Organized by the Indian Ministry of External Affairs and the Federation of Indian Chambers of Commerce and Industry (FICCI) at a cost of more than Rs 22 crores (approximately $49 million), the event was held in one of the largest fairgrounds within the city. All the roads leading to the fairgrounds were festooned with banners displaying the image of the Indian tricolor emblazoned with the words, "Welcome Back, Welcome Home." The event was the celebration of the first ever Pravasi Bharatiya Divas—literally, the "Day of the Indians Abroad," inaugurated by Prime Minister Atal Bihari Vajpayee on January 9, 2003. Over the next three days, panelists from India and sixty other countries spoke at length, making their case for the need to strengthen the "already present" historical and cultural ties between India (the "motherland") and Indians abroad ("her children"). Strikingly, most of the Indians abroad who were being welcomed back home were not Indian citizens. Consisting of first-, second-, and, to a lesser extent, even third- and fourth-generation emigrants, the 20 million strong Indian diaspora was being hailed as India's "national reserves" living abroad, India's *domestic abroad.*

Acknowledging that this move marked a definite shift from the Indian state's past policies toward the diaspora, Deputy Prime Minister L. K. Advani declared that the overdue recognition of the Pravasi Bharatiyas (Indians abroad) had been made possible by the "happy confluence of two historical developments—the coming of age of India and the coming of age of Indians working and living abroad."[10] Just as India had emerged in the new millennium as a "strong, self-confident and rapidly prospering nation, which was set to become a global power," Indians abroad "had collectively acquired the image of a community of high achievers, whose achievements in diverse fields...are becoming the talk of the world." The Pravasi Bharatiya Divas celebrations, as Advani put it, were an acknowledgment by his government of a new phenomenon: Vishwa Bharati (Global India). The subjects being honored by his government, he claimed, did not just represent India to the rest of the world—they *were* embodiments of India in the world. As such, the Indian state was willing to turn its back on a policy that had been in place since Indian independence, introduce dual citizenship legislation in parliament, and set up a separate ministry of nonresident Indians (NRI)/persons of Indian origin (PIO) affairs to facilitate greater interaction between the Indian nation-state and Indians abroad.

What makes this phenomenon noteworthy is that it is not peculiar to just India or Mexico. As even a cursory look at global politics in the beginning of the twenty-first century reveals, a large number of countries, including the People's Republic of China, Russia, Turkey, South Korea, the Philippines, Tunisia, Morocco, Jordan, Haiti, the Dominican Republic, Hungary, Portugal, Ecuador, Poland, Italy, and Greece, are actively involved in constituting sections of their diasporas as not just part of a larger deterritorialized nation, but a new constituency that is connected to, and has claims on, the institutional structures of the state. While this trend has definitely not passed unnoticed by scholars and political commentators, it has generally been seen as part of a larger process—the increasing visibility and political power of diasporas in global politics. An article in the *Economist*, for instance, began by posing a series of questions:

> Why does Macedonia have no embassy in Australia? Why might a mountain in northern Greece soon be disfigured by an image of Alexander the Great 73 metres (nearly 240 feet) high? Who paid for the bloody war between Ethiopia and Eritrea? How did Croatia succeed in winning early international recognition as an independent country?[11]

The answer to each of these questions, the article suggests, lies in the emergence of an influential diaspora—"a community of people living outside their country of origin." Macedonia has no embassy in Australia because of the exertions of the strong Greek diasporic community. Much to the consternation of the Greek population, the monumental Alexander might be carved on a mountain face because of the demands of the Greek Foundation of Chicago, which has had close ties with successive Greek governments and is ready to bear the $45 million estimated cost. Eritrea was able to wage its border wars with Ethiopia because of the 2 percent income tax that it levied on its 333,000 émigrés. And the Croatian diaspora not only raised more than $30 million for the nationalist cause prior to independence in 1991 but also effectively lobbied for early recognition of the new Croatian state by the European Union—efforts that the new state rewarded by granting Croats abroad twelve seats in the 120-member parliament, as against the seven seats set aside for Croatia's ethnic minorities. Each story, the article concludes, points to a simple and unassailable fact of contemporary global politics: "for the first time in history," diasporas are coming "together cheaply and effectively" and are "exerting their influence on the politics of the countries they have physically, but not emotionally, abandoned."[12]

The role of diasporas in global politics, particularly as political and social actors who transcend territorial boundaries, is a subject that has drawn intense scholarly scrutiny in recent times.[13] Focusing on specific diasporas (Haitian, Mexican, Russian, Sri Lankan, Serbian, or Croatian), specific locations (such as the United States, Germany, or Great Britain), and specific kinds of political processes (such as lobbying, participating in elections, or supporting particular factions in civil wars), scholars have made persuasive arguments about the increasing relevance of diasporic activities in making sense of international relations. While there have been debates about the novelty (or lack thereof) of such transnational activities, much of this literature has generally tended to converge on understanding and explaining diasporas as disrupting the narrative of "politics as usual."[14] More specifically, diasporas are presented as complex, hybrid political subjects, whose very existence and actual behavior transcend and thus challenge the authority of the territorial nation-state system. As some scholars have pointed out, however, this focus has had the unfortunate effect of obscuring the role of the state, particularly the "home" state (also designated as "sending countries" in the immigration literature) in making diasporas viable actors in global politics.[15] Consequently, despite the burgeoning interest in the diasporas themselves, the dramatically transforming relationship between nation-states and their diasporas—a transformation that is seemingly driven by state actors—has drawn limited scholarly scrutiny. It is this largely overlooked phenomenon that forms the central concern of this book.

I introduce the concept of the "domestic abroad" to capture this new, widespread form of transnationalism, produced through state policies and initiatives aimed at institutionalizing the relationship between nation-states and their diasporas. To assert the novelty of the domestic abroad phenomenon is not, however, to deny the existence of transnational links in the past. The relationship between diasporas and their homelands, of course, has always been characterized by the existence of informal links. In a few instances, these links even had an institutional dimension, as in the case of the European metropoles and the settler colonies during the heyday of European imperialism, or the Jewish diaspora and the modern Israeli state.[16] However, what we see now is a far more widespread and qualitatively different phenomenon. The production of the domestic abroad rests on the constitution of diasporas as subjects of an expanded, territorially diffused nation. To that extent, it marks a fundamental shift in the way nations are configured. This shift, however, is part and parcel of the political-economic transformation of the state—in a word, what is typically called "neoliberal restructuring."[17] This book makes the argument that these two processes—political and economic, affecting nation and state—far from being distinct, are in fact intimately related. The *differentia specifica* of the domestic abroad can thus be found not only in the ongoing, systematic proliferation of institutional links connecting the "global nation"—the visible surface of the phenomenon—but also in the transformation of the state itself by means of an equally pervasive neoliberal restructuring. In other words, it is not only its policies and actions that are new but also the nature and character of the state itself.

From the standpoint of international relations, the phenomenon of the domestic abroad—manifested through practices that serve to dissociate the nation from a fixed territory and to link the state as a structure of authority and rule to that territorially diffused nation—appears as a paradox. While transnationalism is generally associated with the "retreat of the state" and the "erosion of its sovereignty," this particular form of it appears to be propelled by the state itself and to reaffirm its authority. These state practices, however, far from reinscribing the traditional, functional correspondence between nation and fixed territory, threaten to disrupt it. The task we are faced with is then to make sense of a process that in some respects reinforces the modern nation-state system and the territorial nation-state as its constitutive unit, while in others strikes at its very foundations. To do that, however, we need to begin by clarifying one of the basic conceptual categories used in this book.

Diasporas: A Definitional Caveat

The question of what constitutes a diaspora or what it means to talk about diasporas in the contemporary international system is one that has been the subject of intense debates in the past two decades.[18] Scholars working in the field of diaspora studies have generally tended to acknowledge the historical importance of the Jewish experience of exile, dispersal, and promise of eventual return in giving meaning to this concept. However, in recent years a number of them have argued that, given increased migrations and the formation of new emigrant communities with links to both the host and home societies, it is essential to look beyond the framework established by the Jewish experience and extend this concept in a meaningful way.[19]

In keeping with this line of argument, Khachig Tölöyan, the editor of *Diaspora*, used the introduction of the first issue to claim that the subject matter of the journal was one that encompassed the experience of immigrants, refugees, exiles, guest workers, expatriates, and overseas ethnic communities. To put it slightly differently, the conceptual category of "diaspora," as far as he was concerned, served as shorthand for the all-encompassing "vocabulary of transnationalism."[20] That this editorial policy was not universally accepted is quite obvious in William Safran's contribution to the same issue.[21] In an oft-cited essay, Safran argued that it is important to use the concept of diaspora sparingly, "lest the term lose all meaning."[22] He proposed, instead, a set of specific criteria that could be used to determine what kind of populations should be seen as constituting a diaspora. These criteria include dispersal from a specific original "center" to two or more "peripheral" regions, retention of collective memories of the original homeland, partial alienation and insulation from the host society, a lingering desire to return to the homeland, a commitment to the maintenance or restoration of the "safety and prosperity" of that homeland, and the derivation of a communal consciousness and solidarity from that relationship.[23]

Safran's attempt to delineate the boundaries of diaspora studies, with its more than implicit assumption of the Jewish experience as an ideal type, has resonated with some scholars, who argue that catastrophic origins and forced migration are the main features of a diaspora.[24] Others have taken issue with his treatment of non-Jewish diasporas, to claim that the somewhat oversimplified set of criteria he proposes needs to be amended to account for the histories of migrations undertaken in the service of various empires, which in turn engendered much more ambivalent and contradictory relationships with the homeland than Safran is willing to account for.[25] Moving specifically beyond the catastrophic connotations surrounding many of the other attempts at definition, Robin Cohen, for instance, focuses on the etymology of the word *diaspora* to contend that it is not only possible but also perhaps desirable to conceptualize communities characterized in this manner as encompassing a wider range of originary moments.[26] The importance of this move is that it enables diaspora studies scholars to go beyond an increasingly sterile debate about who truly deserves the nomenclature of diaspora and engage with the dynamics of different kinds of identity communities, especially those that have emerged as important global actors in the past few decades.

Given the proliferation of the term "diaspora," a new set of related terms, and the academic debates surrounding the meaning of those terms, to provide a comprehensive survey is beyond the scope of this book.[27] What this brief discussion should make clear is that much like some of the other central political concepts of our times, "diaspora" defies a single, widely accepted definition. Questions such as what diasporas are, how they emerge, or for that matter, whether the term should be used outside the historical context in which it came into being, all remain contested in the general literature. Despite the lack of agreement regarding the precise meaning of the concept, "diaspora" is used in this book as a way to refer to emigrant communities—populations that originate from a nation-state that is different from the one where they reside. My usage here is similar to that of Tölöyan's to the extent that we both treat "diaspora" as a fairly inclusive category, without being wedded to the nature of originary moments. By doing so, I do not mean to suggest that this subject category refers to a cohesive or, for that matter, static collectivity naturally connected to their real or imagined homelands. Rather, following Brubaker, I would argue that this term itself needs to be understood as part of political projects that produce the links between emigrant communities and their homelands.[28] In contemporary global politics, "diaspora" has become, in both popular and state discourse, the dominant descriptive term to portray emigrant communities that are being constituted as the domestic abroad. It is possible to read in the increased popularity of the term an implicit acknowledgment of the fact that the conceptual category of diaspora succeeds in capturing the essence of a link (however tenuous, ambiguous, or contradictory) between populations perceived (by themselves and others) as living outside the territories of their states of origin and that "homeland." To that extent, when used by those "speaking in the name of the putative homeland state," diaspora becomes a way of "formulating the identities and loyalties of a population" as being intrinsically linked to the homeland.[29] Understanding this link is key to making sense of the production of the domestic abroad. What is fundamental to this production is the reiteration of not only a lasting connection between emigrant communities and their states of origin (constituted as homelands) but also the claim that these connections need to be and deserve to be acknowledged and empowered through the state institutions of the homeland.

The sense of belonging to a common homeland, crucial to the formation of diasporas, does not automatically emerge from the fact that members of emigrant communities trace their journey to a common place of origin. Rather, it is socially as well as politically constructed through the interactions among members of a community, through their being marked as different in their host societies, and through the institutionalization of their relationship with the homeland. While acknowledging the importance of other kinds of practices in the formation of diasporas (especially those centered around social, economic, political, and cultural exchanges among the spatially dispersed populations comprising the diaspora), the focus of this book is on the hailing of the diaspora by the nation-states constituted as the homeland.[30] As such, the use of the singular *diaspora* throughout this book does not stem from the assumption that there exists a cogent political community with a single fixed political identity that can automatically be characterized as *a* diaspora. Rather, it is a working acknowledgment of the state project of attempting to construct a cogent national body.

Explaining the Domestic Abroad

Given that the domestic abroad seems to have emerged on the world stage at a particular moment in history (the current phase of globalization, understood variously as the heyday of global capitalism or the technological revolution), under certain conditions (when diasporas seem to have acquired a critical mass in terms of numbers, earning potential, and the like), it is possible to proffer several intuitive explanations of the phenomenon. Laurie Brand, for instance, draws on the existing immigration and transnationalism literature to provide a typology of a few distinct, plausible explanations.[31] The main type of these is what Brand calls macrohistorical explanations, in which emigration and state responses to it are understood as effects of larger trends, more specifically, a particular stage of unequal capitalist relations between the North and the South that, combined with technological advances and ease of travel, has led to a rapid expansion in the size of emigrant communities. Focusing on a different dimension, the "international politics" explanation highlights the relationship between host and home or sending states, focusing on issues like discrimination against the emigrants in the host state and belief in the lobbying possibilities of diaspora groups that might lead sending states to try cultivating their emigrants. A third set of explanations that can be grouped under the security/stability model primarily focus on the home state's interest in maintaining order and controlling dissent in the communities abroad. However, as Brand rightly points out, none of these explanations provides a comprehensive analysis of what is a paradoxical and complex phenomenon. For instance, it is probably true that the development of state interest in diasporas might be contingent on the presence of a critical mass of emigrants, thus providing some credibility to the main variants of a macrohistorical explanation. At the same time, there is no evidence to suggest that state policies develop in a linear fashion, beginning with a gradual increase in mobility and numbers of emigrants, and followed by a gradual institutionalizing of the sending state's relationship with this group. Similarly, while home state elites might encourage lobbying efforts by emigrant communities in their states of residence, this does not appear to be the sole or, for that matter, decisive motivating factor in the development of the relationship between the two. There are, however, two other types of explanations of the domestic abroad phenomenon that Brand examines, which deserve closer scrutiny.

The Question of the Economy

The economic rationale explanation highlights the increasing financial clout of various diasporas and the importance of remittances for the economies of the homelands as being the main factor driving the greater institutionalization of the state-diaspora relationship.[32] The *Economist* article previously discussed, for instance, refers in passing to the Ghana Homecoming Summit, organized in Accra in July 2001, as an attempt by the government to "get the [Ghanaian diaspora] to cough up" more in remittances and perhaps even investments.[33]

This is an argument that seems to have prima facie validity. In countries such as the Dominican Republic, the remittances sent home by members of the diaspora (amounting to nearly $2 billion annually) are the largest single source of foreign exchange for the home country and nearly 10 percent of the country's gross domestic product (GDP).[34] Even when remittances form a very small percentage of the home country's GDP, as in India and Mexico (approximately 2 percent), the monetary value of the remittances is extremely high ($9.9 billion and $9.1 billion, respectively), leading to conjectures about their importance for not only familial incomes but also the home country's balance of payments.[35] While these examples might make the economic rationale argument seem persuasive, we need to be a bit cautious about drawing a direct link between the financial needs of the state and the resources of the diaspora. It needs to be noted, for instance, that remittances were flowing into the economies of home states like India and Mexico decades prior to any organized endeavors by those states to hail their diasporas as part of the national community. For that matter, the remittances from the Ghanaian diaspora amounted to nearly $400 million annually well before the state decided to welcome them home.[36] Two significant examples—China and Russia—further caution against attempting to establish a direct correlation between the economic clout of emigrant communities and their being courted by the home states.

The Chinese economy has in the recent past received a major fillip from more than $55 billion in annual investments made by overseas Chinese communities. Recognizing the importance of this group, the Overseas Chinese Affairs Office has been quite active in facilitating their interaction with the Chinese state, specifically by maintaining contacts with all overseas Chinese organizations, ensuring a smoother path for overseas investment, proposing and implementing policies at the provincial level to provide educational facilities within China for the children of overseas Chinese, enabling members of the diaspora to reconnect with their ancestral villages, and facilitating their return to the mainland. Notwithstanding these measures, however, the Chinese state has been among the most reluctant to engage its emigrants in any aspect of domestic policy making. Despite having one of the largest modern emigrant populations, dual citizenship is not on the agenda in the People's Republic of China.[37]

Russia, on the other hand, seems to have made the cause of the Russians in the "Near Abroad" a centerpiece of both its domestic and foreign policy agendas. Emerging almost overnight in the aftermath of the collapse of the Soviet Union, the 25-million-strong Russian population in nearby countries is clearly perceived as a crucial subject group by the Russian nation-state, despite the fact that "their political and intellectual influence" on the "historic homeland has been minimal thus far."[38] More important, this dispersed group of Russians, treated as "national minorities" in the newly independent former Soviet states, has not been a source of noticeable remittances or investments in Russia. In fact, as Igor Zevelev argues, given the post–cold war scenario (especially Western support for the post-Soviet states), embracing the issue of the "Russian diaspora" carries substantial potential economic and political costs for the Russian state. Despite an implicit acknowledgment of these costs, there seems to be a broad consensus within the political spectrum that the Russian state has some sort of a moral obligation to protect its diaspora in the Near Abroad.[39]

In highlighting the examples of China and Russia, the point here is to not completely dismiss the importance of remittances per se or, for that matter, assert that states are essentially uninterested in ensuring a continuing flow of remittances from their emigrant communities.[40] Given the current crisis of the global economy, it would be hard to argue that nation-states (especially those that have a harder time attracting foreign direct investments) are not concerned about ensuring a flow of foreign exchange from all sources, especially emigrants. However, while it is important to not overlook the need for remittances in explaining the changing relationship of states and their diasporas, it is also important to not overstate its significance. The ever-present danger of this latter tendency, I contend, emerges out of an implicit assumption that characterizes much of the literature on international migration. This is the assumption that equates economic rationales with the need for remittances.[41] The argument animating this book is quite compatible with and sympathetic to the general idea of focusing on developments in global capitalism to explain the phenomenon of the domestic abroad. But to equate this idea with the need for states to secure potential sources of investment or hard currency, or even the larger question of the push and pull of labor leaves us with a rather desiccated notion of what capitalism is and how it functions. I argue that there *is* indeed a powerful economic explanatory element to the rise of the domestic abroad, an element that is intrinsically tied to the development of capitalism, but it is of a far broader character than has generally been understood. What this means concretely will be elucidated in the next chapter. For now, I wish to note that the manner in which capitalism affects the production of the domestic abroad is not expressed simply by a series of economic indices. Economic phenomena are always, so to speak, embodied in a definite and yet dynamic alignment of social forces that are, moreover, continuously involved in a process of class struggle. In that sense, what counts as the "economic" cannot and should not be seen as distinct from what counts as the "social." An attempt to explain the economic logic of state actions thus requires us to go beyond issues like remittances and balance of payments (important though they are) and analyze the actual social struggles between the bourgeoisie and the other classes that characterize the development of capitalism, at both national and global levels. In the particular case of the domestic abroad, such an analysis can take as its starting point the broader context within which state actors seem to be embracing their diasporas as part of a larger national community.

Discussing the hailing of diasporas as a domestic abroad (even if not quite in those terms), almost all writers on the subject have noted, even if only in passing, the ongoing neoliberal restructuring of the home states. In all cases, the state, in the context of neoliberal economic restructuring (at varying points of time and to varying degrees), has declared its commitment to the cause of a "greater nation" that is not territorially bound by showing its willingness to represent the interests of its "nationals" abroad. It has made changes (or is in the process of making changes) to existing citizenship laws to enable dual nationality and set up specific organizational structures to facilitate the involvement of its new constituency in domestic politics. In the case of Mexico, for instance, Vicente Fox's much-touted "transnationally informed policy making" was made possible by a series of steps undertaken by at least two earlier administrations following the neoliberal turn of the 1980s. This turn, as scholars have noted, was a "break from the historic popular pact by which the PRI had ruled for more than 50 years."[42] In the aftermath of the introduction of sweeping neoliberal economic reforms and a contentious presidential election, the administration of Carlos Salinas (1988–1994) made the first significant break from the past and intensified what came to be known as the policy of *acercamiento*—rapprochement, greater closeness—with Mexican emigrant communities. As part of this new policy, Salinas established the Directorate General of Mexican Communities Abroad (DGMCA) and the Program for Mexican Communities Abroad (PMCA)—offices within the Secretariat of Foreign Affairs that were charged with the task of not only building bridges to Mexican communities abroad but also "improv[ing] the image of Mexican Americans inside Mexico [and]...burying the image of the *pocho*."[43]

These measures were continued during the tenure of Ernesto Zedillo (1995–2000) who made his strategy toward Mexican immigrants a central feature of the new Mexican National Development Program. Launching the *Nacion Mexicana* (Mexican Nation) initiative, Zedillo declared that the Mexican state was willing to acknowledge its responsibilities toward the greater Mexican nation by making changes in citizenship rules and providing more legal rights to emigrants. In 1998, the Congress unanimously passed legislation permitting dual nationality. Mexicans abroad could now not only vote in Mexican elections if they chose to return to the Mexico during that period, but also become citizens of the country they were living in "without sacrificing their Mexican nationality."[44] These measures paved the way for Fox to claim that his constituency extended beyond the boundaries associated with the Mexican state and also that the Mexican emigrant was a symbol of the potential that characterized *Mexicanidad*.

Similar processes of neoliberal restructuring can be observed elsewhere. The Chinese state inaugurated a new phase of its relationship with overseas Chinese around the same period that Deng Xiaoping (1976–1986) introduced the restructuring of the Chinese economy with the promise that market reforms just meant "Socialism with Chinese characteristics."[45] In the same vein, without taking into account the introduction of perestroika and the collapse of the Soviet Union, it would be impossible to analyze the nature of the relationship between Russia and the Russians in the Near Abroad. As I will demonstrate, the introduction of neoliberal reforms in India marked an important turning point in the discursive articulation of the Indian nation-state's links to the Indian diaspora.[46] At one level, the examples of Mexico, China, Russia, and India highlight the fact that domestic political considerations play an important role in shaping the exact nature of state policies toward emigrants—an issue that is discussed in greater detail in the next section. My point here, however, is that notwithstanding the different policy-level outcomes, the various nation-states that are involved in the production of a domestic abroad appear to have something in common at a more fundamental level: their economies are being restructured in ways that make them more aligned with the demands of international capital.[47] The economic rationale animating the domestic abroad phenomenon thus lies in this fundamental commonality. In other words, to understand the economic logic underpinning the domestic abroad, it is essential to focus on the nature and implications of the neoliberal restructuring of the state.

The Question of Domestic Politics

Another plausible explanation of the domestic abroad is suggested by the salient differences in the way it is being produced by different political systems. In surveying state policies that fall within the rubric of the production of the domestic abroad, one finds a broad spectrum of initiatives aimed at extending the boundaries of the nation beyond the territorial limits of the state. Within this panoply of policy initiatives, the granting of citizenship rights—be it in the form of dual citizenship or a more limited version of dual nationality—is a particularly important manifestation of the attempts by states to convey their recognition of their duties toward their emigrants. However, not all states that are involved in the production of the domestic abroad necessarily follow this path. Demarcating the boundaries of the nation, as Benedict Anderson reminds us, is a complex, historically rooted, politically contested process.[48] Citizenship, the main juridical marker of belonging to a political community, while critical in demarcating the authority of the nation-state, is essentially a subset of this process, which is to say, while citizens of a nation-state could by definition be members of the nation as an imagined community, not all members of the nation need to be citizens. In the case of the domestic abroad, the lack of a necessary correspondence between citizenship and national belonging becomes especially obvious in instances

where diasporas consist of second-, third-, and sometimes even fourth-genera-
tion emigrants who are citizens of various host states. This inconvenient fact,
however, does not preclude states involved in the production of the domestic
abroad from hailing such emigrants as part of the larger, territorially dispersed
nation. The growing trend of celebrations in home states that putatively honor
the achievements of the diaspora provides an important insight into how this
process works.

The Pravasi Bharatiya Divas celebrations that are annually hosted by the
Indian government, for instance, are framed as a commemoration of the many
successes of the Indian diaspora of more than 20 million. This annual festival is
open to those who can pay the registration fee—not only Indian citizens but also
"persons of Indian origin" who may or may not be Indian citizens. The latter
category is especially pertinent, given that since the first "Day of the Indians
Abroad" celebration in January 2003, the Indian state has introduced a limited
form of dual nationality, which is available only to a specific cross-section of the
20 million in the diaspora.[49] Notwithstanding the lack of a comprehensive offer
of citizenship, the Indian state falls back on other categories such as "persons of
Indian origin" (a semijuridical category that falls short of even the limited rights
promised by the Dual Nationality Law) to continue framing its diaspora policies
as being applicable to the "global" Indian nation—the Indian diaspora at large.
The Mexican and Chinese states, however, follow paths that are quite distinct
from each other and from that of the Indian state: while Mexico has already provided dual citizenship and voting rights to its diaspora, the Chinese state, despite
its obvious readiness to accept overseas Chinese investments, has been unwilling
to provide political rights to the Chinese diaspora.

These examples might suggest that the key to understanding the domestic
abroad phenomenon lies in the nature of the operative political systems in the
concerned nation-states. It can be argued that the Chinese state does not need to
convince an opposition party (or several opposition parties) to support any
change in national policies. Nor does the Chinese Communist Party need a new
electoral base. Consequently, the issue of providing political rights to overseas
Chinese communities remains marginal in the production of the Chinese domestic abroad. In contrast, the Mexican diaspora is perceived as a potentially important constituency by various political parties that participate in democratic
processes. As a result, not only has it become more common to see Mexican politicians campaign among diaspora communities in the United States but the
Mexican state also appears to be more involved in politically empowering its
diaspora, specifically by allowing members to vote in the presidential elections
and stand for political office if they return to Mexico.

An argument emphasizing the connection between the hailing of diasporas and
democracy is persuasive to the extent that focusing on the nature of site-specific

political systems is indeed an important aspect of analyzing the production of the domestic abroad. It cannot be denied that if the political system in the home state is a closer approximation of a functioning democracy, there is a greater possibility for diasporas (or at least some sections thereof) to be constituted as potentially powerful subjects.[50] However, merely focusing on the question of democracy can be more limiting than analytically useful in making sense of the domestic abroad. To begin with, this approach would demand a clear answer to the notoriously difficult question of what constitutes a democracy. Would Russia under Boris Yeltsin, Vladimir Putin, or Dmitry Medvedev or Haiti under Jean-Bertrand Aristide and then Gerard Latortue qualify as a democracy when we try to analyze the relationship of the Russian and Haitian nation-states to their diasporas? In addition, seeking the explanatory key to the production of the domestic abroad simply in the logic of a specific type of political system may have an even more deleterious effect. The correct and important recognition of similarities at the level of political systems may conceal more important and, in fact, decisive differences in terms of the trajectories of historical and political struggles peculiar to each country. As the later chapters in this book make obvious, making sense of the Indian domestic abroad requires not just taking account of the "fact" of Indian democracy, but a serious engagement with its particular, complex historical and political landscape: the legacy of British colonialism, the nationalist struggles waged against it, the presence of a relatively strong national capitalist class on the eve of independence, and the emergence of a remarkably uneven diaspora, consisting of both unskilled laborers and technically proficient multimillionaires from the Silicon Valley.

At a more general level, in making sense of the domestic abroad across different contexts, it is important to keep in mind that the diaspora policies of sending states are influenced by factors such as sheer number of emigrants, the immigration policies of the receiving states, and the relationship between the two state entities. As such, factors like the size of the diaspora and its location are certainly pertinent to any explanation. However, we need to resist the temptation to elevate any of these factors to the status of an explanatory master key. A quick look at the Mexican and Russian state policies tells us why. The granting of political rights to the nearly 23 million people in the Mexican diaspora is undeniably related to the fact that nearly 97 percent of them are located in the United States, which is geographically contiguous to the territories associated with the Mexican state.[51] However, the Russian state, despite having a diaspora comparable in size and location to that of Mexico (25 million, primarily located in the territories of fifteen former Soviet republics), has attempted to forge a relationship with this diaspora by following a path distinctly different from that of the Mexican state.

While the possible explanations for the production of the domestic abroad that I have outlined in this chapter call attention to several important issues, they stop short of providing a comprehensive analytical framework that would enable us to understand this complex phenomenon. As Robert Smith has argued, to understand the relationship between "sending states and their diasporas," we need a more complete framework that allows us to analyze not only the domestic politics of those states or the ability of the migrant groups to exercise political action, but also the "evolving relations of [the sending states] to the global system."[52] More explicitly, we need a framework that can put into focus the nature of this global system while not losing sight of the historically specific political struggles that help shape the "evolving relations" of nation-states to this system. In crafting such a framework, this book begins with the understanding that the developments of capitalism on a global scale constitute the systemic framework for making sense of a complex, contradictory phenomenon like the domestic abroad. These developments, however, need to be understood in a way that underscores the mutually constitutive relationship between the global and the national, between the nation and the state, and most importantly, between the economic and political realms. This book therefore proposes a heuristic framework that highlights two distinct, though interrelated, sets of processes that bring together these elements. In other words, it argues that the domestic abroad should be understood as the product of two simultaneous ongoing processes: the neoliberal restructuring of the state and the diasporic reimagining of the nation within a particular political, historical context.

Organization of the Book

This book is, at one level, a study of transnationalism engendered by contemporary forms of globalization. Its subject matter—the production of the domestic abroad—is tied to the movement of people, capital, and knowledge across boundaries and the centrality of such movements for the making and remaking of those national boundaries. As such, this book continues a tradition of multidisciplinary (and occasionally interdisciplinary) scholarship that, to paraphrase Aihwa Ong, takes seriously the claim that transnationalism "stimulates a new, more flexible, and complex relationship" between nations, states, and capital.[53] However, this book is also an attempt to take seriously the meanings and implications of the domestic abroad for the discipline of international relations (IR). The next chapter, therefore, begins with an analysis of the dominant disciplinary understandings of transnationalism and identity, specifically within the liberal constructivist tradition. I show that in this tradition, transnationalism is understood as definitively detached from the state and its policies, while identity appears as removed from the material structures of global capitalism. The reductive framing of these two important concepts consequently precludes us from registering and explaining the broad and contradictory interactions that constitute the domestic abroad. To make sense of this phenomenon, what we need is a theoretical framework that helps us understand the peculiar transnational nationalism embraced by state actors at the same time that they embark on programs of neoliberal economic restructuring. To put it differently, what we need is a framework that helps us understand and analyze the ways in which the boundaries of the imagined community of the nation and the nature of the state are intrinsically connected to the development of capitalist social relations, at both global and national levels. The rest of the chapter develops such a framework through a systematic analysis that delineates first the political and then the economic dimensions of the domestic abroad, revealing the manner in which they are related to each other through an elucidation of the concept of hegemony. This framework then sets the stage for understanding the domestic abroad as the product of the processes through which the bourgeoisie, in the context of the development of capitalism on a global scale, continues its attempts to establish a seemingly organic connection between its interests and the interests of the nation at large and to legitimize its hegemonic status.

The remaining chapters of the book present an illustration of this theoretical argument by providing an in-depth analysis of a specific case: the ongoing production of the Indian domestic abroad. Although a comparative analysis of various exemplars of the domestic abroad would undoubtedly be an interesting project, the decision to focus on a single case rests to a large extent on the logic of the theoretical argument that animates this book. To truly make sense of the ways in which the articulation and rearticulation of bourgeois hegemony shapes the nature of the state and the limits of the national community, we need to pay close attention to the unfolding of specific political struggles that underlie the creation and continued existence of a nation-state. These struggles, moreover, need to be contextualized in the historical development of capitalist social relations, at both global and national levels. We need to, in other words, analyze the conditions under which specific nationalist movements emerge, the nature of the social forces that shape them, the type of state projects that are enabled and legitimized at particular historical junctures, and the ways in which these reflect and affect the development of capitalism on a global scale. It is for these reasons that this book provides a close engagement with a specific case rather than a macrolevel comparison. However, I should make it clear that the choice of the Indian nation-state and its relationship with the Indian diaspora as the subject of analysis is not driven by claims about the uniqueness of the Indian domestic abroad. While the book argues that it would be impossible to understand the production of the Indian domestic abroad without paying attention to the specific conditions that led to the creation of the postcolonial Indian nation-state, its larger theoretical argument can be applied to analyzing and making sense of the domestic abroad phenomenon in general.

In a manner similar to other state actors involved in these processes, the Indian state has in recent years engaged in systematic attempts to institutionalize its relationship with its 20 million strong diaspora, marking a distinct shift from its earlier policies toward this group. Chapters 3, 4, and 5 explain the nature and logic of this shift by analyzing how the contraction and expansion of the conceptual boundaries of the Indian nation are intrinsically connected to the changing nature of the Indian state, understood specifically in terms of the articulation and rearticulation of bourgeois hegemony. While not following a strict chronological order, each of the three chapters focuses on specific moments when the existing relationship between nation and state was not only brought into sharp relief but also fundamentally challenged thereby paving the way for the production of the Indian domestic abroad.

At the moment of independence in 1947, the postcolonial Indian state very deliberately adopted a policy of distancing itself from the emigrant communities identified variously as Indians abroad or overseas Indians. What made this move puzzling was that prior to independence, these very groups had been identified by the Indian nationalist movement as an essential part of the nation in the struggle against British colonial rule. Chapter 3 sets up the puzzle of the shift from the transnational nationalism that prevailed during colonialism to the more territorially based nationalism that replaced it following independence. In the tradition of postcolonial scholarship, the chapter begins to address this puzzle by situating the contestations regarding the meaning and extent of the modern Indian nation and state in the context of the historical experience of colonialism. The Nehruvian project of producing modern India as a "sovereign republic" was in part based on upholding the right of all newly independent states to safeguard and develop their national economic resources. This move was cemented through a series of state practices that effectively denied institutional links between the Indian state and overseas Indians. For example, when various African regimes, in the process of nationalizing their economies, expropriated the assets of the Indian diaspora, they were supported in their efforts by the Indian state. When faced with appeals from members of the diaspora, the Indian state responded with an exhortation for them to "associate themselves as closely as possible with the interest of the country they have adopted" and not serve as exploitative agents. In other words, even though a sizable diaspora did exist at the time of Indian independence, the relationship between nation and state (negotiated on the terrain of capitalist social relations) that prevailed at that time precluded its institutional inclusion and political empowerment.

Chapter 4 goes beyond the first approximation at resolving the puzzle of why the Indian state turned away from the Indian diaspora immediately after independence, providing a more focused analysis of the nature of the postcolonial Indian state. The chapter begins with an examination of the controversy

surrounding the takeover bid of two Indian companies by Swraj Paul, an industrialist of Indian origin based in the United Kingdom. It does so in order to put
into focus the making of bourgeois hegemony, particularly in the period leading
up to Indian independence, and its implications for the shaping of postcolonial
India. I argue that the socioeconomic and political agenda adopted by the dominant faction of the Indian nationalist movement, which later took over the reins
of the state from the British—its commitment to state sovereignty, state-
sponsored industrialization, the protection of domestic economy, and so forth—
all of which logically led the independent Indian state to distance itself from the
concerns of the Indian diaspora, revealed the success of the bourgeois hegemonic
project. To maintain its hegemonic position, the Indian bourgeoisie had to constantly strive to make the connection between its particular interests and the
general interests of the nation at large appear seamless and natural. While this
seemed plausible in the early decades after independence, the rapidly changing
conditions of the global capitalist economy—made evident in a number of ways,
including the changing profile of the Indian diaspora and the economic crises
faced by the Indian state—made the task increasingly harder. By the 1980s, the
hegemony of the Indian bourgeoisie appeared increasingly fractured, and it is in
this context that the Swraj Paul incident—which snowballed into a referendum
not just on the legitimacy of the Indian capitalist class but also on the relationship between the Indian state and the diaspora—became especially significant.
The chapter concludes with an analysis of this incident and its implications for
redefining the role of the Indian state and the boundaries of the Indian nation.

Chapter 5 examines the economic liberalization initiated in 1991 to argue
that while the Indian state had instituted earlier structural adjustment programs,
this moment was a significant crisis for postcolonial India. As the analysis of the
intense controversy surrounding the announcement of the structural adjustment program reveals, the main bone of contention among the various political
actors emerged from the general perception that the International Monetary
Fund (IMF) was imposing the reforms. The three main features of the reforms
package—disinvestment from the public sector, a greater openness to foreign
capital, and the initiation of a more institutionalized relationship with nonresident Indians—came under scrutiny despite the fact that similar measures had
been considered and to some extent, even implemented prior to 1991. By this
time, however, given the developments of capitalism on a global scale, refusing to
accept neoliberal restructuring was not really an option. The problem faced by
the bourgeoisie and its political representatives was now of a different order: the
economic reforms proposed in 1991 were seen as being imposed by external
forces, a fact that was symptomatic of the loss of the sovereignty and the legitimacy of the Indian state. To maintain credibility, the ruling elites made virtue
out of necessity, carrying out this economic agenda while making it appear as

not just voluntary but as a choice that actually reflected its strength. It is in this context that we can begin to make sense of the hailing of the Indian diaspora as a natural, indeed *essential*, part of the Indian nation. If the process of economic liberalization was not to undermine the fundamental premise of the bourgeois hegemony that had characterized postindependence India, a subject was needed who could plausibly embody the potential for India to succeed in the global economy, and this was where the newly valorized subject, the "global Indian," came in. In other words, for the Indian state to underscore its continuing legitimacy, for the Indian bourgeoisie to maintain its claim of representing the true interests of the nation at large, what was needed was the production of the Indian domestic abroad.

The final chapter returns to the question of the Indian domestic abroad to trace its continuing unfolding and implications, especially in the context of the ongoing crisis of the global economy. It briefly engages with the question of how the analysis of the relationship between the Indian state and the groups constituted as the Indian diaspora can serve as a model for making sense of state-diaspora politics at a global level. It concludes with a succinct discussion of the broader implications of the domestic abroad for international relations—both as a practice and as a discipline.

2

Reimagined Nations and Restructured States
Explaining the Domestic Abroad

In spirit, I consider myself to be the prime minister of 15 million Hungarians.
—*Prime Minister József Antall, 1990*

Speaking at the seventieth anniversary of the Treaty of Trianon soon after his election, József Antall, the first post-Communist leader of Hungary, declared that he, and by extension the Hungarian state, represented the interests of all Hungarian citizens—not just the 10 million who held Hungarian citizenship, but also of those who were of "Hungarian origin."[1] This latter category mainly meant descendants of the Austro-Hungarian imperial population, on whom the borders had literally moved after the end of the World War I and the signing of the Treaty of Trianon. Constituting this group as national citizens who could have claims on state institutions—in other words, producing the Hungarian domestic abroad—marked a crucial moment of consciously extending the boundaries of the nation beyond the established territorial limits of the Hungarian state. Moreover, it also symbolized an attempt to articulate what the nature of the new Hungarian state would be: a state that was no longer a satellite of the Soviet Union but would instead characterized by a "sovereign and independent foreign policy," a democratic political order, and a market-based economy.[2]

The domestic abroad, as this example reminds us, not only unfolds across acknowledged territorial boundaries of numerous nation-states but is also aimed at the remaking of those boundaries. Whether it is "Hungarians beyond the boundaries," "Indians abroad," "Chinese living overseas," or "Russians in the near abroad," state authorities' constitution of various diasporas as part of an extended global nation is quite clearly a rearticulation of nationhood, a redefining of who can and should belong to the imagined community of the nation. Beyond this, the process also involves a redefinition of the role of the state—the manner in which it presents the nature of its authority, its position in the arena of global politics, and its responsibilities toward members of the national community. These rearticulations, moreover, are contingent on the mobility (both formal and informal) of people, ideas, capital, and institutional capacities. To sum up, the argument made here about the novel, yet widespread phenomenon of the domestic abroad is threefold: first, the domestic abroad is a manifestation of a transnationalism that reflects changes in the very nature of the nation-state; second, it is a form of transnationalism that is intrinsically connected to nationalism; and third, it is a transnationalism driven by the state in the context of developments in capitalist social relations, both at the global and national levels. To make theoretical sense of this phenomenon, we therefore need a framework that not only engages with the conceptual category of transnationalism but also addresses the nature of nationalism, the state and capitalism, and the ways in which they relate to each other. This chapter provides such an engagement.

The structure of the chapter, as well as the crafting of the theoretical framework, reflects the threefold argument about the domestic abroad laid out in the preceding paragraph. The chapter begins with a critical scrutiny of the dominant constructivist tradition that has framed the study of transnationalism and nation-state identities in international relations (IR).[3] As previously mentioned, theoretical debates in the discipline have largely avoided the subject of diasporas. In that sense, liberal constructivist scholarship is no exception. However, given its attention to the conceptual categories of transnationalism and identity, this tradition has cast a long shadow on more recent attempts by IR scholars to take on the question of diasporas in global politics. The first part of this chapter systematically reveals the manner in which the theoretical constraints imposed by liberal constructivism preclude us from understanding the complex and contradictory ways in which the domestic abroad serves as a manifestation of both transnationalism and the rearticulation of national identities. The second section of the chapter builds on this insight by highlighting the question of nationalism to help frame what I characterize as the political dimension of the domestic abroad. This section engages with two distinct trends in a broad spectrum of scholarship that has emphasized the intrinsic relationship between diasporic transnationalism and nationalism—one that views diasporas as essentially embodying a challenge to nationalism and nation-state projects, and another that takes seriously the nationalist logic underlying much of diasporic transnationalism. Through this engagement, I show how a focus on nationalism that avoids the question of the state ends up falling short of providing a convincing analysis of the peculiar transnationalism manifested by the domestic abroad. The final section of the chapter aims to fill this lacuna by turning to the question of the state. The section begins with a concise analysis of the emergence of modern diasporas, highlighting in particular the role of the state in engendering diasporic flows and empowering certain sections of various diasporas. From this starting point, I argue that to make sense of the complicity of the state in engendering the transnational phenomenon of the domestic abroad, we need to understand it as a dynamic and historically evolving structure that is inextricably linked to the development of capitalism on a global scale. Developing this historical materialist conception of the state further, the section concludes by highlighting the ways in which the Gramscian concept of hegemony enables us to understand the nature of the capitalist state while at the same time providing the theoretical space to make sense of the relationship between the state and the nation, as well as the transnational dimensions of the nation-state.

I. Transnationalism, Identity, and the Challenge of the Domestic Abroad

Identifying Transnationalism

While scholars, policy makers, and political analysts continue to disagree on the nature and consequences of transnational movements, it is impossible to deny that these movements of people, capital, and ideas are an intrinsic and highly visible part of contemporary global politics. In fact, the domestic abroad is itself, in many ways, a manifestation of these movements. While the phenomenon has not been the focus of disciplinary scholarship, one cannot really say the same of the larger trend of transnationalism. A growing body of scholarship on the subject, firmly situated in the liberal constructivist tradition, has tended to dominate discussions of the subject within the discipline.[4]

Going beyond the geopolitical imaginary of the nation-state system, liberal constructivist scholars have argued that the international system is characterized by the creation of new political spaces that transcend and essentially challenge nation-state boundaries. These spaces are created by transnational networks (described variously as "principled issue-networks," "norms networks," or "advocacy networks") that include state actors, nongovernmental organizations, regional intergovernmental organizations, and private foundations. These networks are "driven primarily by shared values or principled ideas" and attempt to create new links between "actors in civil societies, states and international organizations."[5] The fundamental premise of these networks is a shared belief that sovereignty does not entail full and exclusive state jurisdiction within a defined territory. Issue areas, identified by transnational activists such as human rights,[6] the environment,[7] women's rights,[8] labor rights,[9] and the rights of the indigenous nations, are regarded as legitimate areas of concern. In these matters, state behavior is seen as open to scrutiny and challenges by other states and nonstate actors.

The logic of transnationalism unfolds within these dominant disciplinary narratives in a straightforward manner. Driven by agents who seem to exist outside systemic structures, transnationalism emerges as a process that challenges, and is in fact ranged in opposition to, the nation-state. To the extent that state actors figure in these narratives, they are usually the targets of the network's criticism and pressure to reform. At best, they play the role of facilitating the mission of the main actors—that is, the nonstate networks that make up transnational civil society.[10] Furthermore, notwithstanding the definition of transnational civil society as "an imagined community," the invocation of the term associated with Benedict Anderson's seminal work on nationalism is quite ironic in the context of this scholarship.[11] What unites the actors in the networks and gives meaning to their mission—the constitutive element of transnationalism, as it were—are norms about the nature of civilized community that are not based on narrow conceptions of nationalism or restricted to any individual state.[12] Understood as the antithesis of territorial and imaginative provincialism, transnationalism is thus presented as twice divorced from the constitutive unit of the international system—separated not only from the state and its policies but also from nations and nationalisms.

From this standpoint, the biggest obstacle in using this framework of transnationalism to make sense of the domestic abroad should be immediately apparent. At the most obvious level, the transnationalism manifested by the production of the domestic abroad is driven by state actors and premised on a notion of belonging that is essentially national in scope and aspirations. Even if one were to overlook this fact and treat nation-states and nationalism as elements that could be added unproblematically to this framework, several other issues would arise. The picture of the international system that emerges from liberal constructivist scholarship is one in which the dominance of the nation-states and the territorial logic of the nation-state system is steadily being eroded by the actions of transnational actors.[13] In large part due to the consistent reiteration of their role as the harbingers of change, these actors and the transnationalism they embody appear to stand outside existing systemic structures. As a result of this emphasis, most scholars ignore the ways in which transnational movements might be embedded within those very systemic structures, serve the purpose of reinscribing specific kinds of authority, or for that matter, contribute to the reconstitution of the state itself.[14] It should be obvious that this framework has had serious implications for not only the kind of transnational phenomena that have been studied in IR but also the manner in which they have been studied. To account for these blinders, it is crucial to keep in mind that the literature on transnationalism in IR fits within a broader field of the study of norms and identity in global politics and that it is the latter that shapes the ontological commitments of the former.

Generally speaking, identity within the rapidly expanding constructivist scholarship refers to the images of "self" that actors construct and project, in and through their interactions with "others." Notwithstanding the caveats about the dangers of anthropomorphizing, this approach translates into understanding the international system in terms of the construction and projection of a collective identity at the levels of both nation (nationalism) and state (enactment of state sovereignty). This, of course, brings up the question of how one might understand the processes through which such constructions take place. In the schema put forth by Alexander Wendt, perhaps the most influential scholar in this tradition,[15] the task of analyzing identity formation is made simpler by taking apart the concept even more.[16] Identity, Wendt argues, should be conceptualized as having two basic forms: that which is intrinsic to an actor ("corporate") and that which can only be constructed intersubjectively in a social structure ("social"). Making himself ever clearer, Wendt asserts that all states have four "national interests" that exist outside social context: to preserve and further physical security, autonomy, economic well-being, and collective self-esteem. These are what constitute a state's "corporate" identity and are thus above and beyond the requirement of scholarly scrutiny. The problems with this distinction, even from the standpoint of a consistent constructivism, should be immediately apparent.

Even if we accept that "autonomy" and "economic well-being" are basic interests of state actors, what they mean across different contexts—spatial and temporal—is far from self-evident. For instance, when Hungary declared that it was accepting its responsibilities toward "Hungarians beyond the border" by amending the national constitution and setting up a separate government department to oversee "internal" and "external" minority affairs, these state practices were certainly an expression of the autonomy of the Hungarian state. That understanding of autonomy, however, was quite different from the notion that guided the Hungarian state's action when it was a member of the Eastern bloc. Similarly, while the expressed commitment to the "economic well-being" of the nation might be something common to Hungarian governments through the near century of the existence of the Hungarian state, what this meant, how it could be achieved, and who belonged to the nation that needed to be safeguarded are all questions that have distinctly different answers across time. In this context, to assert that autonomy or economic well-being is some sort of suprasocial attribute all states possess does not enable us to understand the processes through which these different rationales become meaningful for the social actors concerned and the ways in which identities of both the nation and state are expansively rearticulated in the context of the production of the domestic abroad.[17]

To make sense of the essential dynamism of nation-state identities across time, we need to begin with the acknowledgment that every aspect of the construction of identity is irreducibly social. But having done that, the question becomes one of determining how these intersubjective, social aspects should be analyzed. When faced with this question, liberal constructivist scholarship has

generally tended to fall back on reiterating the main difference between constructivist and the rationalist approaches (such as neorealism and neoliberal
institutionalism) that dominate the discipline. Constructivist scholarship, in
other words, has tended to present itself as embodying a critique of the materialist ontology and empiricist methodology that have dominated the field.[18] A good
illustration of this response can be found in a prominent effort to articulate a
comprehensive constructivist position on national security.[19] In the introductory
essay of *The Culture of National Security*, Peter Katzenstein argues that in terms
of analysis, rationalist theoretical frameworks have meant an understanding of
reality as something that was "out there," as something that could be easily
accessed by the analyst through a "three-step process":

> First, there is the specification of a set of constraints. Then comes the stip-
> ulation of a set of actors who are assumed to have certain kinds of interests.
> Finally, the behavior of the actors is observed, and that behavior is related
> to the constraining conditions in which these actors with their assumed
> interests, find themselves.[20]

This, as Katzenstein points out, is a framework that "highlights the instrumental
rationality of actors" and is common to neorealism and neoliberal institutionalism.[21] In contrast to this "economic mode of theorizing," he argues that the task
of the constructivist tradition should be one of presenting a framework that
privileges "social factors":

> The effort to test sociological, culture-based explanations *against economic,*
> *interest-based explanations* centers on identifying and describing problems
> overlooked by existing scholarship and specifying the social factors, here
> state-identity and the cultural-institutional context, that shape concep-
> tions of actor interest and behavior.[22]

However, in their attempt to distance themselves from this mode of analysis,
Katzenstein and, by extension, his fellow constructivists effectively embrace the
notion that explanations focusing on economic factors are necessarily interest-based
ones in the narrow sense of the term. Consequently, they understand identity construction as a process taking place in a normative, cultural context that is distinct
from any material context, and their notion of state identity is one wherein the
"social" is essentially distinct from the "economic." To put it differently, their attempts
to distance themselves from the positivist epistemologies and structural analyses of
mainstream IR have led constructivists to a point where, in emphasizing the social
construction of identities and interests, they have generally tended to ignore the constitutive role of structures such as the global capitalist economy in these processes.

It is precisely this commitment to emphasizing the importance of norms-based explanations as against interest-based ones, highlighting cultural, social, normative factors as against material factors in making sense of the contemporary international system, that has shaped the content and direction of the study of transnationalism in IR, undermining it in two important ways. First, highlighting the normative basis of transnationalism within this literature takes place at the expense of an analysis of how these processes might be embedded within systemic structures, such as that of the global capitalist economy. This, in turn, leads to a skewed representation of transnationalism as a set of processes that not only undermine state sovereignty but also lead to the building of a putatively progressive global civil society.[23] Second, notwithstanding the initial reiteration of the distinction between "norms" and "interest-based" explanation, much of the scholarly work on transnationalism tends to treat this distinction as a sort of harmonious two-step—first come the norms, and then comes the strategic interest-based action. To the extent that transnational networks are conceptualized as emerging out of commonly held principles, scholars present them as an intrinsic part of a "normative" explanation of global politics. To understand the emergence of transnational networks, it is argued, one has to pay attention to the emergence of norms. However, once they are formed, the explanations of how these networks function and the conditions under which they succeed make them appear to be a transnational version of interest groups—groups that act across borders (much like domestic interest groups) in a strategic manner to affect and, hopefully, alter state policy. To that extent, the dominant disciplinary conception of transnationalism remains, at its core, an extension of the liberal conception of state politics—a point I will return to in the following section.

Mainstream IR debates on transnationalism and identity, as the brief preceding discussion should make obvious, have certainly not focused on the subject of diasporas per se. Despite that, and notwithstanding some of its obvious blinders, this scholarship has shaped some of the more prominent attempts to theorize the nature and role of diasporas in global politics.[24] For this reason, we are compelled to take seriously the claim that liberal constructivism can provide the theoretical tools needed to understand the role of diasporas, and by extension the domestic abroad, in global politics.

A Case of Mistaken Identity: Liberalism, Constructivism, and Diasporas

In the summer of 2003, *International Organization*, the leading journal in the discipline, published two articles dealing with the subject of diasporas. While one of the essays dealt with the specific issue of the Chinese diaspora in Southeast

Asia, the lead article sought to fulfill the more ambitious goal of articulating the broader theoretical significance of diasporas for IR.[25] This publication in a prominent journal marked the acceptance of diasporas into the disciplinary mainstream as an important object of study. The significance of this fact was not lost on the authors, who begin by noting that despite "increasing recognition of the importance of diasporas in international affairs, there has not been, to our knowledge, any serious attempt to incorporate this phenomenon into international relations (IR) theory. This article seeks to fill this void."[26] Coauthored by Yossi Shain, perhaps the most prolific scholar in the discipline on the issue of diasporas, the article is structured around the contention that in order to understand "diasporic activities," a theoretical framework that emphasizes the "shared space" between constructivism and liberalism is required.[27] The authors' argument is quite straightforward: diasporas are important actors in global politics because of their peculiar identity, and their role can be understood by treating them as yet another transnational interest group. To understand the manifold complexities of diasporic politics, the authors then propose a liberal constructivist theoretical framework that not only helps account for "actors' identities, motives and preferences" but also provides an explanation "for their actions once their preferences are settled."[28] As I have shown, the dominant disciplinary understanding of both concepts—identity and transnationalism—suffers from serious drawbacks. Not surprisingly, those shortcomings are reproduced in Shain and Barth's attempt to employ these concepts to the study of diasporas.

Starting with the by now routine claim about the distinction between "constructivist" and "rational [sic] approaches," Shain and Barth begin by asserting the importance of national identity—"a variable, shaped by international and domestic forces."[29] More specifically, the authors turn to William Bloom's discussion of identity to claim that there is something called a "national identity dynamic" that provides a way to understand diasporas:

Because national identity is *both a variable and a resource* (the authority to direct policy), it stands to reason that different groups attach varying importance to it. *A resource is usually more valued by those lacking in it.* In this case, diasporas—outside the state but inside the people—often attach more importance to national identity than those inside the state. While the insiders experience their national identity in their day-to-day life, diasporic distinctiveness tends to be fluid and more tenuous. Diasporas thus engage in efforts to shape national identity not so much to gain through it leverage over (material) interests, but mainly because it is *in their interest to sustain an identity* that perpetuates and nourishes their self-image.[30]

Apart from the strangeness of presenting the diasporic subject as a container that is not quite filled with "national identity," this argument illustrates a major conceptual flaw.

Shain and Barth repeatedly assert that diasporas are "inside the people," rather than tracing the processes through which the boundaries of the imagined community of the nation are given meaning. This, at the very least, undermines their claim of conceptualizing identity as socially constructed. Should not the construction of the boundaries demarcating the "inside" from the "outside" itself be a subject of inquiry rather than an assumption for scholarship within the constructivist tradition? As the discussion in the previous chapter should make clear, diasporas have not always and certainly not unequivocally been considered to be "inside the people." In fact, in many cases such as that of Mexico, diasporas have been ignored and delegitimized by their homelands at certain historical junctures precisely because they are considered to be denationalized—outside the imagined community of the nation. Furthermore, the question of what this has meant has differed across space and time. For instance, when India became independent in 1947, Prime Minister Jawaharlal Nehru offered what was at best a qualified acceptance of India's relationship to overseas Indians, instructing them to either adopt Indian citizenship or remain "good citizens" of their country of residence. In essence, as I explain in the next chapter, the effect of the Nehruvian stance that remained in place through the next two decades was to put the diaspora "outside," rhetorically, institutionally, and politically. That changed somewhat in the 1970s, when Indian Foreign Minister Atal Bihari Vajpayee declared that "everyone of Indian origin overseas is a representative of India...though our sons and daughters have gone abroad to work or to reside there, India will never disown them," at least paying lip service to the notion that members of the Indian diaspora were "inside the people."[31] But given that this assertion was not backed by any changes in the institutional structures of the Indian state, what being "inside the people" meant for members of the Indian diaspora and the Indian state at that juncture is quite different from what that means in the context of the ongoing production of the Indian domestic abroad.[32]

Beyond their discussion of the question of identity, the limitations of importing existing conceptual categories is also apparent when we take a second look at the manner in which the two scholars attempt to theorize the role of diasporas in global politics. Though the notion of what holds diasporic networks together (i.e., a particular norm of belonging to a national community) may make them seem unlike the networks discussed by the transnationalism literature, this difference is superficial, for the theoretical logic guiding the two is the same. Within the conceptual framework proposed by Shain and Barth, diasporas, much like the transnational networks discussed earlier, exist across the territorial boundaries of nation-states and work to effect changes in state policies. They do so by behaving like domestic interest groups, the only difference being that these are transnational interest groups that influence domestic political agendas.

Diasporas, Shain and Barth claim, are "independent actors" that should be "viewed as one of the many domestic interest groups" struggling to have an influence on foreign policy. In making this assertion, they add the caveat that in this context, "domestic" does not stand in for that which is "non-international."[33] Put differently, diaspora networks are transnational actors that are seen as independent in the sense of being outside the systemic structures they are affecting, but still working across boundaries to influence the foreign policy decision-making processes of states. In delimiting the effectiveness of this influence, the authors turn to the question of the state. They argue that diasporas are most effective in shaping the foreign policy of their homeland when the latter (as well as the "hostland") is a "weak" state, in the sense that it is "highly permeable to societal influences on its decision-making process."[34] The authors conclude their discussion of weak states by arguing that democracies are generally weak and therefore are (along with "some non-democratic weak states") susceptible to the influence of diasporas. Even if we accept their claim, the question still remains as to why democracies such as Mexico and India are turning to their diasporas at this particular historical juncture, and not before.

The authors skirt this question in part because of an implicit liberal-pluralist understanding of the state: a political arena that is a passive construct, a terrain in which the real agents of civil society, the interest groups, compete to gain control of political institutions.[35] At a general level, this conception is problematic in overlooking the intrinsically *political* and *historically situated* character of the state as a structure of rule. By this, I mean that the liberal-pluralist understanding of the state precludes Shain and Barth from conceptualizing it as a dynamic entity that is constituted in relation to other evolving structures, particularly those of global capitalism. This in turn leads the authors to a vacillation between ignoring the historical dimension of state-diaspora relations altogether or merely asserting its "increasing" importance.[36] Even in the latter case, this "increase" is unaccounted for (beyond a reiteration that weak states are more open to the influence of diasporas) and certainly not presented as a marked qualitative change that has occurred under specific historical and political conditions.[37]

At this juncture, I should make it clear that I am quite sympathetic to Shain and Barth's general project. Like them, I argue that the subject of diasporas is both important and undertheorized in IR. It is a subject that requires, at some level, an analysis of the relationship between the nation and the state, transnationalism and identity. Having said that, the weakness of Shain and Barth's endeavor makes it clear that embracing the prevailing disciplinary theoretical frameworks does not really serve as a means to work through these analytical knots. If anything, these frameworks act more as straitjackets that preclude us from making sense of the manifold complexities of the domestic abroad.

For instance, while the domestic abroad is undoubtedly a manifestation of transnationalism, it is a peculiar form of transnationalism in that it poses a serious challenge to the predominant conception about the nature and effects of this process on global politics. Furthermore, it is a form of transnationalism that is very much rooted in circuits of global capital, is driven by the state, and is national in origin, character, and aspirations. It is aimed at extending not only the boundaries of the imagined community of the nation but also the extent of the state's authority. Its paradoxical effect is therefore to strengthen, rather than undermine, the foundations of the nation-state system.[38] Similarly, while the domestic abroad signifies a remaking of both national and state identities, these processes of reconstruction take place in the context of fundamental political and economic transformations of the state, in the context of its relationship to structures of global capitalism. Therefore, to understand these shifts, it is essential to conceptualize nation-state identities as dynamic and historically constituted in and through a relationship to global capitalism.[39] Thus, the task of analyzing the domestic abroad requires at the very least a rethinking of transnationalism and identity beyond disciplinary confines.

As we develop the requisite theoretical framework, it is important to remember that implicit in the institutionalized acknowledgment of diasporas as being "inside the people" are questions regarding the boundaries of the nation, the economic and political authority of the state, and the continuing relevance of the territorial nation-state as the constitutive unit of global politics. In other words, the domestic abroad is a product of changes that are taking place at the level of the global and the national, in the nation and the state, and in the economic and political realms. To understand the processes through which such changes result in the production of the domestic abroad, the rest of the chapter develops a heuristic framework that takes seriously the mutually constitutive relationship between these elements, while bringing together the conceptual categories of transnationalism and identity. In doing so, it provides the theoretical bulwark for the book's larger argument that the domestic abroad can be made sense of only as the product of two concurrently occurring, distinct yet interrelated processes: the diasporic reimagining of the nation and the neoliberal restructuring of the state. To make this argument, the next section lays out the relationship between diasporas and nationalist projects. It begins by discussing the logic of the common prevailing tendency to treat diasporas as posing a challenge to dominant nationalisms embodied in the territorial nation-state and shows the pitfalls of such an argument. Building on this analysis and drawing on the broader interdisciplinary literature on transnationalism, the section concludes by explaining the manner in which transnational nationalisms serve as a crucial platform for the diasporic reimagining of the nation.

II. Diasporas, Nationalism, and the Political Dimension of the Domestic Abroad

Imaginary Postnationalisms

Diasporas exist outside the territorial limits of the states designated as the "homeland" and are held together by the notion of belonging to an extended community that is essentially connected to that homeland.[40] As such, they seem to challenge the cogency of the modern territorial nation-state project at home and abroad and do so by appearing to disrupt the very notion of "home" and "abroad." Given this ability of diasporas to embody an in-between space, it is not surprising that their relationship to nationalism in general and the nation-state system in particular has been subject to much scholarly scrutiny. Scholars like Paul Gilroy, Lisa Lowe, and David Palumbo-Liu have focused on the historical conditions that led to the emergence of a specific diaspora to interrogate modernity, while others including Stuart Hall and Arjun Appadurai have attempted to provide an overarching theorization of the nature and role of diasporas. Writing under the umbrella of cultural studies, these scholars have, to a large extent, set the tone for conceptualizing diasporas as the embodiment of the most viable challenge to the existing nation-state system. It is this particular view of diasporas as hybrid subjects who challenge the very logic of a territorially cogent nation-state entity and the grip of dominant state nationalisms that has tended to frame much of the discussion of the subject in diaspora studies.

In an argument that is a well-known illustration of this trend, Arjun Appadurai contends that the contemporary world is characterized by a "rupture."[41] If the modern world was dominated by the imagined communities of the nation (and its corollary, the territorial state), the contemporary world, according to Appadurai, is characterized by "images and viewers" that do not "fit into circuits or audiences that are easily bound within national, regional or local spaces."[42] In other words, "the nationalist genie, never perfectly contained in the bottle of the territorial state, is now itself diasporic."[43] The task of studying diasporic public spheres becomes, then, one of spelling out the processes of deterritorialization—the "unyoking of the imagination from place"—that characterize the present.[44] Despite his occasional protestations to the contrary, Appadurai highlights these relationships and their unforeseeable consequences precisely because he sees in them the potential for ways "to think ourselves beyond the nation."[45] The "modern governmental apparatuses," he argues, "are increasingly inclined to self-perpetuation, bloat, violence and corruption."[46] They have persistently tended to use nationalism as an ideological alibi for exclusion and eventually some form of totalitarianism. To be more precise, a singular, official nationalism has generally become the "ideological alibi of the territorial state" and "the last refuge of ethnic totalitarianism."[47] Implicit in this process has been a flattening of different kinds of imaginings of political communities that are not necessarily territorially bound. However, in the modern world, such alternative imaginaries do exist and can be found mainly in the diasporic public sphere, the groups of mobile populations, connected by mass media and deterritorialized imaginations. It is in them that one can find the possibility of a transformed, postnational world order.

What makes Appadurai's analysis noteworthy is not only its omnipresence in the general literature but also the fact that one can find similar arguments across the spectrum of loosely defined cultural studies scholarship dealing with the question of diasporas. Paul Gilroy, Homi Bhabha, and Stuart Hall, to name a few outstanding examples, deploy tropes of imprisonment and liberation in their descriptions of the dominance of territorial nation-states in modern vocabulary and imagination and the challenge posed by diasporas to that dominance. In fact, the conceptual category of the nation-state emerges in these scholarly narratives as restrictive and fundamentally suspect.[48] This view of dominant nationalisms and the nation-state form is not surprising, given that much of the cultural studies–oriented discussion of diasporas is indebted to a tradition of postcolonial theory. It is this tradition that has been at the forefront of challenging discourses of colonialism, modernity, and nationalism.[49] In particular, postcolonial theory has mounted a stringent critique of the dominant nationalism embodied in the postcolonial nation-state as well as its earlier anticolonial incarnation. Theorists in this tradition have argued that despite the important role played by nationalist movements in ending colonial rule, both anticolonial and postcolonial nationalisms are driven by the same violent, exclusionary logic.[50]

Paul Gilroy, for instance, begins his scrutiny of the problems faced by black Britons by analyzing the manner in which the construction of the nation rests on notions of "cultural insiderism" that present the national community as "an ethnically homogeneous object."[51] In the context of British politics, this translates into a view of British history (shared, as Gilroy says, by "the right and left, racist and anti-racist, black and white"[52]) that treats the historical emergence of black social groups in Britain as a result of the collision between two fully formed cultures—the indigenous (and therefore "real") culture of a Britain that was inhabited only by white citizens and the external (and consequently never "authentically" British) culture brought in by the slaves and their descendants. This process of conceptualizing the historical constructions of national communities in simple ethnic terms is, as Gilroy points out, a project that is common to all sorts of nationalisms. Nationalist projects have always been concerned with the definition of the national community, not only in terms of constantly striving to draw the boundaries of what constitutes a genuine national culture and who the members of the nation are but also in terms of delimiting the geographical boundaries of this community. In and through this process of "territorializing"—producing the space of the nation-state—dominant nationalist discourses attempt to delegitimize and discipline transterritorial identities that do not necessarily respect the frontiers of the nation-state.[53] It is in this context that diasporas have served as an important site as well as mode of postcolonial critique.

Within the postcolonial tradition, diasporas generally come into play as a referent for the idea of cultural dislocation connected to human displacement. Postcolonial diasporas thus reflect complex histories of slavery and exile and challenge any claims to stable meanings of identity.[54] While dominant nationalist discourses try to deny the hybridity that is constitutive of national identity, migrants and diasporic subjects embody the hybrid history of the nation. They are the true postcolonial subjects—"neither new nor old"—who challenge the construction of a homogeneous national space that travels through empty time from a pristine past (the "old") to a future (the "new") not overwhelmed by external influences. Diasporas thus become the sites showing the limitations of nation-state forms that rest on narratives of a cogent political community of people with a shared historical past.

Appadurai, for instance, argues that among the implications of the postnational diasporic world order is "the possibility that, while nations might continue to exist, the steady erosion of the capabilities of the nation-state to monopolize loyalty will encourage the spread of national forms that are largely divorced from territorial states."[55] The notion that nations *might* continue to exist is already a concession for a scholar who generally tends to emphasize the obsolescence of the nation-state form. But what is more striking is the contention that the potential alternatives to the nation-state would be deterritorialized, free-floating forms of political organization that no longer have any necessary connection to a territorial state.[56] Appadurai makes this claim by using the "hard case" example of the United States. He contends that what initially appears to be a "triumphant example of the territorial nation-state" is but "one node in a postnational network of diasporas."[57] Accepting this claim requires a leap of faith that rests on the hardly novel claim that there now exist diasporic populations embodying "extraterritorial nationalisms" who "love America, but are not necessarily attached to the United States" and that the "challenge of diasporic pluralism is global." The crux of Appadurai's meditations on the United States has to do with the nature of the hyphen that connects various diasporas to "America." As he puts it succinctly, the "formula of hyphenation (as in Italian-Americans, Asian-Americans and African-Americans) is reaching the point of saturation, and the right-hand side of the hyphen can barely contain the unruliness of the left-hand side."[58] These communities, in Appadurai's view, constitute a "de-localized transnation" that is not really connected to the territory of either the nation-state that was their ostensible point of origin or the United States itself.

At a superficial level at least, diasporas do have a certain instinctive appeal as subjects that could transcend the limitations of nations and states. In that sense, their celebration as being somehow *postnational* is understandable. For scholars like Appadurai, the territorial nation-state is the entity that has imprisoned our imaginations and actively tried to discipline alternative geographies of "frontiers and borders." As Katharyne Mitchell rightly notes:

> The identification of peoples who have multiple loyalties, move between regions, do not occupy a singular cultural space, and who often operate in some sense exterior to state boundaries and cultural effects, has proven attractive for theorists who have sought to disrupt normative narratives and understandings of nation and culture. Those in literal motion in-between nations or outside of proscribed, static cultural locations become vaunted as the potential locus of cultural understandings that resist hegemonic norms of both race and nation.[59]

Notwithstanding its own peculiar logic, such an orientation ultimately effaces a crucial aspect of the role of diasporas in global politics. The increasing visibility of diasporas does not necessarily indicate a corresponding decline in the relevance of either nation-states or struggles over territories. While scholarly commitments might lead one to wish for the gradual fading away of the territorial limits to our imagination, the emergence of a borderless world, populated by postnational diasporas, is quite unconvincing. Far from being agents embodying the emergence of a "pre-" or "post-" national order, diasporas are playing a critical role in reinscribing both nationalisms and the nation-state structure itself.[60] Rather than give in to the two main impulses that seem to characterize much of the existing cultural studies scholarship on the subject—to find in diasporas both the transcendence of the territorial nation-state and the alternative to the dominant nationalisms associated with it—the complicity of diasporas in nationalist projects needs to be subjected to more critical scrutiny. Only by taking this important step can we begin comprehending the paradoxical and complex phenomenon of the domestic abroad in contemporary international relations.

Transnational Nationalisms and the Diasporic Reimagining of the Nation

Diasporas, though far from being monolithic entities, are conceptually held together by the notion of having a common origin, belonging to a specific community, and hailing from a particular nation. While diasporas assert their connection and trace their roots to national communities that are associated with a definite physical location, what sets them apart from the more traditional national communities is that they do not physically inhabit that particular space. Given that their very existence reveals the arbitrary and redundant nature of territorial boundaries, one might be tempted to focus (as much of the kind of scholarship discussed earlier does) on the notion of diasporas going beyond—and thus embodying an alternative to—the territorial nation-state form. However, such a focus, as discussed in the preceding section, remains essentially limited and serves only to efface important facets of contemporary global politics. On the one hand, the plight (for the want of a better word) of diasporas—their need for specific travel and citizenship documents, their being marked as different in the host countries, their symbolic and material connections to the home country—serves as a clear reminder of the continuing relevance of the nation-state form. On the other hand, and more important for our purposes, diasporas—for better or for worse—continue being very visibly involved in the perpetuation of ongoing nationalist projects.

In the past decade, a growing interdisciplinary group of scholars have focused on specific diasporas, such as the Russian, Kurdish, Tamil, Haitian, and Croatian (to name but a few), to provide insight into their relationship with their presumptive homelands, shining the spotlight on the "national" dimension of transnationalism.[61] The formation of national identities in these cases (as in any case) is, of course, far from automatic or natural. However, the very emergence of a diaspora community—through the teaching of a common history and language, newspapers, and regular cultural events, to name but a few types of community networks—rests on the presumption, reassertion, and ongoing construction of a certain coherent political identity. As such, diasporas constitute a fertile soil for the blooming of a nationalist consciousness. Given that the origins of diasporas are often traced to a notion of exile, persecution, and systematic deprivation of opportunities in the home state, it is not surprising that analyses of the nationalisms embodied by diasporas have more often than not fallen within the rubric of what has been called "ethnic" or "minority nationalism."[62] In that sense, the relationship between diasporas and nationalism is generally perceived as being framed by notions of secession and working against the existing territorial nation-states.

Secessionist movements have long found diasporas to be an invaluable resource in terms of both attempting to build the legitimacy of their nationalist projects and acquiring the actual material support (men, money, arms) needed to sustain a political struggle in the home state. This is even more pertinent when the diaspora itself (or at least a significant part of it) was created as a result of that struggle. For instance, a large section of the Tamil diaspora living in India, Western Europe, and North America fled Sri Lanka during the course of the nearly three-decade-long struggle for an independent Tamil homeland led by the LTTE (Liberation Tigers of Tamil Eelam).[63] As Sarah Wayland has shown, the role played by this diaspora has been essential to the maintenance of the high level of political mobilization we have seen in the Sri Lankan Tamil nationalist movement.[64] Despite being dispersed across the Asia Pacific region, Western Europe, and North America, Tamil elites have worked toward mobilizing ethnic networks through a combination of methods.[65] These included providing information exchange among members of the diaspora by means of Tamil newspapers and Web sites, organizing conferences and marches, and fund-raising through legal as well as illegal channels. These measures, as Wayland points out, have been extremely successful in keeping Tamil expatriates aware of the LTTE's struggle and providing the LTTE with much-needed funds.[66] This last feature of diaspora activities has been constantly reiterated by the Sri Lankan government, which estimates that the Tamil diaspora raises an average of $80 million per annum.[67]

Despite the peculiarities of the Tamil case—the context of a long-standing Tamil nationalist movement and the conditions under which the diaspora itself was created—the construction and sustenance of national identity in this manner, as politics of so-called minority nationalism, is far from being exclusive to it. During the last two decades of the twentieth century, the Kurdish nationalist movement took root among the "Turkish" diaspora in Europe through a similar series of efforts by political elites.[68] Drawing on resources that were made available by the existence of satellite and communication technology, Kurdish nationalists spread out across Europe pooled their expertise to broadcast Kurdish-language programming that was crucial in standardizing a Kurdish language, a particular rendering of Kurdish history, and the production of a specifically Kurdish (as opposed to a Turkish) national culture.[69] The politicization of the Kurdish diaspora has, as scholars have argued persuasively, in turn helped sustain the Kurdish nationalist movement based in Turkey.[70]

These two examples serve as an illustration of an important point: even for scholars who take the national dimension of transnationalism seriously, the nationalism embodied by diasporas has a certain oppositional tinge. To put it simply, even while acknowledging that the end goal of such movements is the establishment of an independent nation-state, much of this analysis tends to frame diasporic nationalism in terms of the challenge it poses to established territorial nation-states. The logic of this trend can be traced to the very foundations of this "transnationalism project" that has informed such studies. In an oft-cited, agenda-setting article that defined transnationalism as a new, interdisciplinary field of study, Alejandro Portes, Luis Guarnizo, and Patricia Landolt argued that the sustained interactions between migrant communities and their home states had created a truly original phenomenon calling for a more rigorous analysis of the diverse economic, political, and sociocultural activities that fell within this transnational rubric.[71] The authors went on to argue that the phenomenon of transnationalism should be understood as a grassroots *reaction* to the initiatives and policies of state actors at national and local levels. In elaborating this claim, they essentially ended up demarcating the boundaries of transnationalism as a field that was distinct from (albeit related to) the institutional structures of the state.[72]

Despite the acceptance of "state-sponsored transnationalism" as a valid category, this agenda setting seems to have had a general effect of occluding the role of the state in most analyses of transnational phenomena. This certainly seems to be the case in the study of transnational nationalisms. While the role of diasporas in nationalist projects has certainly not been ignored by scholars in this field, their scrutiny has to a large extent highlighted the role of various diasporas as agents of specific kinds of nationalism.[73] This, more often than not, has come at the cost of analyzing the role of state actors in the process.[74] From the standpoint of putting into focus the domestic abroad phenomenon, this lack of attention becomes a serious issue. The construction of particular historical national narratives characterizing the production of the domestic abroad, in which diasporas appear in one way or another as a seamless extension of the nation and the embodiment of its many virtues, is a process that is primarily driven by the state. Diasporas are, of course, an essential part of these state projects. It would be impossible for the state to merely assert the importance of diasporas without some semblance of participation from some sections of the concerned communities. However, they are far from being the main agents in the process.

The reimagining of the nation manifested by the domestic abroad is, fundamentally, a state-driven phenomenon. It is produced by state policies and initiatives that are aimed at institutionalizing the relationship between states and their diasporas. These policies and initiatives, as I mentioned earlier, can take and have taken varied forms, ranging from establishing special ministries that deal with diaspora affairs to reserving seats for members of the diaspora within state legislative bodies. What holds these initiatives together is that they serve to acknowledge the rights of the various diaspora groups and the duties of the concerned state toward these groups, even if this acknowledgment remains purely rhetorical, as it does in many cases. In other words, these initiatives are all aimed at extending the boundaries of the nation beyond the territorial limits of the state. To that extent, in acknowledging the claims of a territorially dispersed "global nation" on its institutions, state policies take on a *transnational* form. To make sense of the domestic abroad, then, we need to understand the political economic transformations that set the stage for the transnational nationalisms embarked on by states in the contemporary international system. In other words, what we need is to not just bring the state back into the study of transnationalism, but to do so in a way that helps us comprehend the nature of its transformation. We turn to this task in the final section of the chapter.

III. States, Capitalism, and the Economic Dimension of the Domestic Abroad

Diasporic Capitalism

Most scholars would agree that there exists a definite economic dimension to the relationship between diasporas and nation-states. At the more obvious level in the contemporary international system, this dimension manifests itself in the form of the push and pull of labor and the need for and supply of remittances. As important as those trends are, it is crucial to keep in mind that they are merely symptoms of the deeper systemic structure of capitalism.[75] Therefore, to make sense of the economic rationale underpinning a phenomenon like the domestic abroad, we need to focus our attention on the historical development of capitalism on a global scale.[76] More specifically, we need to begin by analyzing the ways in which the emergence of modern diasporas and the various roles they have played in global politics are inextricably tied to this dynamic systemic structure.

The development of capitalism on a global scale, particularly from the eighteenth century onward, was made possible and sustained by imperialism as a system of rule. While one aspect of this system involved sending men and women from the imperial metropole to govern the colonies, creating what Robin Cohen has called "imperial diasporas," this was just a small proportion of the migration engendered by imperial imperatives.[77] Larger and, for our purposes, more important diasporas were created by the forced migration of people from the eighteenth century to the early twentieth century. This migration, specifically from Africa and Asia, was facilitated by imperial authorities primarily to serve the needs of the early colonial capitalists.[78] The Indian case is illustrative of this point. By the mid-nineteenth century, the British Empire, much like other European imperial powers, was facing a labor deficit. The main cause for the crisis was the 1833 Act of Abolition, which banned slavery across the British Empire.[79] The end of this institutionalized supply of cheap labor meant that the colonial powers had to look elsewhere to meet the needs of both colonial settlers and metropolitan capital.[80] It was in this context, as a result of the attempts to avert one of the first major crises of British capitalism, that the story of the modern Indian diaspora actually began.

A series of emigration acts in the mid-nineteenth century enabled the British Indian state to supply Indian indentured labor bound by contract to work in the plantations owned by British settlers all across the empire.[81] Notwithstanding the fact that many of the migrants "voluntarily" chose indenture (if one ignores the dire economic conditions that drove them from their homes), the system itself was propped up by state-sanctioned violence.[82] This was one of the main reasons for the strong public outcry against the indenture system, leading to its official demise by the early part of the twentieth century. By this time, however, the labor diaspora was being joined by a qualitatively different group of emigrants, consisting of petty merchants and traders who helped create "Indian" enclaves—spaces that retained traces of the language, culture, and traditions of various parts of India—in their new lands of settlement.[83] The colonial authorities permitted this migration for two main reasons: the traders provided some of the basic services needed by both the colonial settlers and the families of the indentured laborers; more importantly, they played a mediating role between the colonial rulers and the native populations, more often than not supporting the former against the latter.[84] As we will see in the next chapter, this had a profound effect on how anticolonial movements and the nation-states they gave rise to in Asia and Africa perceived the nature and role of diasporas. At this point, it suffices to reiterate that sustaining capitalist economies and running an imperial system of governance would have been impossible without the assistance—voluntary or otherwise—of the various migrant communities. Various imperial authorities were well aware of this fact, which is why the heyday of European imperialism saw the creation and growth of numerous modern diasporas.

Formal independence for Asian and African colonies by the middle of the twentieth century did not in any way sever the link between the development of capitalism and diasporic flows. At a broader level, imperial rule had rested on the systematic restructuring of colonial economies to serve the needs of metropolitan capital.[85] The destruction of indigenous industries (such as the Indian textile industry), the reorienting of agricultural systems in Asia and Africa so that they would produce cash crops (such as cotton, indigo, and cocoa) needed by metropolitan industries, and the channeling of the wealth of the colonies back to imperial centers like London, Paris, and Lisbon are but a few examples of how this system operated.[86] Among the main consequences of this system was that it not only created a connection between the imperial centers and the colonies but also ensured that formal independence would not imply an automatic erasure of imperial relations. The former colonies continue to occupy a structurally disadvantaged position within the global capitalist economy,[87] and they remain to this day the main source of contemporary diasporic flows.[88] The connections between various imperial metropoles and their colonies (a colonial heritage) ensured that much of this flow in the mid-twentieth century was generally westward bound—primarily to Europe. However, the boom in petroleum prices, with the consequent strengthening of the Organization of Petroleum Exporting Countries (OPEC) economies in 1970s, and the predominance of the United States in the global capitalist economy ensured that parts of both North America and the Middle East served as host states for numerous diasporas.

As I have argued elsewhere, there is a highly visible continuity between the types of diasporas that existed in the heyday of European imperialism and today.[89] Much like in the past, there is today a significant labor diaspora of unskilled and semiskilled laborers who migrate from the global South to the North, oftentimes lured with promises of a better future by government-authorized agents. While reviled by right-wing nationalists within host states for taking away jobs from the natives and in general acting as a drain on national resources, this exploited and politically disempowered group of diasporic actors is the contemporary incarnation of the indentured laborers of the past. Like those who "voluntarily" chose indenture, these new migrants, too, are driven by dire economic conditions in their homelands and a desire to find new means of subsistence. By taking up forms of employment that often render them invisible to the state and by providing a virtually uninterrupted supply of cheap labor, they, too, serve the demands of the capitalist system.[90] In ways that bear a striking similarity to the earlier mercantile diaspora, today we have the diaspora constituted by knowledge workers—technically skilled doctors, engineers, academics, lawyers, and software professionals—who provide the services essential for the maintenance of social and economic systems in their host countries. The economic successes of this layer of diasporas and their identification in many cases with the political projects of the advanced capitalist host states make them unique in the sense of being potentially valorized in both home and host states.[91]

This is, admittedly, a brief retelling of the complex history of the formation of diasporas.[92] However, it suffices to make a vital point: the emergence of modern diasporas and their socioeconomic and political roles has always been constitutively linked to the development of capitalism on a global scale. More importantly, it also reveals that this relationship has always been mediated by structures of the state, be it the colonial or the postcolonial state. But how do we understand the nature of the state that performs such a function? Even at the most superficial level, states are obviously not ahistorical, unchanging, fixed entities. In the context of the domestic abroad, the question of these changes becomes even more pressing. What are the conditions under which state actors consciously turn to their emigrant communities, attempting to validate them and empower them institutionally? In other words, how do we make sense of the move from the state as an enabler of emigration to the state as a prime mover in the production of the domestic abroad? To address these questions, we turn next to the question of the state.

Hegemony and the Neoliberal Restructuring of the State

The role of diasporas in contemporary global politics cannot be understood without paying attention to the involvement of states in the production and empowerment of diasporas as specific kinds of actors. Going against the grain of much of the interdisciplinary scholarship on diasporas, this book argues that it is necessary to "bring the state back" into the study of transnationalism. Since being popularized by Peter Evans and Theda Skocpol in the mid-1980s, this expression has generally been associated with the neo-Weberian approach to the state. While I agree with these scholars insofar as underscoring the continuing relevance of the state in contemporary international relations, the approach of this book differs from theirs in an important way.[93] The neo-Weberian approach posits the independence of the state both as an analytical variable and as a political agent, occluding the historicity of the institution.[94] This book, in contrast, follows the historical materialist tradition in arguing that the modern state, far from being independent in that sense, is a dynamic and historically evolving structure that is inextricably linked to the development of capitalism on a global scale.

At this juncture, it is important to emphasize the fact that while capitalism can be understood as an abstract system at a certain level of analysis, it is not a disembodied monolithic systemic structure that merely acts on ontologically prior state entities. As Marx famously remarked, capital is at its core a set of social relations.[95] These relations unfold on the complex landscape of social classes. The classes, moreover, are not frozen in time and cannot be captured by a merely sociological analysis. They are themselves subject to historical development and are thus dynamic. Finally, classes are not simply analytical categories, however complex and historically nuanced, but are instead living social forces engaged in a process of political struggle.[96] But what do these historical, sociological, and political complexities mean in the context of our attempts to theorize the nature and function of the state? To address that question, it is necessary to take one more analytical step and bring into the picture the concept of hegemony.

Hegemony, as Antonio Gramsci explains, is the historical balance between force and consent that constitutes the political power exercised by a particular ruling class.[97] The domination or force exercised by this class is manifested most directly in its control of the state apparatus. This ruling class is singular and cohesive in terms of sharing certain fundamental principles (such as defending the right to private property) and in its relationship to subordinate groups. However, in and of itself, it is far from a monolithic entity, as various factions differ in how they extract and accumulate surpluses (for instance, industrial versus financial bourgeoisie). The internal equilibrium between these factions is a product of historical development, with different factions rising or fading in relative importance at different points of time.[98] This in turn means that institutions of the state can be configured and reconfigured on the basis of the changing relations of forces between various factions of the ruling class.[99] The control of state institutions does indeed set the stage for the relationship between the ruling classes and what Gramsci calls its "enemies," in the sense that the former "tends to 'liquidate' or...subjugate" the latter "by the use of armed force."[100] But it is important to keep in mind that the exercise of hegemony requires more than use of force. Even before winning control of state institutions and, in fact, as a necessary precondition to winning such control, the ruling class needs to exercise "intellectual and moral leadership."[101] This task is carried out successfully to the extent that the ruling class is able to translate its distinct social interests into the general interests of society at large.[102]

Understanding the nature of the state and the exercise of state power therefore requires an analysis of the complex and historically evolving production of hegemony.[103] In carrying out such an analysis across different times and places, we need to keep in mind an important caveat. As Gramsci himself made clear in his classic explanation of the Italian Risorgimento, while it is possible to talk in general terms about the historical impediments to the establishment of bourgeois hegemony, understanding the process through which it is produced (especially in new political orders) requires us to pay close attention to the particular moments of relation of forces.[104] In other words, though we have a template to understand the nature of the capitalist state in general, it is vital for us to not lose sight of the historical specificities of various struggles for hegemony. Thus, the concept of hegemony enables us to understand the nature of the capitalist state while providing the theoretical space to make sense of the relationship between the state and the nation.

Gramsci's close engagement with the travailed history of bourgeois nationalism in the Italian Risorgimento serves not only as a generic theoretical template (the structural weakness of the native bourgeoisie, the necessary outcome of a passive revolution, etc.) but also as a model exactly for its historical concreteness and attention to the peculiarities of the Italian case, down to the "molecular" level.[105] Out of this concrete analysis, it is possible to draw theoretical concepts that resonate outside the Italian context. What gives concepts like "war of position" or "passive revolution" meaning is not an abstract, preordained, linear unfolding, but the contingent political struggles that delineate the historical conditions of possibilities of particular hegemonic alliances. Partha Chatterjee, for instance, draws on these concepts to provide one of the most sophisticated analyses of the nature and consequences of the Indian nationalist movement. He argues that the main purpose of the anticolonial nationalist struggle was to end the political rule of the colonial power and establish an independent nation-state. To achieve this end, a series of alliances were created within the nationalist movement between the bourgeoisie and other classes. These alliances provided the moral, intellectual, and political leadership of the movement, which then attempted to mobilize "mass support from the subordinate classes," in the name of a *nationalist* ideology that claimed to speak for a specific, well-defined political community.[106] As Chatterjee argues persuasively, it was the "content of [this] nationalist ideology," particularly in terms of what it claimed to be possible or legitimate, that shaped the politics of the postcolonial Indian state.[107] As we will see in the coming chapters, this had far-reaching consequences for the ways

in which the postcolonial Indian state dealt with the demarcation of the boundaries of the Indian nation, especially in the context of defining its relationship to
the Indian diaspora at large. However, despite the coalescence around a particular set of policies that kept the diaspora at a distance in the early decades after
independence, the relationship between the Indian state and the Indian diaspora
remained far from settled. To understand why this was the case, it is useful to
return to the question of hegemony.

Understanding the struggle between social forces, the formation of alliances,
and the production of hegemony allows us to make sense of the processes by
which the state emerges as a "relatively unified ensemble" of socially embedded
institutions and social forces that are involved in "making collectively binding
decisions for an imagined political community."[108] Intrinsic to this project is
defining who belongs to, who should be counted as part of that imagined political community. In that sense, the processes of imagining and diasporic reimagining of the nation are not parallel or incidental to, but rather an essential part of
the processes through which the ruling class captures and exercises state power.
It is, to state it baldly, an intrinsic element of the reconfiguring of hegemony.
Notwithstanding the appearance of coherence at particular moments in time—
of what the purpose of the state is or who is a member of the political community represented by the state—hegemonic projects are not what can be regarded
as done deals. While the hegemony of a particular class can be established as a
result of certain political struggles, it is not established in toto and forever. It can
be maintained only to the extent that the ruling class successfully continues presenting its particular interests as the general interest, against the challenges posed
by other social forces. The constant and ongoing project of the rearticulation of
bourgeois hegemony becomes even more complex when we bear in mind that
capitalism itself is dynamic in nature. It is in this context that we need to focus
on the question of neoliberalism.

Scholars, policy makers, and political commentators alike have generally
regarded the second half of the 1970s as a landmark moment in the development
of the global capitalist economy. During this period, China under Deng Xiaoping
took its first step toward liberalizing its economy, Britain under Margaret
Thatcher moved toward a sustained policy of attacking stagflation through
curbing union power, and the United States prepared itself for economic revital-
ization as envisaged by Paul Volcker and adopted by Ronald Reagan. The effect of
these changes occurring in different epicenters has, according to David Harvey,
been so profoundly transformative that "future historians might well look upon
the years 1978–80 as a revolutionary turning-point in the world's social and
economic history."[109] Although we might argue about the exact nature of this
revolution, it is undeniable that the socioeconomic policies associated with
Thatcherism and Reaganomics are today truly global in scope—to the extent

that they are often seen as part of the inexorable development of neoliberalism. The neoliberal ideology (also often described as "economic globalization") presents private property rights, free markets, and free trade as elements essential to the well-being of individuals. In this context, the state is supposed to have the minimal role of providing and guaranteeing the required institutional framework, facilitating but not intervening in the functioning of the market. In terms of state policy, to put it very simply, this has translated into the deregulation of finance, liberalization of trade, privatization of state-owned industries, undermining of labor rights, and withdrawal of the state from social welfare functions. It is these broad policy shifts that are grouped under the umbrella category of "neoliberal restructuring."[110]

At one level, the neoliberal restructuring of the state has been understood as the implementation of a set of economic policies by the state. In fact, much of the scholarly discussion about these processes has revolved around the question of the effect of these policies on the state. On one side of the debate are neoliberal scholars who argue that the powers of the state and its ability to govern have been largely diminished in the context of expanding transnational capital.[111] On the other are neo-Weberians, who not surprisingly have insisted that reports regarding the state's demise have been greatly exaggerated.[112] Each group of scholars in turn produced exhaustive studies of particular areas of governance, attempting to support their claims that the state no longer controls or still continues to control (depending on the camp they belong to) how particular policies are decided and implemented within its territories. As Jim Glassman points out in an incisive intervention, what these studies have revealed is that, notwithstanding their differences, both camps treat the state as an entity that is "anchored firmly in social forces within [its] own national territories."[113] To that extent, regardless of their analytical orientation, scholars involved in the "state debate" begin with the ontological assumption that states (and their powers) are "contained within the bounded territories over which they have formal sovereignty."[114] Consequently, the debate between the neoliberals and the neo-Weberians remains stuck around the question of the extent to which the implementation of neoliberal restructuring leads to a diminishing of state power—the latter camp making the argument that the actual extent is much less than what the former claims. To make sense of the broader meaning and implications of neoliberalism for states, it is essential that we go beyond the narrow scope of this particular debate.

As the latest phase in the development of capitalism on a global scale, neoliberalism (as has been accepted across the board) is characterized by greater "internationalization of capital." The increased mobility of capital, brought about by the general loosening of financial regulations, has resulted in greater exploitation of national labor by international capital.[115] However, at the same time, there is also greater communication and coordination of activities among the various classes. The main implication of this set of processes is a more elaborate and calculated transnational reorienting of social forces beyond the territorial limits of the nation-state.[116] As state apparatuses become "increasingly oriented towards facilitating capital accumulation for the most internationalised investors, regardless of their nationality,"[117] there is a concomitant ongoing creation of a "like-minded international business and government elite."[118] What holds this nationally diverse group together is not just a "a common language (English)" and "common technical training skills and training," but a worldview that keeps them attuned to the "broader international capitalist consensus."[119] Occupying positions of authority within various nation-states, members of this group, aided and abetted by the demands of international agencies such as the International Monetary Fund (IMF) and the World Bank, act in a way that suggests not just the "internationalization of capital," but the "internationalization of the state" itself.[120]

At this juncture, it is important to sound a cautionary note. While the expansion of capitalism on a global scale is real, so is the persistence of the territorial nation-state system. Therefore, to extend the logic of the internationalization of the state to imply the creation of a transnational capitalist class that supersedes and replaces national bourgeoisies is, to put it mildly, a theoretical exaggeration that misses the contradictory and paradoxical character of the development of capitalism.[121] Given that they have to deal with the pressures of the global economy, capitalists across nation-states can and do coordinate their policies, especially in terms of pushing for the opening up of new markets through the institutional framework of agencies like the IMF. To that extent, state actors, particularly in the Third World, face demands made by a seemingly coherent international capitalist class that works sometimes in tandem and sometimes against the interests of domestic capital. These coalitions, however, are at best a contingent coming together of social forces, forming an unstable equilibrium that in turn provides the context and the impetus for the renegotiation of bourgeois hegemony at the level of the nation-state. Losing sight of this important fact leads to an overly structuralist account of the neoliberal phase of capitalist expansion and, consequently, an inability to account for the national distinctiveness and historical particularities in the international system.[122] As I illustrate in the following chapters, it is not possible to understand the nature and consequences of the ongoing neoliberal restructuring of the Indian state without taking seriously the specificities of the Indian experience and, in particular, the legacy of the Indian nationalist movement.

Emphasizing the distinctiveness of specific national contexts, however, does not mean that neoliberal restructuring (which is, in a technical sense, connected to a specific set of economic policies) can be understood as measures that are peculiar to a particular regime or political party.[123] In the case of India, for instance, the Congress Party was in power when the highly contested neoliberal reforms were introduced in 1991.[124] These reforms were strongly opposed by numerous political parties, such as the right-wing Bharatiya Janata Party (BJP) and the left-wing Communist Party of India (Marxist), who were at that time part of the parliamentary political opposition. In the decade and a half since that initial introduction of the reforms, both the BJP and CPI(M) have been part of ruling coalitions at the center and in complete control of various local state governments. Notwithstanding their initial vociferous opposition, when presented with the opportunity, both parties have in fact embraced neoliberal policies.[125] This serves to underscore the larger point that processes of restructuring, once set in motion by a particular regime (perhaps, as in the case of most Third World states, under pressure from the IMF or the World Bank), cannot be rolled back willy-nilly by a different regime, given certain political parameters. Undeniably, there are important differences among the various political parties at the level of domestic politics. However, in the context of the development of capitalism on a global scale, these differences do not translate into a fundamental challenge or outright repudiation of the principles of neoliberal restructuring. It is to highlight this important theoretical point that in the later chapters of this book, I use the umbrella categories of "Government" and "Opposition" (rather than discussing specific political parties that were in power at various points of time) while discussing the crafting of state policies.

The neoliberal restructuring of the state, as I have shown, marks a critical moment in the reconfiguration of hegemony. It is this transformation that provides both the logic and the milieu for the production of the domestic abroad. Given the changing capitalist relations at the global level, as ruling elites approach the task of rearticulating their interests, they are faced with a bigger challenge—that of reasserting their legitimacy and credibility in the national context. In other words, they are faced with the task of rearticulating their hegemony, of reinscribing the correspondence between their particular interests and the general interest in a way that makes sense to their "audience." The success of hegemonic projects, as discussed earlier, rests on the ability of particular alliances of social forces to present themselves as seamlessly emerging from and legitimately representing the interests of a broadly defined imagined political community. An essential element of this project is demarcating the very boundaries of this community. It is in the context of addressing the challenges of neoliberal restructuring that state elites have turned toward their diasporas, constituting them variously as "newly valorized subjects" of the state, as essential elements of the national body politic, and as members of a broader political community that have the right to institutional protection. In other words, the neoliberal restructuring of the state enables and, in fact, necessitates the diasporic reimagining of the nation, leading in turn to the production of the domestic abroad.

Conclusion

The phenomenon of the domestic abroad, as seen in the hailing of "Hungarians beyond the boundaries," "Indians abroad," "Chinese living overseas," or "Russians in the near abroad," quite clearly involves both a rearticulation of nationhood and a redefinition of the role of the state. To make sense of this phenomenon, we began by taking seriously the ways in which the conceptual categories of transnationalism and identity have been theorized within the dominant liberal constructivist tradition in international relations. In engaging with this tradition, this chapter revealed the reductive framing of both these concepts and showed how it precludes us from detecting and explaining the broad and contradictory interactions that constitute the domestic abroad. As a first step in building a heuristic framework to understand these interactions, this chapter cast the spotlight on the transnationalism manifested by the domestic abroad, highlighting in particular the relationship between diasporas and nationalisms. Building on a well-established interdisciplinary scholarship on the subject, it revealed the manner in which diasporas, far from being harbingers of a postnational world order, can and do serve the purpose of reinforcing nationalist projects and the authority of nation-states. However, the diasporic reimagining of the nation that characterizes the production of the domestic abroad is not a process that is driven by diasporas themselves. It is, as even a cursory look at global politics reveals, a peculiar form of transnational nationalism that has been embraced by states at the same time as they embark on programs of neoliberal restructuring. To put it differently, in the context of the domestic abroad, it is the state that institutionally anchors the [re]imagining of the nation and does so in ways that are linked to developments in global capitalism. Therefore, as the next step in the theoretical process, I proposed "bringing the state back" into the analysis of diasporic transnationalism. The final section of the chapter began with a brief analysis of the emergence of modern diasporas, highlighting in particular the role of the state in engendering diasporic flows and empowering certain sections of various diasporas. Using this brief retelling of a complex story as a springboard, I argued that to make sense of the complicity of the state in the shaping and regulating of modern diasporas, we need to understand it as a dynamic and historically evolving structure that is inextricably linked to the development of capitalism on a global scale. Developing this historical materialist conception of the state further, I showed how the Gramscian concept of hegemony enables us to understand the nature of the capitalist state, while at the same time providing the theoretical space to make sense of the relationship between the state and the nation. Intrinsic to the production of bourgeois hegemony—the establishment of a seamless and organic correspondence between the particular interests of the bourgeoisie and the general interests of an imagined political community—is defining who belongs, who should be counted as part of that imagined political community. In that sense, the processes of imagining the nation are not parallel or incidental to, but rather an essential part of the processes through which the ruling class captures and exercises state power. It is, however, important to keep in mind that the hegemony of the bourgeoisie, even once established, is never quite a done deal, for it needs to be constantly rearticulated, particularly in response to extensive transformations of the world economy. It is in the context of this rearticulation that we can make sense of the simultaneous economic restructuring of the state and the redrawing of the boundaries of the nation that produce the domestic abroad.

3

Putting the Diaspora in Its Place
From Colonial Transnationalism
to Postcolonial Nationalism

Indians abroad, it may look like a paradox to say so, paved the way really for Indian emancipation within the frontiers of India. It was the gospel of passive resistance that was conceived, developed and implemented in Transvaal in 1908 that paved the way for the development of non-cooperation, passive resistance, civil disobedience and *satyagraha* in the years 1920 to 1945, and it was really the implementation of the teachings of Mahatma Gandhi, subject to the principles of truth and non-violence over a quarter of a century that made Indian freedom possible. We therefore owe all that we *are* to the initiative, the originality, the daring and the sacrifice of Indians abroad.

—*Pattabhi Sitaramayya, President of Indian National Congress*

We have left it to the Indians abroad whether they continue to remain Indian nationals or to adopt the nationality of whichever country they live in. *It is entirely for them to decide.* If they remain Indian nationals, then all they can claim abroad is favourable alien treatment. If they adopt the nationality of the country they live in, they should associate themselves as closely as possible with the interest of the people of the country they have adopted and never make it appear to function in any way that they become an exploiting agency there.

—*Jawaharlal Nehru, Prime Minister of India, September 1957*

In September 1957, more than a decade after India had attained independence from British rule, Prime Minister Jawaharlal Nehru declared in the Indian parliament that his government had successfully resolved the question of Indians abroad. While acknowledging that people of Indian origin were facing discrimination in different parts of the world, the prime minister framed the Indian government's postindependence policy in terms of a choice that had to be made by the Indians abroad themselves. Indians abroad, Nehru asserted, were at a crossroads. They could choose to claim Indian citizenship, thus officially becoming a part of the independent Indian nation-state. In that case, while the Indian state would accept its duties toward them and strive to protect their interests through the means of traditional diplomacy, they could not expect anything other than "favourable alien treatment" outside Indian territory. As for those who chose to accept "the nationality of the country they live in," the Indian state wished them well and, in that spirit, exhorted them to comport themselves in their new countries as true citizens and not exploitative agents.[1]

At one level, the prime minister's declaration took no one by surprise, for it was the clearest articulation yet of a policy that Nehru's government had been following since independence in 1947. However, within the broader milieu of the anticolonial nationalist struggle that had led to India's independence, this declaration did mark a dramatic turnaround. The fact that Gandhi, adulated by millions and institutionally revered by the state as "Father of the nation," had himself been an "Indian abroad" was not lost on the leadership of the nationalist movement. Many of them, like Pattabhi Sitaramayya, the president of the Indian National Congress, openly acknowledged and praised the critical role played by Indians abroad in India's independence struggle.[2] To be fair, such acknowledgments were not merely a nod toward Gandhi's special place in Indian politics. The leaders of the Indian nationalist movement had in fact first articulated their demands for complete freedom from British rule by establishing a direct link between the discrimination faced by people of Indian origin in various British colonies and India's lack of sovereignty. In that sense, Indians abroad had indeed been an essential part of the development of Indian nationalism. Given this context, it was commonsensical to expect that once independence was attained, the Indian state would actively protect the rights of Indians abroad, especially in former British colonies. But the policies adopted by postcolonial India seemed to consciously go against these expectations, with Nehru's government offering not protection, but rather the choice of Indian citizenship to Indians abroad and somewhat stern, paternalistic advice to those who chose not to accept Indian citizenship. In other words, far from acknowledging the diaspora as India's domestic constituency residing abroad, the independent Indian state deliberately turned its back on the expansive transnationalism that prevailed prior to independence. Instead, it systematically embraced the idea of a bounded nation that was territorially congruent with the limits of the state's authority.[3] Why did the postindependence Indian state go against expectations and distance itself from the Indian diaspora? More importantly, how do we make sense of these counterintuitive state practices, in terms of the contemporary production of the Indian domestic abroad? It is these questions that form the central concern of this and the following two chapters.

This chapter sets up the puzzle of independent India's relationship with the Indians abroad. It begins by putting into focus the processes of early emigration from British India and the development of the relationship between the emerging Indian nationalist movement and the groups hailed as the Indians abroad. In doing so, it illustrates three important aspects of the broader theoretical argument of the book. First, it highlights the crucial role of the state (in this case, the colonial state) in creating and sustaining diasporas. Second, it shows that these state actions make sense only if we take into account the logic of capitalist developments. Finally, it illustrates the politically contingent, historically produced relationship between nation and state, between political belonging and a definite territory. The processes of imagining the Indian nation, particularly in a form that challenged the legitimacy of the colonial state, required the existence and participation of the Indians abroad. As leaders of the Indian nationalist movement themselves acknowledged, the Indian diaspora was crucial for the development of nationalist consciousness. To that extent, even prior to the establishment of the postcolonial Indian state, India was imagined as a transnational nation. Despite this, however, as the second part of the chapter reveals, the moment of independence marked a definite closing in of the boundaries of the nation and a distancing of the state from the concerns of the Indians abroad. The chapter concludes by arguing that to make sense of this dramatic turnaround and its connections to the contemporary production of the Indian domestic abroad, we need to begin by analyzing the political struggles that were productive of the specific set of relationships between nation and state in modern India.

I. The "Indians" Abroad

Despite the fact that over 60% of the population even wants for minimum necessities, the migratory instinct is practically non-existent among the Indian peasantry, free emigration beyond the seas being unthinkable.[4]

When Nehru made his declaration regarding Indians abroad in the parliament, it was patently clear to both him and his audience that the subjects he was referring to were the persons of Indian origin, numbering more than 4 million, living primarily in former British colonies around the world.[5] A significant percentage of this population consisted of members of the Indian peasantry and business communities. However, as sociologist Lanka Sundaram notes in an almost bemused tone, these social groups were not really known for their "migratory instincts." Despite this, by 1933 (when Sundaram wrote his account of "Indians Overseas") their total number had already surpassed 2.5 million.[6] Given that the migration of Indians in the late nineteenth century and early twentieth century was hampered not only by the social limits on their imagination but also by the material and social costs of traveling overseas, how do we make sense of the emergence of a dispersed and fairly large group of Indians abroad? Answering this question requires a closer look at a specific event that has been justifiably regarded as an important and progressive step in the history of Western civilization.

In 1833, the British Parliament passed the Act of Abolition, banning slavery across the British Empire. France followed suit in 1849.[7] The end of this institutionalized supply of cheap labor required the colonial powers to look elsewhere to meet the needs of both colonial settlers and metropolitan capital.[8] In 1859, the governor of the South African province of Natal made an urgent appeal to the Government of India for a shipment of Indian peasants who could be absorbed into the local population. In response to the request, British authorities sent a group of 342 Indians on board the S.S. Truro, which arrived in Durban on November 16, 1860.[9] Thus began the story of modern Indian emigration that was initially "assisted" by the colonial state.[10] The nature of this assistance can be found in the series of emigration acts beginning in 1842,[11] along with the various conventions with France (1861), Denmark (1863), and Holland (1870) that permitted the supply of indentured Indian labor not only to the various British colonies but also to those of other European powers. Legalizing the system of indenture basically meant that the state oversaw supplying cheap Indian labor that was bound by contract to work in the plantations owned by settlers all across various European empires.

In a dispatch of May 1877 to the secretary of state for India, the policy of the British Indian government with regard to emigration was described as "that of seeing fairplay between the parties to a commercial transaction, whilst altogether abstaining from the bargain."[12] This statement, of course, overlooked the complicity of the colonial government of India in procuring the required labor for colonial plantations in return for annual subsidies as in the case of the £10,000 paid to it by the Natal authorities.[13] The role of the colonial government as an impartial overseer, who facilitated but did not necessarily encourage emigration, was institutionalized through specific practices. The government appointed "persons of approved character" to conduct the oversight of emigration on its behalf. These agents then selected recruiters whose appointments had to be approved by the Government Protector of Emigrants.[14] The recruiters had the task of "persuading" people to emigrate. Once persuaded, the emigrants were taken to local magistrates, who would record the transaction. They were then moved to licensed collection houses in the port towns of Calcutta, Madras, and Bombay, where they would live under the watchful eyes of the migration agents until licensed ships carried them to their destinations. The licensing of the ships to ensure that "they are equipped in every respect with what is needed to ensure the safety of the passengers on their long voyage" marked the end of the colonial government's direct involvement in the transaction.[15]

Contrary to the description of bureaucratic controls and governmental impartiality in the dispatch, the colonial state did play a very critical role in shaping the character and direction of Indian emigration. While rules existed on paper, they were bent with impunity whenever there was need for labor on the plantations. Furthermore, the official end of the government's direct involvement once the ships filled with emigrants left Indian shores only meant that plantation owners and managers could violate the contracts without fear of governmental reprisals. The peculiar character of Indian migrant labor in Malaya provides a good illustration of both the complicity and the hands-off attitude of the imperial government with regard to early emigration.

Unlike the more plausibly voluntary Chinese migration to Malaya (and Southeast Asia in general), the migration of Indian labor was planned and executed by the colonial authorities with a view to aiding British manufacturers by providing a cheap source of raw materials and potential markets and also keeping a check on the growing Chinese population. Colonial migration thus was tailored to satisfy the demands of British capital (as it was invested primarily in the plantations), a process that transformed the very structure of Malayan society. The colonial state very consciously chose the migrants from the South Indian untouchable/Adi Dravida castes—65 percent of the total migration during the colonial period was from these groups—as it deemed it far easier to convince the untouchables to move away from the places where they were subjected to caste oppression.[16] The very nature of the indenture system (and its variants, the Kangani and Maistry systems) ensured that wherever they were sent—be it the West Indies, Natal, Mauritius, Burma, Fiji, Ceylon, or Malaya—laborers from India were the subject of systemic oppression.

As state complicity in perpetuating and maintaining various systems of recruitment became more obvious, the image of the colonial state as a distant, though fundamentally benevolent, structure of authority became more than a bit frayed. It was at this juncture that eminent political activists like Gopal Krishna Gokhale, and C. F. Andrews took up the cause of the emigrants. Popularizing tales of the miserable plight of the Indian laborers in various public fora around the country, they occasionally and temporarily succeeded in pressuring the government to ban recruitment[17] and appoint commissions to investigate the charges against the plantation and mill owners.[18] One such commission appointed to look into the abuses taking place in British Guiana (1871) reported that "immigration, as far as the coolies are concerned, has failed to fulfill its purpose, if after being acclimatized, after learning their work and paying for their passage out, they must still be brought under indenture after indenture, and not encouraged to take their station in the country as free labourers."[19]

The consequences of these commissions and the solutions regarding the problems of emigrant labor that emerged from their findings created a piquant situation. The colonial state in India, reconstructed as a paternal structure of authority, fought battles on behalf of emigrant labor and often became entangled in tense relations with not only other dominions but also the Colonial Office in London.

One of the solutions proposed for resolving many of the problems involving early Indian emigrant labor was to provide them with the right to own land and work as freed men once they had served their indenture. This step initially found favor in crown colonies, such as Natal, that were suffering from a severe lack of labor. However, as the laborers began settling in the land as free men, white plantation owners began petitioning the colonial office to ensure that they were forced to return to India once they had served their indenture.[20] The rejection of this petition led to the proposal of several innovative measures to ensure either that the emigrant laborers were forced to leave the colony after having served their indenture or that they continued to live there under conditions of abject poverty and humiliation. Among these measures were the attempted extension of the indenture so that the contracts would officially end only after the laborer returned to India, the imposition of a residence tax on those who chose to remain behind, and a ban prohibiting employers from hiring emigrants who might show an inclination to stay back. For instance, in 1893, the Government of Natal proposed that all "free Indians" should pay a special annual tax of £25, which was beyond most workers' means. Under pressure from the viceroy of India, Lord Elgin, this amount was reduced to £3 (a sum that could be earned by a worker in six months) but was imposed not only on the male laborer but also on his wife and children over the age of sixteen. Furthermore, all ex-indentured laborers were supposed to buy a special license for £25 in order to work, and all fresh immigrants were supposed to pass a European language test. In case these measures were not sufficient to stem the tide of Indian immigration, in 1894 the Natal authorities also introduced a bill disenfranchising all "Asiatics" whose names were not already on the voters' lists.

Mohandas Gandhi, then a young Indian lawyer in Durban, came to know about the disenfranchisement bill at a farewell party thrown on the eve of his departure to India. Postponing his return, he organized the first ever resistance by Indians abroad against a discriminatory regime. As a result of Gandhi's intervention, the 1894 bill was disallowed by the secretary of state for the colonies, who declared that "the British Empire could not agree to the establishment of a colour bar in its legislations."[21] The success of the movement led by Gandhi in South Africa was temporary, as the Natal authorities soon after passed a new bill that disqualified Indians on unspecified grounds. However, it served the important purpose of bringing the horrors of indenture, as well the institutionalization of discrimination in places like Natal, to the attention of the Indian public. Gopal Krishna Gokhale, the well-known moderate nationalist leader, actually visited South Africa and on his return publicized the conditions of abject misery under which Indian emigrants were forced to live, highlighting the fact that to pay for the licenses needed to work, Indian women were often driven to prostitution. The resulting outcry in India led the British Indian government to prohibit emigration of indentured labor to Natal in 1911.[22] Over the next ten years, the system of indenture gradually came to an end as it was banned in Mauritius (1915), the West Indian islands (1917), and Fiji (1920).

The Nationalist Movement and the Imagining of "India"

In the early decades of the twentieth century, the demands made by Indian leaders on behalf of their expatriate countrymen fit well within the liberal discourse of the moderate nationalists. The colonial state was still seen as a legitimate source of authority that would ensure better treatment of Indians abroad, especially unskilled laborers, through institutions such as its legal systems and bureaucracy. Hence, initially the emphasis was to bring to the attention of the state a particular case and maintain constant pressure by building up public opinion until the government machinery sprang into action, setting up committees to investigate the alleged incident, and suggesting measures for redress. This faith seemed to be justified by the attitude of various emigration committees that recommended the suspension of labor emigration to places like Mauritius, Natal, and the West Indian islands on the basis of constant violations of the rights of emigrants.[23]

In addition to the illiterate bonded laborers, the voluntary middle-class emigrants faced their own problems of institutionalized discrimination and often open hostility from the white communities. This discrimination put into question their livelihoods and their continued survival in their places of settlement. In support of their cause, Indian nationalists added their voices to the demands to end racial inequality. However, these demands were not based on any claims of Indian independence. Rather, moderate leaders demanded that Indians be treated on par with their British "compatriots," for they were all citizens of the same empire and, as such, entitled to the same rights. An extension of this argument to the case of Indians abroad implied that it made perfect sense for the government of India to demand in the imperial conference of 1917 that "British Asiatics, that is Asiatics of British nationality, should at least not be less favourably treated than other Asiatics."[24] Similarly, when the Union of South Africa made continuous demands that descendants of the formerly indentured Indian laborers be repatriated to India, the government of India pointed out the implausibility of those demands on the grounds that the Indians were an important part of the fabric of South African society and that they had certain rights as *British* citizens:

Nearly 63 per cent of the resident Indian population was born in South Africa, and the majority of that element regard the country as their home, and hardly likely to return to India unless compelled to do so. We question whether this Indian population…can justly be regarded as an alien element. [The] bulk of them have settled in Union for long periods, have in their own respective spheres contributed to the development of the country, and proved their value to the other elements in the population. They have acquired vested interests and established manifold associations, severance of which will be a source of distress to many and great economic dislocation and loss. As British subjects in South Africa they, we submit, are entitled to look upon the Union Government as the trustee of their interests equally with other elements of the population.[25]

The support of the colonial government of India for the cause of the emigrant Indian populations is not hard to understand. Its leading lights (the viceroy, Lord Chelmsford, and the secretary of state for India, Lord Montagu) were among the small section in the British ruling elite who, in the aftermath of the Bolshevik Revolution, argued that unless the contributions of subject nations like India to the war effort were recognized and rewarded, the potential of a revolutionary movement would be greatly increased. Furthermore, the "moderates" of the Indian national movement were recognized as their natural allies in attempts to defend the empire. Unlike the revolutionaries (also known as the "extremists"), the moderates still believed not only in the possibility of equality and justice within the empire but also in the empire itself.[26]

This argument, most forcefully articulated by Montagu, was lost neither on the new viceroy of India, Lord Reading, nor on the British prime minister, Lloyd George, when the demand for equality was made for the first time by an Indian, Srinivasa Sastri, at the imperial conference of 1921. When it seemed as though the South African opposition to equal treatment of Indians might carry the day, Lloyd George stepped in to strongly advocate the Indian position. Entreating his fellow delegates to do justice to the Indian cause, the British premier warned that sending the Indian delegates back with empty hands might create a situation "which would make India simply flow with the blood of men who only a few years ago were willing to give that blood for the Empire and the flag under which they live."[27] Lending weight to the plea was an assurance that adopting the Indian resolution would not commit any of the dominions to any action. Despite this, South Africa registered its disagreement with even a nominal acceptance of Indian claims to equality.

Soon after this conference, a new turn of events cast a further shadow on the aspirations of the moderate nationalist leaders. Five decades of assisted emigration, supplemented by the voluntary migration of certain business communities, had led to a substantial increase in the number of overseas Indian communities in East Africa, as well as a change in their profile. While legal provisions had been put in to enable some sections of the emigrant population to transition from indentured labor status to that of free men, they faced strong opposition to their presence from the local population—usually the white communities.[28] This opposition became very obvious in East Africa, where Indian emigrants actually had played an important role in sustaining imperial rule until the end of World War I. In part, this supportive role was acknowledged in a proposal during the Treaty of Versailles negotiations to offer ex-German possessions in East Africa (Tanganyika) as a special preserve for Indian colonization, especially for demobilized sepoys.[29] Rather than strengthening the position of the Indian community, this proposal (which in any case came to naught) stirred up trouble for Indians in Kenya and elsewhere. The European community in East Africa strongly resisted any attempts to provide land rights to the Indians on the grounds that such measures would lead to the disenfranchisement of the native Africans. As the Convention of White Associations in East Africa declared: "In the fair name of Christianity,... [we] would have the world believe that these colonies were held by them as a trust for the native inhabitants and that the presence of the Indians in the country constitutes a menace to the African race in the land of their birth."[30] On the basis of this claim, the white settlers demanded further restrictions on Indian emigration. In response to their demands, the Foreign Office in London published a White Paper in 1923, the Devonshire Declaration, which held that "the interests of the African natives must be paramount... if and when those interests of the immigrant races should conflict, the former should prevail."[31]

The Devonshire Declaration revealed the limits of the liberal discourse of equality within the empire to even the most committed moderate leaders. It drove home the fact that, even as imperial conferences were being held regularly, laws against Indian emigrants (as well Indian emigration) continued to be enacted with impunity around the Commonwealth. Moreover, it became quite evident that the problem was not just that some British citizens were more equal than others, but that the rights of some citizens were contingent on the exploitation of others. Even moderate leaders realized that legislative acts such as the Devonshire Declaration of 1923, which purported to uphold the rights of native Africans against those of Indian settlers, were mere smokescreens for preserving white dominance. In this context, claims regarding the possibility of Indian progress as part of the British Empire began to sound quite hollow. Following the blow dealt to the hopes of Indians in Kenya by the imperial rulers in 1923, the Indian National Congress for the first time introduced a resolution advocating separation from the empire. Underlying the resolution was an argument that would frame the emerging movement for independence. The colonial state had neither the desire nor the ability to safeguard the rights and the resources of the Indian nation. Part of what enabled the nationalists to make this argument was the connections that had been established with the political struggles of the Indian emigrant communities and the hailing of these communities as Indians abroad.

Unlike the Indian immigrants in Southeast Asia or the West Indies, the settlers in East and South Africa included middle-class Indians who were ready and willing to make vocal demands for equality with white settlers. It was in the process of making those demands that the overseas Indian communities established a connection with the mainland nationalists, who saw in their plight a reflection of the larger problems faced by the Indian nation. In South Africa, Mohandas Gandhi, who had initially supported the British during the course of the Anglo-Boer wars, fought for the rights of the Indian community by fashioning a unique form of civil disobedience.[32] The immediate provocation was the new British ordinance that demanded that all Indians in Transvaal (including women) obtain certificates of registration containing descriptions of body marks and fingerprints, and also that they carry such certificates on their person at all times. Failure to produce these certificates on demand could result in imprisonment, fines, or even deportation. In 1908, as a response to this ordinance, as well as the Transvaal Immigrants Restriction Bill, Gandhi organized the first *satyagraha*—a nonviolent civil disobedience movement that involved groups of Indians courting arrest by crossing the Natal-Transvaal border, hawking without licenses, and refusing to register. Though in this particular case it failed to produce the desired outcome, this method was used more successfully by Gandhi in 1913, when he called for a miners' strike in Natal to oppose a new rule invalidating all Indian marriages and imposing a £3 annual license fee on all Indian indentured laborers who had settled in South Africa.[33] During the period of his leadership of the South African Indian struggle, Gandhi visited India twice, addressing the Indian National Congress (INC), the Chambers of Commerce, and other organizations and drawing their attention to the appalling conditions faced by their fellow countrymen not just in South Africa but around the world.

Soon after World War I, Indian expatriates in East Africa set up the East African Indian National Congress, drew up a list of grievances that were presented to the local and imperial governments, and sent delegations to establish contact with the INC. In India, the cause of the East Africans found support with INC stalwarts like Gopal Krishna Gokhale and Sarojini Naidu, who reiterated the demand for an Indian protectorate in Tanganyika.[34] In the decades that followed, Indian leaders consistently raised the issue of the sufferings of Indians abroad at annual imperial conferences, as well as at meetings of the League of Nations.[35] The main issue was the racist nature of immigration policies that were being put in place in the former colonies to restrict Indian migration, be it in Canada or

South Africa.[36] To show solidarity with their fellow countrymen, as well as to keep up the pressure on the government of India to take a firm stand against institutionalized discrimination in the colonies and Commonwealth, the INC also sent a series of missions to South Africa, Fiji, Malaya, Ceylon, Kenya, and Zanzibar.[37] These missions not only served the purpose of creating associations that were tied to the INC, as in the case of Malaya,[38] but also underlined the INC's conviction that the problems faced by the Indian nation were not restricted to the territory of mainland India.

While the indenture system and its variants had ensured that the early emigrants completely depended on the goodwill of the colonial state for their very survival, the situation had not really improved, even as assisted emigration was giving way to voluntary migration by members of the middle class. Wherever they went, emigrants from India were facing institutionalized and often brutal discrimination. Although members of various emigrant communities struggled against constant indignities and often succeeded in making small political gains, even these could be overturned at the will of the colonial ruling classes. Equality, which the moderate nationalist leaders believed should have been the right of the emigrants, had become a matter of intense political struggle in which the colonial state played an ambiguous role at best. As such, the emigrants embodied the plight of the Indian nation—they were, in every sense of the term, *Indians* abroad. As the nationalists argued:

> Wherever they may be and howsoever difficult their existence, they constitute little bits of India and take to the lands where they live the culture and the religion, the traditions and the ways of their great motherland. Neither the passage of centuries nor in some cases, the complete break with the past, has made them forget the glory that was India.[39]

Making a direct connection between the problems faced by the emigrant communities and British rule, they further claimed that Indians abroad faced institutionalized discrimination because India was a colonized nation and could not really respond to the needs of her people. Writing about the Canadian reactions to the moderate successes of the Indian emigrants, Lanka Sundaram remarked in 1933: "The fact that India is a subject country has a lot to do with the recrudescence of race prejudice, and since the people of India cannot be expected to protest even if they were hit under the belt, the Canadians scored numerous technical triumphs."[40] The colonial state was not representative of the "people of India" and did not particularly care if they "were hit under the belt." This was why other countries could, with impunity, enact discriminatory legislative acts against Indians abroad. The contrast that was usually drawn was with China. Some nationalists argued that prior to the Japanese occupation, even though China was not necessarily regarded as a great power, it could still afford to look after the interests of its citizens because of its independence. The impact of being a subject nation could be seen even as the colonial state tried to provide institutional spaces to address the plight of Indians abroad. In 1936, the government of India established a separate Department of Overseas Indians that was headed by Dr. N. B. Khare. However, the department could do little for Indians abroad, other than making sure that the imperial government was aware of their problems. Further limiting its ability to function was the express need to ensure cooperation between various parts of the empire and the Commonwealth during the course of World War II. Consequently, the government of India remained a mute spectator as the Union of South Africa continued to enact rules such as the Pegging Act of 1943, which sought to restrict the amount of land that could be purchased by Indians in Transvaal and Natal. As a result of this act, 24,000 Indians would be confined to 200 acres, and 7,000 whites would have mores than 5,000 acres at their disposal.[41] Referring to this demeaning legislation, Dr. Khare remarked that had "India been independent, she would have considered it a *casus belli* against South Africa."[42] Public outrage in India reached a peak with the Council of the Imperial Indian Citizenship Association suggesting openly that since appeasement of the South African government time and again had resulted in only greater hardships for Indians, it was time that India took steps to "safeguard her honour abroad."[43] However, even after conveying the dismay of the Indian people, the Government of India did not take any action. The reason for this inaction, the nationalists argued, was that the government was not truly representative of the Indian people. After all, "since the British Government [was] unwilling to concede Indians absolute freedom…in their own country, they can hardly be expected to prove themselves vigorous champions of Indian rights in other countries."[44] Colonial subjugation thus came to be regarded as the main reason for not only government inaction but also the manner in which the members of the diaspora were looked upon in their new places of settlement. As long as India was to remain a colony, Indians, wherever they lived, would be treated as second-class citizens.

II. The Moment of Independence

India's uniqueness as a nation required an independent nation-state…no alien power could possibly represent and fulfill the aspirations of the Indians as a people.[45]

Soon after its formation in September 1946, Jawaharlal Nehru's interim government announced its presence on the international stage by confronting South Africa in the United Nations.[46] The immediate reason for this confrontation was the latest anti-Indian measure announced by the Union of South Africa. In January 1946, Marshall Smuts announced the Asiatic Land Tenure and Indian Representation Act, which not only restricted housing even more than the Pegging Act but also ensured that Indians were unable to represent themselves in any of the legislatures.[47] In retaliation, the Viceroy's Council decided unanimously to terminate India's trade agreement with South Africa, the first ever imposition of any form of economic sanctions against the apartheid regime. When that measure failed to induce the South Africans to agree to a conference to discuss the issue, the Indian government threatened to refer the matter to the newly established United Nations (UN). The stage therefore had been well prepared for the first nationalist government to act on behalf of its "subjects" living abroad. Nehru, the member in charge of External Affairs and Commonwealth Relations, appointed Vijayalakshmi Pandit to lead the Indian delegation to the UN. Despite South African attempts to remove the Indian complaint from the UN agenda on the grounds that it was a domestic issue, the UN General Assembly not only discussed the matter but also resolved that any issue concerning South African Indians had to be a subject of discussion between India and South Africa. Insofar as the future of India's relationship with Indians abroad was concerned, the UN affair of 1946 indicated two things: first, the Indian government would not hesitate to use all available means to protect the interests of overseas Indians,[48] and second, while not yet a great power, India was already emerging as an actor "whose potential contribution to the Commonwealth [and the UN] will be great, and her potential nuisance value will be correspondingly high."[49]

In an act that seemed to further underline the nationalist commitment to the cause of the larger nation, the Government of India wrote to the India Office requesting permission to send missions and appoint agents to those colonies with a sizable Indian population, namely, East Africa, British West Indies, Fiji, and Mauritius. The India Office did not welcome the request, arguing that:

> The danger of Indian representatives or agents is, of course, that their appointment in colonies where there is a substantial Indian population would be liable to encourage the local Indians to think of themselves as a self-contained national community and to discourage the process of assimilation, which we have been trying to foster in the Colonies.[50]

Ultimately, the Colonial Office's opposition was overcome by the arguments of the Indian viceroy, Lord Mountbatten, who pointed out that negotiations for Indian independence were well under way at that juncture, and all assurances of cooperation from the British government on colonial matters would be welcome. By July 1947, Nehru was informed that Great Britain supported the appointment of Indian agents in certain colonies, at least in principle, as long as the Government of India undertook to instruct its agents not to encourage separatist tendencies among the Indians settled in the colonies.

Within a month, on August 15, 1947, India became formally independent. Indian nationalists had always emphasized that no alien power could truly "fulfill the aspirations" of the Indian people. Now that state power had been obtained, the newly independent India could focus on representing the interests of "its" people. Prior to independence, the nationalists had argued that the colonized status of the Indian nation was the main reason for the sorry plight of Indians abroad. Post-1947, it seemed intuitive to expect that the aspirations of the Indians abroad would at last be represented by an independent India, for were they not part of the Indian people? Furthermore, the contributions of Indians abroad to the independence struggle could not be easily forgotten. As Congress President Pattabhi Sitaramayya had pointed out, the path to Indian independence was in a way shaped by the sufferings and the actions of Indians abroad.[51] To that extent, the newly independent Indian state owed them a serious debt. As India moved into the first decade of its independence, there were many opportunities to repay the debt.

In 1947, there were nearly 4 million people in the Commonwealth who emigrated from undivided India, and the practice of describing them as "Indians abroad" largely continued.[52] This practice was further reinforced by the new Indian government's eagerness to strengthen bonds with the overseas communities, as it picked up where the interim government had left off. Of the Indians abroad, the largest communities, numbering around 750,000, were in Ceylon and Burma (see table 3.1). A brief survey of the problems faced by these communities will give us an idea of the issues that would test the new Indian nation-state's commitment to the cause of its diaspora.

On January 4, 1948, Burma became independent. Even before actual independence was declared, relations between the Indian community (roughly 4 percent of the total population) and the local Burmese population had been quite tense. Indians in Burma were laborers (both plantation and urban, the latter commonly known as "coolies"), clerks, businessmen, and railway workers, whose migration had been facilitated by the fact that Burma was an Indian province until 1937.[53] For the most part, Indian labor took the jobs that were considered too menial by the Burmese. However, as the economy slowed down and jobs became scarcer, the nationalist movement in Burma took on an anti-Indian tinge. Separation from India began to be seen as the first step toward independence. The first major manifestation of this sentiment was the anti-Indian riots of 1930, which resulted in more than 30,000 Indians fleeing Rangoon. The next came soon after Burma was separated from India in 1937. The Burmese nationalist politician U Saw used the publication of a book that criticized Buddhism to provoke another anti-Indian riot in 1938.[54] This time, more than 11,000 Indians were repatriated to

Table 3.1.   Overseas Indians at a Glance: 1948

Country	Number of Persons of Indian Origin*	As Percentage of Total Population
Ceylon	750,000	NA
Burma	750,000	4%
Malaya	520,000	11%
South Africa	285,260	3%
Mauritius	265,000	65%
Trinidad	195,747	35%
British Guiana	163,434	42%
Fiji	125,000	47%

The Indian community in East Africa numbered more than 175,000 but constituted a very small, though growing, section of the population.
* All figures except those for Fiji are based on the 1946 census. The figures for Fiji are based on the 1948 census.
Source: Tinker, Separate and Unequal, 313–314.

India after having lost all their material goods. Interestingly, even while some Burmese nationalist politicians were organizing "Indian bashing groups,"[55] others like Aung San were looking toward the Indian national movement as a prototype for the Burmese struggle and welcoming Nehru to Rangoon.

South Asia became yet another battleground for World War II with the Japanese invasion of Burma in 1942, which resulted in a large number of evacuees, mostly of Indian origin, fleeing to India. With the end of the war, most of these wartime refugees were looking forward to returning to their homes and businesses in Burma. However, they faced certain structural difficulties. The nationalist interim government led by the same Aung San who had welcomed Nehru to Rangoon as the "leader of millions" passed the Emergency Immigration Act of 1947, which restricted the reentry of the evacuees by placing the Indians in the category of "foreigners."[56] This categorization and the kind of Burmese nationalism it reflected had a serious effect on the political and socioeconomic status of Indians in Burma, even as India awoke to independence.

Indians in Ceylon were not necessarily in a better situation. From the early nineteenth century onward, there had been a steady migration of laborers (especially from South India) to the tea, coffee, and rubber plantations in Ceylon.[57] The descendants of these laborers, along with newer migrants, were the "Indian" community in Ceylon at the time of Indian independence. The condition of the laborers who were bound to the Kangani and the local middlemen had been a source of concern for the Indian government even prior to independence. Despite the appointment of an agent to look after the welfare of the Indian workers in Ceylon in 1924, their material conditions continued to deteriorate. However, the issue that was becoming more critical was the controversy surrounding the political status of the Indians in Ceylon. Until the mid-1920s, the nature of the forty-nine-member legislative council ensured that the Indians, who had merely two representatives, did not really play a role in Ceylon politics. Things, however, began to change when the Donoughmore Commission of 1928 released a report recommending the extension of the franchise to Indians who had been living in Ceylon for at least five years. The proposed admission of the Indian coolies to the general electorate created an unforeseen furor among the Sinhalese leaders, who argued that this would put Ceylonese politics at the mercy of the nationalists in mainland India who could sway the Indian community. Furthermore, the Indian immigrants were not *Ceylonese*. Don Senanayake, a young Sinhala politician who was to later play an important role in Sri Lankan politics, articulated this point most forcefully: "We are told that if anyone of us went to England it would not be difficult for him to get the vote. But I wonder what the people of England would say if every year, hundreds of thousands of people were recruited from abroad into England."[58] Responding to the demands of the Sinhalese, the governor recommended that to qualify for the vote, Indians should either fulfill the existing property or literacy qualifications or obtain a certificate of permanent residency. The former criterion automatically ruled out the plantation laborers, who were neither rich nor literate. The latter was an almost impossible demand, for obtaining permanent residency would automatically lead to the Indians losing the rights guaranteed to them under various agreements between the two governments. This move provoked a strong reaction in India. The Central Legislative Assembly not only debated the "anti-Indian" measures but also engaged in a drawn-out struggle with the Colonial Office through the India Office. Ultimately, the Ceylon governor was told that any measure that might be a detriment to the position of Indians would have to be discussed with His Majesty's Government before taking the shape of law. This episode tended only to convince Sinhalese leaders that their fears of Indian intervention were not unfounded.

As in Burma, the economic depression of the 1930s saw the strengthening of the anti-Indian lobby in Ceylon. Cheap Indian labor was seen as taking away more jobs from the indigenous population. Though the Government of India discontinued immigration to Ceylon as an official policy, in 1934 the Ceylon legislature introduced a policy of "Ceylonization" in all branches of the public services, including the employment of daily wage workers. This policy was aimed not only at stemming the tide of immigrants but also at edging out those Indians who were permanently settled in Ceylon, for the category "Ceylonese" did not even include those Indians who were born in Ceylon if their parents had not obtained a Ceylon domicile certificate at the time of birth. The expressed desire of the Ceylon government to impose this policy strictly—retrenchment of Indians and their eventual repatriation—led to the prohibition of all unskilled immigration from India in 1939. Even as Nehru visited Colombo in 1939, all discussions for a proposed round table conference to settle the issue of Indians in Ceylon fell through when the Ceylonese government refused to treat the matter as an issue of institutionalized discrimination. Matters took a turn for the worse when the Indian laborers in Ceylon formed trade unions on Nehru's advice. The plantation owners reacted by sacking the union leaders, which in turn led to a wave of strikes and violence between Indians and Ceylonese police. Ceylonese leaders used this event to underline the "alienness" of the Indian presence in their country. As Ceylon moved toward dominion status and eventual independence, the Colonial Office tried to sidestep potential problems by insisting that any issues arising out of the Indian presence in Ceylon needed to be discussed and resolved by the Indian and Ceylonese governments. However, Sinhala nationalism "seemed to have found its principal expression in fear of, and hostility to, Indians."[59] Its premise, in Senanayake's words, was that the Indian presence was a "treacherous variety [of allegiance], which gives its entire devotion to the country of origin and bestows on the country of residence mere lip-service, vilification and misrepresentation."[60] Given this context, it was not surprising that the "Indian question" remained unresolved.

In 1947, India under Nehru was immediately faced with the task of resolving the problems faced by Indians abroad. As explained in the previous section, the plight of this social group had, after all, been seen as a manifestation of the Indian nation's subservience to a foreign empire. Nationalist leaders from the 1920s onward had argued that the situation would be different once the colonial state was replaced by a *national* state. Ceylon and Burma, neighboring countries that attained independence around the same time as India, presented important test cases for the Indian government. As early as December 1947, Nehru met with Ceylonese Premier Don Senanayake to discuss the issue of the "Indian" population. At the end of the meeting, the two sides jointly presented a six-point program that was supposed to serve as the basis of an agreement. However, none of the questions about actually granting political rights to this group of people were even discussed. While the Ceylonese side held on to proof of domicile and a nine-year residence period for families as a prerequisite to granting citizenship, Nehru refused to even discuss those terms. Over the next two years, despite ongoing correspondence between the two prime ministers, Ceylon unilaterally tried to decide the fate of the Indians through a series of legislative measures.

The first of those was the Citizenship Act (No. 18, 1948), which defined the scope of Ceylonese citizenship as a form of belonging that could be claimed on the basis of indigenousness or registration. It was followed by the Indian and

Pakistani Residents Act (No. 3, 1949), which defined the process through which Indians could attain citizenship. Since the process required substantial documentation, which most of the plantation labor force did not possess, it automatically ruled out citizenship as an available option for most persons of Indian origin (PIO).[61] As a final measure, the Ceylonese government passed the Ceylon (Parliamentary Elections) Amendment Act (No. 48, 1949), which removed all voters of Indian origin from the electoral list.[62] These moves were met with strong protests from the Indian government, but little else. The Indian stand on the issue was that, though they were of Indian origin, the Indian component of the Ceylonese population was essentially made up of citizens of Ceylon. Most were born there, and even those who had moved to Ceylon from India had gone there to establish a new life and not as temporary immigrants. All had contributed enormously to the development of the Ceylonese economy. Hence, to deny them citizenship on the grounds that they had come to the island merely for temporary employment "would be contrary to the facts of history."[63] Based on these very "facts of history," India refused to discuss Ceylonese proposals to repatriate persons of Indian origin, leading to a standoff that continued to plague Indo-Sri Lankan relations till the 1980s.[64]

The impasse over Indians abroad was not restricted to Ceylon. Even though anti-Indian sentiment had been gathering force prior to Burmese independence in January 1948, the Constituent Assembly that met in 1947 made one final attempt to deal with the "Indian issue." It provided citizenship to those Indians who could claim at least one "indigenous grandparent," had resided in Burma for at least eight years since 1932 or 1937, and intended to become permanent residents of Burma. After independence, this provision was slightly altered by the Burmese constitution, which provided automatic citizenship to all those who claimed indigenous origin but demanded a formal application for citizenship, coupled with a stated desire for permanent residency and renunciation of all other citizenship, from the nonindigenous (Indian and Chinese) population.[65] Soon after, the government declared its intention of reducing the number of governmental positions that could be held by nonnational Indians and reducing the granting of import licenses to Indian firms, so that Burmese firms might have an advantage in various sectors of the economy. The actions of the Burmese government took on added urgency because of emerging threats of rebellion. Making common cause with the Communists, the government announced a "Leftist Unity Plan." In keeping with the plan, the Burmese parliament passed the Burma Land Nationalisation Act, which authorized the government to appropriate all capitalist interests, including landed estates. The most obvious target of this measure was a group that originated in India, the Chettiars, who owned more than 70 million acres of land in Burma.[66] Realizing that the Burmese government's actions were aimed mostly at persons of Indian origin, Sir G. S. Bajpai strongly advised Nehru to exert pressure on the Burmese government to protect the interests of the Indian capitalists.[67] Going against this counsel, Nehru not only refused to bring up the matter with the Burmese government but also went to the extent of assisting them with military supplies in their battle with insurgents. India's special role in helping the Burmese government consolidate its position was recognized in the Indo-Burmese Treaty of Friendship (1951), soon followed by a trade agreement.

In both Burma and Ceylon, persons of Indian origin were facing the kind of institutionalized discrimination that had so rankled Indian nationalists prior to independence. Counterintuitively, the independent Indian nation-state seemed to be doing very little to improve the lot of its "nationals" abroad. In the case of Ceylon, the desire to establish friendly relations with neighboring countries, coupled with unwillingness to entertain questions of possible repatriation at the early stages, led to the creation of a new category of "stateless persons" with no civic rights.[68] With regard to Burma, the Indian government actually turned away from an early opportunity to exert pressure on the Burmese government—a move that contributed in no small measure to the deterioration of the position of the Indian community in Burma. How do we make sense of these moves in the context of the earlier nationalist expressions of solidarity with overseas Indians and commitment to the cause of improving their lot?

The disavowal of Indians abroad by the newly independent Indian state, M. C. Lall argues, primarily stemmed from an "ideological rubric" that emphasized respect for territorial notions of sovereignty. Prior to independence, the moral bulwark provided by "Indians abroad" had helped build the case for a deterritorialized subject nation. However, after 1947 the Indians abroad no longer fit within the dominant statist discourse that emphasized the sovereign right of former colonies to govern over explicitly demarcated territories. Furthermore, the ideological commitment of the new Indian leadership to anticolonial struggles blinded them to the potential of the Indians abroad as an economic and political resource. Hence, "they were simply ignored."[69] The ideological rubric of postcolonial India did indeed shape the newly independent nation-state's relationship with the Indians abroad, but the complexities of this relationship went beyond an inability to acknowledge economic potential or a simple turning away. Strangely enough, India continued negotiations with Ceylon and Burma over decades (more so with the former), set up rehabilitation schemes for those Indians who did come back,[70] and consistently raised the issue of the treatment of Indians in places like South Africa and Fiji in fora like the UN and the Commonwealth. To that extent, the postindependence Indian state was still concerned with the status of overseas Indians, but the framework of that concern had changed with the taking over of institutionalized state power.

III. The Making of Postcolonial India

The preamble of the constitution that came into effect on January 26, 1950, declared that India was a "sovereign, secular, democratic, republic." However defined, the space of modern India could not be created through a constitutional diktat. It had to be produced through a series of state practices that made sense only in the context of particular historical-geographical experiences. The process of "coming into being" for the Indian *nation-state* was fraught with violence. "India" was born amid the bloodshed of partition, through a ripping apart of the territories of the British colony. The almost immediate border conflicts with the new neighboring state of Pakistan and the forcible integration of the former princely states made imperative the process of territorializing "India." One aspect of this process was the demarcation of the physical boundaries of the new nation-state, a task that was seen as both urgent and incomplete, given India's "creation-by-amputation."[71] The other was the spatial organization of social groups that would define the scope of the state's authority.[72] This latter task was far from easy, given that it brought to the forefront the question of not only the large groups of people who had been forcibly and violently displaced due to the partition of the subcontinent, but also those who had been forced to migrate under colonialism.[73]

Independent India's first citizenship laws came into effect with the adoption of the constitution of 1950. Coming to grips with the legacies of colonialism, the citizenship clauses of the constitution appeared to be, at first glance, fairly liberal. As Article 5 made clear, Indian citizenship could be obtained virtually by anyone who might consider himself or herself Indian, because of residence, birth, or descent.[74] Specifically addressing the question of persons of Indian origin living overseas, Article 8 of the constitution declared that any person who was born in India (or whose parents or grandparents were) as per the definition of the Government of India Act of 1935, had the right to be "deemed as a citizen of India" if he or she had been registered as a citizen by the Indian diplomatic or consular office in the country in which they were "temporarily" residing. This right, as Article 6 made clear, also applied to those who had relocated from the territories of Pakistan after August 1947. However, state practices related to the definition of who belongs to a political community always also serve as exclusionary tools.[75] Consequently, there were some exceptions to the liberal citizenship rule. Article 7 denied Indian citizenship to people born in the territories of undivided India if they had immigrated to Pakistan before March 1947. Article 9 denied citizenship to those who voluntarily acquired the citizenship of any other country. Although the laws themselves seemed to exclude only those who voluntarily chose other citizenships, there was a deeper underlying assumption about the nature of modern nation-states at work: the idea of "the nation-state as the only expression of sovereignty…with distinct territorial boundaries within which the sovereign state [represents] the nation-people."[76]

Apart from the right to decide *who* the citizens were, the sovereignty of the modern nation-state also implied the right to determine *how* the prosperity and progress of the nation-people could be ensured.[77] In fact, the latter was more of a duty. In the nationalist rendering of the economic history of India, the colonial state had failed precisely because it could not fulfill this duty.[78] During the colonial period, the state was structured to satisfy the demands of metropolitan capital and not the well-being of the nation. This pattern was fairly obvious in the history of early Indian emigration, when the demands of British plantation owners led the state to sanction the mass export of Indian labor. The struggle against colonialism therefore necessitated a different kind of state—one that would not only dismantle existing exploitative economic relations but also steer the productive forces of the nation in a manner that would promote the welfare of the people. Consequently, after 1947 the economic policy of the sovereign Indian nation-state was characterized by an emphasis on state planning and the promotion of self-reliance (*swadeshi*). This basically implied nationalization of industries, state-sponsored economic development, and cultivation of an indigenous technological base.[79] Given the nature of the Indian nationalist movement, this understanding of the role of the state and its relationship to the nation, however, went far beyond the determination of postindependence domestic economic policy.

By the time India was on the verge of attaining independence, the leadership of the Indian national movement had come to see its efforts as something larger than a limited struggle for national freedom. In one of its early resolutions after independence, the ruling Congress Party declared:

> The National Congress has, even while it was struggling for the freedom of India, associated itself with the progressive movements and the struggles for freedom in other countries. India's liberation was viewed as a part of the larger freedom of all the countries and the peoples of the world. In particular, the Congress has stood in the past for the ending of all imperialist domination and colonial exploitation of any country or people.[80]

Given this emphasis, it was not surprising that one of the main foci of Nehru's government was building an alliance among the newly independent states of Asia and Africa.[81] Nehru argued that notwithstanding the differences in specific foreign policy goals, the formerly colonized states had a common interest in ensuring true economic development and, more important, the complete end of the colonial system of rule. It was with the goal of arriving at a clear articulation of these interests that the Indian state took the lead in calling for a meeting among the leaders of newly independent states in Asia and Africa. The resulting conference that was held in Bandung, Indonesia, has drawn the somewhat desultory attention of scholars of international relations mainly because of its foundational role in the now-defunct Non-Aligned Movement.

The 1955 Bandung conference was undoubtedly a critical moment in the attempt to articulate a common Afro-Asian vision that would not be bound by the binary politics of the Cold War. But as Itty Abraham points out, this conference had an equally important role in legitimizing the very contours of the newly independent states.[82] The attempt to acknowledge critical differences in the goals and worldviews of the various state members, while arriving at a common minimal statement critiquing the continued presence of colonial rule, also served "to elevate national sovereignty to the highest level" and allowed members "to insist on being sole masters of their own domain."[83] The main effect was that state members agreed implicitly to "consign the fates of 'their' people—people who had migrated, moved, traveled—to the decisions of another state."[84]

As the declarations and practices of Nehru's government leading up to and during the Bandung conference made obvious, the foreign policy of the Indian nation-state was predicated on the principle of supporting the sovereign right of other newly independent states to decide who their citizens were and to take the steps they considered necessary to end the exploitative legacy of colonialism. Consequently, even as the government of Ceylon refused to accept persons of Indian origin (PIO) as citizens, Nehru argued that his government should focus on attempting to remove the "fear and apprehension" that Ceylon had of India—"a fear that this great and big continent of a country might overwhelm them"—for, "in the ultimate analysis, each country decides for itself who its citizens should be."[85] India, he argued, was definitely concerned about the plight of the PIO not because they were "Indian nationals"—to the contrary, they were Ceylonese—or because it was a "political dispute," but because "the welfare of a large number of human beings is involved."[86]

By contrast, the attitude toward the PIO in Burma was not even cast in the light of a "human welfare" problem. Though the Indian government claimed willingness to offer repatriation benefits to those Indians who returned from Burma, it did not consider itself obligated to make demands on behalf of the shopkeepers and landowners who were being affected by policies of nationalization. The argument that the Indian state made was that the nationalization policies were being applied without discrimination, and the PIO had no grounds to object, either as Burmese citizens or as Indian nationals.[87] To be good Burmese citizens, the onus was on the PIO to ensure that they "associated themselves as closely as possible with the interests" of the Burmese people and not become an "exploiting agency there," which in this case implied acceptance of the Burmese government's nationalization policies. If they chose instead to give up Burmese citizenship and accept Indian citizenship, then as Indian nationals, "all they could claim abroad [was] favourable alien treatment," which in turn meant that they could not expect the Indian state to take special steps to safeguard their properties.[88] Underlying both choices, however, was a particular understanding of what constituted Indianness—an understanding that went beyond a legalistic notion of citizenship.

The production of the sovereign, modern Indian nation-state called for a certain positioning of the Indians abroad as politically distant from India, unless they had adopted Indian citizenship, and more importantly, as subjects whose Indianness (even if only cultural) underscored the need for them to be "non-exploitative agents." Given the ongoing nature of this production, it is not surprising that the positioning of the Indians abroad remained a terrain for contestation. Even at a time when his brand of postcolonial (inter)nationalism was the dominant discourse, Nehru had to clarify his position by insisting that PIO citizenship in other countries would not sever India's cultural connections to them.[89] The weak gesturing toward cultural links proved less than satisfactory, as events around the world signaled greater crises for India and the PIO in the 1960s.

The surprise Chinese attack and India's humiliating defeat in the war of 1962 was seen as a great blow to Indian pride and Nehru's foreign policy.[90] The subsequent treatment of the PIO in Asia, especially in Burma, was seen as a direct reflection of government inaction and India's lowly position even among Asian nations. In an interesting echo of arguments that had been made by the nationalist leaders less than four decades earlier, opposition members declared that the plight of Indians abroad was a reflection not so much of the choice they had made in terms of citizenship, but of the Indian nation-state itself. As an opposition member declaimed rather dramatically in Parliament: "What [has the Government] been doing here? India is being kicked by Ceylon; India is being kicked by Burma; India is being kicked by Pakistan; India is being kicked by China. What are they doing there—sitting and moping?"[91] The question of what the government was doing was asked more intensely and much more frequently as events unfolded in Africa through the decade. After initiating discussions in the United Nations about the racially discriminative policies of the South African government, India continued to raise this issue at every possible international forum. However, the Indian state's interest in the matter stemmed not simply from the presence of Indian nationals in South Africa, but from its opposition to racial inequality. The government made it very clear that though there were South Africans of Indian origin, there were no *Indians* in South Africa—thus preempting any move on the part of the South African government to demand repatriation. As the struggle against apartheid intensified, the Indian government held up persons of Indian origin in South Africa as models to be emulated in the rest of Africa. Through their cooperation with the African National Congress, they embodied India's views that in "Africa, the interests of the Africans must be paramount and it is the duty of the Indians there to cooperate with them and help them to the best of their ability."[92]

However, the picture of the PIO cooperating with Africans was soon disturbed by the anti-Asian protests that broke out in newly independent countries like Kenya, Tanzania, and Uganda. In the case of Tanzania, the initial measures taken by the new government were mild forms of affirmative action—the so-called Africanization of the bureaucracy and the economy. When the matter was raised in the Indian parliament, the government, not surprisingly, pleaded its inability to do much, on the grounds that it recognized "the sovereign right of an independent state to enact measures concerning ownership of property, within its limits."[93] This argument became harder to apply in the case of Kenya, where African leaders seemed to embrace President Jomo Kenyatta's exhortation to the PIO to just "Pack up and Go." Not quite the colonizers, but never quite identifying themselves with the Africans, the position of the PIO in Kenya had always been an ambiguous one. This had been exploited by the white settlers, who in their representations to the imperial authorities during the early decades of the twentieth century had always portrayed the Indian presence as detrimental to African interests.[94] Insofar as the anticolonial resistance movement of the 1950s was concerned, this assertion was highly credible, especially in the context of the alliance between sections of the Indian community and the British during the course of the Mau Mau rebellion. Soon after Kenyan independence in 1963, relations between the PIO and African Kenyans further deteriorated, as more than 80,000 PIO opted for British citizenship, compared with the 30,000 who chose to officially become Kenyan. Anti-Indian sentiments manifested themselves not only through policies of "Kenyanization" but also through riots, toward which the new Kenyan government turned a blind eye. Given these conditions, it was not surprising that a large percentage of the PIO were forced to "pack up and go." This was the context for a series of stormy debates about the nature of the Indian nation-state.

In one of the earliest discussions on the African question, opposition members argued that the goodwill and prestige that had been associated with India because of its leadership in the struggle against colonialism had worn off. The treatment of the PIO in East Africa reflected this loss of prestige.[95] The Indian government, they further argued, had made a big mistake by distancing itself from the PIO on the basis of notions of citizenship, which though acceptable in "legalistic terms" was a problem in the context of "Indian nationhood." Not treating the PIO as part of the nation had projected an image of India as neither wanting nor caring about people who were originally Indians. This was detrimental

to both India and the Indians abroad. Contrary to the current government position, some members of parliament argued that "the image we should present to
every country in the world is that every Indian, even if he has accepted some
other nationality, is rooted in the culture, the soil and in the traditions of India,
and that he is our brother."[96] Translated into state practice, this position would
imply that the Ministry of External Affairs would take care of all *Indians*, regardless of their citizenship. This in turn would create a stronger India, not only
through shoring up its overseas image but also by creating bonds between all
Indians. The latter was a particularly urgent task in the light of the divisive effects
of the Indian government's emphasis on presenting the PIO in South Africa as
models to be emulated by other communities.[97]

In responding to this attack, the Congress government found an ally in the
Communist Party of India (Marxist). The CPI(M) stalwart, Indrajit Gupta, rose
to the occasion by insisting that members of an *Indian* parliament should not
be exercised over policies of "Africanization." India itself had rightly embraced
policies of nationalization soon after independence. The newly independent
African countries were "backward, undeveloped, poverty-stricken and much less
mature than India on the eve of her independence." Under these conditions,
wanting to "Africanize" state institutional structures was a "healthy national sentiment." Furthermore, the Indians who were being affected by these measures
were the "economically better-off section" who had openly sided against the
Africans (and with the British) during the struggle for independence and,
through their actions, threatened to destabilize the newly independent African
states.[98] On the eve of independence, these were the people who had queued up
outside the British Embassy to acquire British citizenship—not Indian or of the
countries where they resided. Hence, they had no right to look to India for help.

Bolstered by this support, the government's case was made through a statement that had been tabled by Lakshmi Menon, the minister of state for external
affairs. Refuting the argument that India needed to change its position vis-à-vis
Indians abroad, the minister argued that those who were being forced to leave
the newly independent African states had brought their troubles on themselves.
Going against the long-standing advice of the Indian government, the Indians in
Africa had never identified with the Africans. They had "spent their lives in the
pursuit of wealth, were not progressive and were completely devoid of the *kind of
feelings that free India stood for.*" This debate is important for several reasons. For
one, it exemplifies the kind of political contestations that became more common
in the next two decades. More importantly, it also reveals the way in which the
positioning of the Indians abroad helped articulate and legitimize "what free
India stood for."

The main opposition demand was, at this juncture, an acknowledgment of
the responsibility of the Indian nation-state toward the Indians abroad. While

seemingly driven by concern for the Indians abroad, the more fundamental issue at stake was the position of India. For those who demanded a change in the state policy, the maltreatment of Indians abroad was a manifestation of the "corrosion" of India's prestige and position in the world. In and through its inaction on behalf of its own "nation-people," independent India was being perceived as a weak actor—an actor who was unable to act even when it was "kicked around" by everyone else. Accepting the responsibility for "every Indian" regardless of nationality, therefore, was a necessary step in reasserting the strength and vitality of the Indian nation-state.

Supporters of the government's policy, however, argued that India stood for certain principles—to fight against colonization, to challenge all forms of exploitative socioeconomic relations, and to uphold the right of each country (especially the poorer ones) to nationalize state institutions during these battles. The PIO who were suffering in places like Burma and East Africa were the kind who had lived their lives contrary to these principles: they were landowners, shopkeepers, and middle- to upper-class bureaucrats who, at least in the East African case, had aligned themselves with the colonizers. Supporting them in ways that were not already institutionalized would undermine all that "free India" stood for. The production of the modern Indian nation-state at that historical juncture necessitated a policy that would be based on these principles and not one based on the "origin of people."[99]

The latter position won the day. India did not make any special representations to the Kenyan government on behalf of the PIO. However, acknowledging the "cultural connections" of the PIO to India and doing its part to help avoid a "human tragedy," the Indian state did permit those who had British citizenship to use any port in Indian territory as a transit until they were allowed into the United Kingdom.[100] Within a few years of the Kenyan crisis, Idi Amin's regime in Uganda unleashed a reign of terror, targeting the PIO in particular. The Indian government rode out the crisis by condemning the brutality of Amin's regime and offering support to the small section of Ugandan Indians who did not possess British citizenship, while at the same time pointing out the complicity of the PIO in the construction of the "ugly Indian" image that made such crises possible. To that extent, despite the challenges posed primarily by the non-Congress opposition, the Nehruvian doctrine of keeping the Indian state at a distance from the diaspora, both literally and figuratively, remained dominant even a decade after his death.[101]

I have argued in this chapter that the development of the relationship between the postcolonial Indian state and the Indian diaspora poses a serious conundrum. Immediately after acquiring state power, leaders of the Indian nationalist movement turned their backs on the expansive transnationalism that helped develop and sustain their struggle against British colonialism. Rather than embracing the cause of the Indians abroad and offering them the unqualified support of the Indian state, the new leadership instead offered a critique of their comportment in their states of residence, while upholding the sovereign political and economic rights of *those states*. In every way, the relationship between the Indian state and the Indians abroad marked a dramatic renegotiation of the boundaries of the nation. As the latter part of the chapter makes obvious, postcolonial theorists have tended to explain the demarcation of the boundaries of the Indian nation by focusing on a series of factors: the trauma of partition, causing what Sankaran Krishna has described as "cartographic anxiety," Nehru's commitment to a particular kind of socioeconomic political order, and most important, the logic of his internationalism. To the extent that these explanations underscore the constitutive role of colonialism in the making of modern India, it is important for us to take their insights seriously. At the same time, however, the emphasis on colonialism cannot be a substitute for critically interrogating the social character of anticolonial nationalist movements and the nation-state forms that they engendered. Scholars in the postcolonial tradition would undoubtedly concur with the claim that the struggle against colonialism was not waged in a social vacuum. However, their analyses largely tend to rest on a very specific, and in my view, inadequate understanding of what constitutes social relations. The result of this commitment is the sort of analyses that unfortunately tend to reduce both the struggle against colonialism and the postcolonial nation-state engendered to either a matter of the psyche (albeit framed in social terms) or present it as a supra-class affair. To go beyond these limitations, it is crucial that we return to questions that have been largely treated as being settled or passé. To put it differently, while the idea of state policies being guided by a "cartographic anxiety" in the aftermath of partition might seem to make sense, it is vital to ask questions about who exactly amongst the general Indian population suffered from such anxiety, when and under what conditions it was engendered, and what particular agendas were furthered through its production. For it is only by asking and addressing these questions that we can move beyond abstract claims about the meanings of modernity and postcoloniality toward a critical analysis of the material basis of the postcolonial Indian nation-state. We turn to this task in the next chapter.

4

The Making and Unmaking
of Hegemony
Indian Capitalism from Swadeshi to Swraj

A person of Indian origin who renounced deliberately his Indian citizenship
but who was rewarded with Padma Bhushan for his so-called invisible service
to our country, is now strutting the stage of the corporate sector like a
buccaneer trying to grab what are called well-established industries as if they
were lollipops, under benign dispensation.

—*Somnath Chatterjee (CPM), Lok Sabha Debates, August 24, 1983*

In 1983, Swraj Paul,[1] a London-based businessman of Indian origin was awarded
the Padma Bhushan, one of independent India's highest civilian honors, by Prime
Minister Indira Gandhi. In the same year, interpreting the provisions of the
newly introduced Non-Resident Indians (NRI) Portfolio Scheme rather loosely,
he spearheaded an attempt to take over two of India's biggest industrial firms.
Despite Paul's success in acquiring 10 percent of the shares of the two companies—Delhi Cloth Mills (DCM) and Escorts Ltd.—the board of directors at both
refused to recognize him as a legitimate shareholder. At one level, the matter was
a technical one concerning the legality of Paul's share purchases under the NRI
Portfolio Scheme and was, on that basis, taken to the Bombay High Court (and
later, the Supreme Court of India) by Escorts management. Surprisingly for the
Escorts board, they found themselves fighting not only Paul and his companies
but also the Indian government, which fully supported Paul's efforts to have his
shares registered.

This struggle between prominent members of the Indian bourgeoisie, on the
one hand, and a rather loose alliance of an NRI and representatives of the Indian
state, on the other, continued for slightly more than two years and was waged on
the terrains of political and civil society. Interestingly, in debates within the
Indian Parliament, as well as in public fora around the country, the matter

snowballed from a discussion on the specifics of an attempted industrial take-over to a referendum on the status of the Indian bourgeoisie, the future of Indian economic policy, and the relationship of the Indian nation-state to nonresident Indians.[2] What was the logic of this shift? How did the debates surrounding the legality of shares purchased by a single NRI businessman get so easily translated into a critique of the role of the Indian bourgeoisie in postindependence India? And more importantly, what was the connection between that critique and the attempts to rearticulate the relationship between the postcolonial Indian nation-state and the Indian diaspora? This chapter addresses these questions through an analysis of the making and unmaking of bourgeois hegemony in the postcolonial Indian state and its implications for the boundaries that delineated both the extent of the nation and the role of the state.

The chapter begins by analyzing the nature of the state that replaced the colonial state in 1947. It does so by putting into focus the making of bourgeois hegemony, particularly in the period leading up to Indian independence, and its implications for the shaping of postcolonial India. I argue that the socioeconomic and political agenda adopted by the Indian National Congress (the dominant faction of the Indian nationalist movement, which later took over the reins of the state from the British)—its commitment to state sovereignty, state-sponsored industrialization, the protection of domestic economy, and so forth—revealed the success of the Indian national bourgeoisie in establishing its hegemony.[3] However, this was not a process that ended with the attainment of Indian independence in 1947 and the institutionalization of the INC's agenda. As Gramsci reminds us, the making of hegemony is an ongoing process. In order to maintain its hegemonic position, the Indian bourgeoisie had to constantly strive to make the connection between its particular interests and the general interests of the nation at large appear seamless and natural. Although this seemed plausible in the early decades after independence, the rapidly changing conditions of the global capitalist economy, manifested in a number of ways, including the changing profile of the Indian diaspora and the economic crises faced by the Indian state, made the task increasingly harder. By the 1980s, the Indian bourgeoisie faced new challenges that revealed the fissures in its hegemonic position and opened up space for the renegotiation of the boundaries of the imagined community of the nation.

The latter half of the chapter spotlights one such challenge. Following its successful negotiation of an International Monetary Fund (IMF) loan to stave off an economic crisis in 1980, the Indian state introduced the NRI Portfolio Scheme, which relaxed the strict controls on the entry of foreign capital, so long as it belonged to persons of Indian origin. It was under the rubric of this scheme that Swraj Paul, a British citizen of Indian origin, attempted to acquire control of two prominent Indian companies. This was a curious case indeed, with the Indian government actually supporting an ostensibly "foreign" capitalist against sections of the "national" bourgeoisie. The actual controversy surrounding Paul had a rather anticlimactic ending, with the Supreme Court of India stepping in to facilitate a negotiated settlement between the concerned parties. However, this struggle had consequences beyond the resolution of a simple case, for it revealed the final limits of the old economic and political model of the Indian nation-state that had been dominant since the final phase of the Indian nationalist movement. In doing so, it brought back to center stage questions regarding the imagining of the Indian nation and the role of the Indian state that were far from resolved. As the struggle unfolded and moved toward a rather tepid ending in the hallways of the Indian justice system, Paul himself remained a socially and politically ambiguous figure. However, it was exactly this ambiguity that made him such a pivotal figure in the Indian political arena, for Swraj Paul embodied the changing conditions that challenged the hegemony of the Indian bourgeoisie and then revealed its fracturing. This in turn made imperative the rearticulation of the hegemonic project in ways that redefined not only the connection between the particular interests of the bourgeoisie and the general interests of the nation but also the very boundaries of that imagined political community.

I. The Postcolonial Capitalist State

In the decades prior to independence, the Indian capitalist class emerged as a strong force, especially in the realm of the economy vis-à-vis foreign capital. This, as Aditya Mukherjee argues convincingly, was a result of a "process of economic and political struggle" that was facilitated in part by the two world wars, the Great Depression, and the crisis faced by British imperialism during that period.[4] However, the emergence of this class was also inextricably tied to the growth of the Indian nationalist movement. This is not surprising, given that the struggles leading to its constitution were waged particularly against the metropolitan bourgeoisie and the colonial state. Moreover, the "notion of an *Indian* capitalist class could not emerge so long as the notion of India or the Indian 'people' did not begin to take root and the capitalist class did not begin to identify with it."[5]

At the institutional level, early nationalist leaders like M. G. Ranade were at the forefront of organizing regional industrial associations and ensuring that they were organically connected to the Indian National Congress (INC).[6] Even as the political agenda of the INC gradually moved from "equality within the empire" to "*poorna swaraj*" (complete freedom), the various regional commercial and industrial conferences were brought under a single national-level umbrella organization in 1927. Perceived from its inception as articulating the opinions and demands of Indian capitalists, the newly formed Federation of Indian Chambers of Commerce (later renamed the Federation of Indian Chambers of Commerce and Industry and commonly known by the acronym FICCI) was portrayed by its founders not only as an organization that would act as the "national guardian of trade, commerce and industry" but also as one that would actively support the cause of Indian nationalism. As leading industrialists like G. D. Birla and Purshotamdas Thakurdas argued, political freedom was absolutely essential to ensure the economic prosperity of the country as a whole as well as that of the capitalist class. The rationale for this argument was quite straightforward. As Indian traders and industrialists attempted to make inroads into domains dominated by Europeans in a colonial economy, such as shipping, banking, and locomotives, they had to face the competition posed by foreign capital and were forced to do so within the constraints imposed by the colonial state. As the leaders of big business in India saw it, the fate of Indian industry and commerce was inextricably interwoven with the future of Indian nationalism.

However, the question of what form this nationalism would have to take to serve the interests of the Indian bourgeoisie, or who best represented the future leadership of this movement, was far from settled. Given the dominance of the Indian National Congress within the mainstream nationalist movements and the long-term involvement of various industrial families like the Tatas and the Birlas in this political organization, it was not surprising that the dominant section of the Indian bourgeoisie represented by FICCI decided to formally declare its support for the Jawaharlal Nehru–led Congress.[7] This move, however, did not remain unchallenged. In 1934, a vocal section among the Indian capitalists led by A. D. Shroff, vice president of the Indian Merchants Chamber, and the well-known industrialist Walchand Hirachand raised a banner of revolt against Nehru through the publication of the Bombay Manifesto, which challenged his vision for India's future.[8] The twenty-one signatories of the manifesto accused Nehru of being a "whole-hearted communist," who in articulating his "immoral" opposition to private property was inciting popular violence and creating conditions wherein "industrial enterprise" could not thrive. They further argued that there was no reason to believe that the rest of the Congress leadership could control Nehru's dangerous ideas and, consequently, that it was necessary for the Indian capitalists to carefully reconsider their relationship with the Indian National Congress.[9] While the signatories of the manifesto were skeptical about the eventual outcome, even they acknowledged that there were deep cleavages among different sections within the Indian National Congress itself, particularly between Nehru on one side and Gandhi and the rest of the Congress Working Committee (CWC) on the other in the early 1930s.

As Bipan Chandra points out, this period marked the high point of Nehru's flirtations with Marxism, culminating with his declaration during his presidential address at the Lucknow session of the Indian National Congress (1936) that the problems faced by India were but "a part of the world problem of capitalism-imperialism" and could be addressed only through embracing socialism, which he defined as ending the system of profit making and private property.[10] Nehru's views did not find much favor with the majority of the CWC, who along with Mahatma Gandhi were against the adoption of policies that would alienate the "more far-sighted leaders" of the Indian capitalist class. Primary among these leaders was G. D. Birla, who rebuked the signatories of the Bombay Manifesto for losing sight of their long-term interests and inadvertently strengthening the hands of "communists."[11] As he pointed out, it was indeed "very crude for a man with property to say that he is opposed to expropriation in the wider interests of the country," for it revealed the extreme self-interest of the propertied classes.[12] This critique did not imply that Birla was sympathetic to Nehru's positions. To the contrary, he remained convinced that "expropriation was against the higher interests of society," but he understood that to be persuasive to the masses, this argument could not be made by men of property. Instead, he persuaded his fellow industrialists that the best way to combat Nehru's Marxist tendencies would be to strengthen the hands of the Congress "right wing"—respected leaders such as Vallabhbhai Patel, Bhulabhai Desai, Rajendra Prasad, and Rajagopalachari, who were sympathetic allies in the fight against socialism. Most importantly, Birla pointed out that despite his rhetoric, Nehru did not necessarily seem committed to pushing the Congress in a direction that would give it an overtly socialist character. Therefore, it was equally important for Indian capitalists to nurture their connections with Nehru, who, after all, seemed to be positioned to lead the Indian nationalist movement.

Although the extent of Nehru's commitment to "radical Marxism" is a matter of debate, it needs to be noted that the combined exertions of a section of the INC leadership (led by Mahatma Gandhi) did ensure a gradual shift in Nehru's public stance, moving from a more radical leftist position in the mid-1930s (when he argued that class conflict was a reality and that political action ought to be geared toward exposing and ending the exploitation of some classes by others) to a more moderate—albeit left-leaning—position by the end of the decade.[13] This shift was brought about in part because of Nehru's troubled, but ultimately respectful relationship with Gandhi (who at this point in time dominated the Indian national movement) and also his own conviction that the Indian National Congress was, despite its shortcomings, the organization best suited to lead India to independence.[14] The Nehruvian "socialism" that eventually became the dominant ideology of the nationalist movement still carried within it rhetorical elements of Nehru's tryst with Marxism, but was a system of thought that facilitated the interests of the Indian capitalist class and ultimately reflected the establishment of bourgeois hegemony.[15] Understanding the processes through which this hegemony was established is thus crucial for making sense of the Indian nation-alist movement as well as the nature of the postcolonial Indian state that came into being after independence.

In his insightful analysis of the development of the Indian nationalist move-ment, Partha Chatterjee makes the argument that the final phase of the inde-pendence struggle was characterized by the "ideological reconstruction of elements of nationalist thought" under Nehru's leadership.[16] The importance of this "ideological reconstruction," as Chatterjee points out, was that it made pos-sible the establishment of a particular kind of postcolonial state—an interven-tionist state that laid the foundations "for the expansion of capital" by "entering the domain of production as mobilizer and manager of investible resources."[17] It is in this reconstruction, I would argue, that it is possible to see the successful establishment of the political hegemony of the Indian bourgeoisie. At one point during the struggle for independence (in the late 1920s and early 1930s), the very real prospect of a growing Communist movement in the country and the simultaneous emergence of Nehru (a well-known member of the Congress Left) as one of the most prominent nationalist leaders was seen as a cause for alarm by many sections of the Indian capitalist class. However, recognizing that attempts to directly challenge the Left might prove to be counterproductive, industrialists like Birla and Purshotamdas developed a strategy they argued would be beneficial to the Indian bourgeoisie in the long run. One part of this strategy, as already mentioned, involved strengthening the position of more right-wing Congress leaders.

An even more important part of the strategy adopted by bourgeois leaders was to discourage any attempts by Indian capitalists to make common cause with the colonial state, for as Purshotamdas argued, they could not afford to forget: "We are Indians first and merchants and industrialists afterwards."[18] Moreover, being perceived as pro-imperialist by the masses (as the feudal landlords and rul-ers of the princely states were) would serve only to strengthen the Indian Left. Going even further, the leadership of this social group argued that the best way to combat the threat of Communism was to address the root cause of poverty and inequities in India. To that end, they called for the abolishment of the feudal landowning class (which they argued could take place through a program of nationalization in which the state could acquire land after the payment of "due compensation") and the enactment of a series of measures that would result in the "scaling down of rents" and the "liquidation of rural indebtedness."[19] However, only a strong state that assumed a central coordinating role could ensure the promulgation and implementation of these measures.[20] As it existed, the colonial state was clearly not willing to take up this role. Therefore, they argued, the prin-cipal task facing the nation was the establishment of a sovereign nation-state. The importance of these moves cannot be overemphasized, for they enabled the members of this class to present themselves as wedded to the greater national cause rather than to their particular interests. Even while having differences with some sections of the Congress leadership, and even while occasionally support- ing the more right-wing elements within the Congress, Indian industrialists thus managed to present themselves as an intrinsic part of the nationalist movement.

More importantly, perhaps, even in their initial formulations, these proposals helped the Indian bourgeoisie establish common ground with Nehru, whose vision of socialism (despite the qualms of some) was not premised on the idea of a mass revolutionary uprising against existing socioeconomic relations. While he believed in the importance of the nationalist movement having a social and eco- nomic agenda, Nehru was committed to ensuring the primacy of the political objective of establishing an independent Indian nation-state. As Chatterjee shows in his analysis of the Nehruvian moment in the Indian national movement, despite his allegiance to the Congress Left and his seemingly heartfelt espousal of Marxism, Nehru was firmly convinced that "attempts at social reforms could be successful *only after* power had been captured and a national state established."[21] This conviction emerged from an understanding of Indian society as character- ized by a deep schism between the nationalist leadership and the (predominantly peasant) masses they were supposed to lead. While acknowledging that the peas- ant masses needed to be involved in the nationalist movement, Nehru's under- standing of their role was shaped by the belief that the Indian peasantry was "poor and ignorant, unthinking and subject of unreasonable excitements."[22] It was a social group that had to be controlled (though not by violence) and "led by responsible leaders who would show them how they could fit, entirely in accor- dance with their true and rational interests, into the national movement."[23] In Chatterjee's terms, this meant that the

> Split between two domains of politics—one, a politics of the elite, and the other, a politics of the subaltern classes—was replicated in the sphere of mature nationalist thought by an explicit recognition of the split between the domain of rationality and a domain of unreason, a domain of science and a domain of faith, a domain of organization and a domain of spontaneity.[24]

According to Nehru, it was the inability of the Communist movement in India to grasp the nature of this schism that made it both unsuitable for Indian condi- tions and eventually unsuccessful as a mobilizing force. It required the genius of the Gandhian intervention to drive home the fact that peasants could be mobi- lized only by putting aside the notion of a rational political program (while not losing sight of it) and "reaching into their hearts."[25] Once this crucial step was taken, the peasants could be mobilized by the nationalist leadership, who could then highlight the main agrarian issues facing the nation. However, the gap between the "real objective interests" of the peasants and their "unreasonable subjective beliefs," coupled with the constraints put in place by the colonial state, meant that there could be no real socioeconomic transformation of the primarily agrarian Indian society prior to independence. Therefore, to Nehru it seemed patently clear that what was needed to ensure the success of any program of social justice was the establishment of a strong, sovereign Indian nation-state.

As World War II drew to a close, leaders of the Indian nationalist movement became increasingly convinced that Indian independence was only a matter of time. At this juncture, in late 1945, some of the most prominent Indian industrialists came together to put forth their economic vision for an independent India. This vision, which came to known as the Bombay Plan, remains the best known articulation of how exactly the Indian bourgeoisie understood not just their interests, but the role that the state could play in helping them achieve those interests.[26] The Bombay Plan began with the assumption that "on the termination of the war…a national government will come into existence at the centre which will be vested with full freedom in economic matters."[27] However, the mere coming into being of a "national government…free of imperial domination" would not ensure the growth of the Indian economy. Such growth, according to the authors of the Bombay Plan, would, to a large extent, depend on the ability of the state to play a leading role in the process.[28] The reasons for this conviction are not hard to understand. The Indian capitalists, as Mukherjee argues, realized that the growth spurts they had experienced during the Great Depression and the two world wars were neither sustainable nor sufficient to guarantee long-term productivity. What was needed was something more—the "economy had to undergo significant growth in a large number of sectors *simultaneously*, if a *structural* break from the past had to be made."[29] The first step in this direction was to ensure the production of the means of production. In other words, it was crucial to invest in and give high priority to basic industries that would serve the dual purpose of propelling India's industrial development and reducing dependence on foreign countries to supply Indian industries with the machinery they needed. This proposal, however, required a massive outlay of capital that would not have high returns, as well as long-term holding power that was beyond the abilities of the Indian capitalists. Hence, they turned to the state as the most viable source of financing these operations. But the state's role was not to be limited to deficit financing. To mobilize and channel the resources of the country, it was argued that all credit and investment institutions in the country should be publicly owned. This realization meant that the Indian capitalists would support a policy of nationalization of major banks and insurance companies in the country.[30] The plan did foresee that these means of financing basic industries might lead to state ownership. At a theoretical level, this was a phenomenon antithetical to the interests of capitalists who, after all, remained attached to the notion of private enterprise. However, the proponents of the plan argued that an interventionist state was essential, especially in the early stages of economic development in a country like India.[31]

The Indian state, within the framework of the Bombay Plan, would be responsible for mobilizing national resources for sustained industrial growth and would actively protect national industries from the threat of foreign capital. Fulfilling this responsibility in part entailed the acquisition or nationalization of key parts of the agricultural and industrial sectors, which had significant foreign investments.[32] While emphasizing the need to have an economy that was free from imperial domination, the Indian capitalists were aware that India might still need an inflow of foreign capital in the decades after independence. To ensure that this need did not translate into an overwhelming dependence, they argued that the state should strictly regulate the flow of foreign capital. In this vein, the plan proposed that the only way in which foreign capital should be allowed into India was in the form of credits or loans that were raised by the Indian state itself.

The signatories of the Bombay Plan argued that on the eve of independence, the Indian economy was at a critical stage. Although it had potential for dynamic growth, this could be achieved only under conditions that were strictly regulated by a sovereign Indian state. At this juncture, it is crucial to note that the leaders of the Indian capitalist class did not perceive the creation of an interventionist state as eventually paving the road to socialism in India. For them, the idea of a state that played an important controlling and coordinating role was simply a feature of modern, advanced industrialized economies.[33] To make a decisive break from its colonial past, the Indian economy had to be a mixed one in which the most crucial role would be played by the Indian state, not only as the force behind a large public sector but also as the patron of the private sector. This vision lay at the heart of the proposal that Indian capitalists brought into the meetings of the National Planning Commission (NPC). Not surprisingly, this vision tallied remarkably well with the Nehruvian understanding of the role of the postcolonial Indian state.

The dominant nationalist ideology during the final phase of the Indian struggle for independence was characterized by an emphasis on the role of an autonomous and independent state in ensuring progress and social justice. As discussed in the previous chapter, Nehruvian nationalism envisaged a modern state that would be fundamentally different from the colonial state in the sense of being committed to the protection and development of the nation and national resources. To fulfill this commitment, the first step would be for the state to "embrace the whole people, give everyone the right of citizenship irrespective of sex, language, religion, caste, wealth or education."[34] However, merely embracing the right to universal suffrage was not enough. For Nehru, the state had to embody the scientific spirit of the age and guarantee the "primacy of the sphere of the economic in all social questions."[35] In other words, to fulfill its historical role, the postcolonial state would have to lead the development of the national economy. In Nehru's understanding, the concept of economic development in the modern world implied not only the building of scientific and technical expertise but also a process of rapid industrialization. History, as far as Nehru was concerned, had adequately demonstrated that the only way to meet the needs of all sections of the population was through industrialization. Unfortunately, given its colonization by the British, India was lagging behind in this process. What India needed to do was catch up with the rest of the world, and this could be done if, and only if, the independent Indian state played a controlling role in industrializing and channeling the productive resources of the nation. Nehru's vision of modern India was predicated on the notion of a state that would, above all, provide political focus to the programs that were needed to ensure the rapid movement of the Indian nation on the path of modernity and progress. Despite the underlying assumption that such a state would "represent the balanced aggregate interest of the people as a whole" and "would not be dominated by any particular group or class," the Nehruvian vision of the postcolonial Indian state converged remarkably well with the proposals of the Bombay Plan.[36]

To explain this convergence, it is important to put into sharper focus the distinctly bourgeois nature of the Indian nationalist movement on the eve of independence. By consistently supporting the nationalists in their struggle against imperialism and by strengthening the hands of those in the nationalist movement they believed would be their best representatives, the Indian capitalists succeeded in establishing and maintaining "bourgeois ideological hegemony over the Indian National Congress, the leading organ of the Indian National Movement."[37] At important moments during the final two decades leading up to Indian independence, the Indian bourgeoisie had strategically put aside its narrowly perceived class interests and embraced the national cause. For instance, in 1928–1929, the viceroy, Lord Irwin, sought the support of Indian capitalists in passing the Public Safety Bill. Ostensibly aimed at containing the spread of Communism in India, the bill sought to give the colonial government extraordinary powers to deal with any challenges to its authority. Despite acknowledging that they were interested in keeping "communism and Bolshevism out of India," the Indian capitalists refused to support the bill, leading to its failure in the Legislative Assembly.[38] Given that this cost them the goodwill of the colonial state and potentially strengthened political movements that were fundamentally opposed to their interests, the stance of the Indian bourgeoisie vis-à-vis the Public Safety Bill did mark a denial of their particular social interests. However, as Gramsci reminds us, dominant social classes defend and further their interests through a complex set of processes that cannot be framed too mechanistically.[39] In fact, the occasional sacrifices made by bourgeoisie are crucial to the larger project of establishing its hegemonic position in society. In this case, by highlighting their opposition to the colonial regime that was widely and rightly understood as oppressive, the Indian bourgeoisie was able to frame its interests as being concomitant with the interests of the nation at large. Without a broad-based violent class struggle, this social class had assumed a hegemonic position in the Indian nationalist movement, and it was this hegemony that shaped the nation-state that emerged after independence in 1947.

As foreseen in the Bombay Plan proposals, the independent Indian state played a critical role in setting up public-sector industries, supporting the private sector, and laying the foundations for the general expansion of capital. One of the major initiatives taken by Nehru, in his official capacity as the first prime minister of independent India, was to ensure the passage of the Reserve Bank of India (Transfer to Public Ownership) Act of 1948.[40] The act laid the grounds for the transfer of the privately owned Reserve Bank of India (RBI)—which had served as the Central Bank for the colonial state as well as the Dominion of India—to the Government of India, effective January 1, 1949.[41] While some of the board of directors expressed their reservations about the pace of the nationalization, the actual process itself was fairly smooth, with board members retaining their positions but now as employees of the Government of India.[42] In 1955, this was followed by the nationalization of the Imperial Bank, the largest private banking institution of the country, which was renamed the State Bank of India.[43] At the same time, the government also nationalized insurance companies and established financial institutions that were charged with the task of channeling expansion funds into major industries.[44] These measures had the effect of ensuring that most of the industrial capital available in the country was concentrated in the hands of the Indian state, making it the major shareholder in India's biggest industries.[45] However, this scenario did not lead to any major standoffs between the Indian state and the national bourgeoisie for nearly three and a half decades after Indian independence. This apparent harmony was in part due to the fact that financial institutions holding the major stake in various Indian industries had declared they would not seek to convert their shareholding power into management control. Their role would be to finance Indian companies, to support the management, and to stabilize the functioning of those companies. In addition to these measures aimed at promoting industrial development, the Indian state also played an active role in protecting domestic industries from the potential threat of "foreign domination" by enacting a series of stringent regulations governing the inflow of foreign capital and investments in India. Indian capitalists were seen as an intrinsic part of the nation that had to be protected from foreign exploitation and sustained by the state. The net effect of these state practices was to produce a state that emphasized and upheld the political and economic significance of territorial boundaries.

The processes of territorializing an independent, modern India, as discussed earlier, had the very important effect of situating the Indian diaspora at a distance from the Indian nation-state. The constitution of a strong, sovereign nation-state rested on defining the boundaries that separated the outside from the inside and the foreigner (the exploiter) from the national (he who needed to be protected from exploitation). In making this distinction, policy makers and state elites did, without question, embrace a certain understanding of what constituted the modern Indian ethos. For instance, as the last chapter makes obvious, parliamentary debates of the early 1960s that dealt with the East African crisis were shaped by a certain understanding of the Indian nation-state's post-coloniality—being "Indian" meant embracing a particular worldview that opposed foreign exploitation of all sorts. More than that, however, the bourgeois nationalism that lay at the heart of state ideology emphasized the territorially limited, legal-juridical aspect of statehood in making the distinction between those who could be counted as Indian and those who ought not to be counted as such. The main argument made by successive Congress regimes after independence regarding the Indian state's attitude toward the diaspora was quite straightforward: members of the diaspora had been given the chance to embrace Indian citizenship, which they chose not to accept; under these circumstances, the newly independent Indian state did not have any legal responsibilities toward them. And since as part of the modern system of nation-states India respected the sovereignty of other countries (especially the newly independent nation-states), it could not intervene in their domestic affairs. Despite intermittent struggles, the logic underlying the drawing of the boundaries of the nation and the delineation of the role of the state remained more or less dominant until the eruption of the controversy surrounding the Swraj Paul case. To understand the significance of the Swraj Paul case, however, we need to take a closer look at the global economic changes that helped shake the foundations of bourgeois hegemony in the Indian state, even while helping create a qualitatively different type of Indian diaspora.

II. The "Foreign Indian"

The preceding chapter showed how the debates surrounding the Indians abroad in the immediate aftermath of independence concerned those communities that had migrated during colonial rule and settled in various parts of the British Empire. The issue of their civil and political rights in general and their relationship to India in particular was played out within the larger framework of decolonization and the imperative to territorialize the newly independent nation-state.

It was in this context that the Nehruvian doctrine of maintaining a certain distance from the diaspora became a cornerstone of the Indian nation-state's foreign policy. Although it had been contested, particularly during the East Africa crises, this policy remained firmly in place and framed the interactions of successive Indians governments toward persons of Indian origin. However, the 1970s and 1980s saw a distinct change taking place in the nature of the Indian communities living abroad. For one, the trickle of highly skilled professionals to the West (primarily to the United Kingdom and North America), which had already been visible in the 1960s, had become a steady flow (see appendix table A.2). As is obvious from table 4.1, a large proportion of the immigration to North America during this period consisted of dependents. But a different picture emerges if we focus on the number of immigrants with reported occupations, that is, those who did not fall in the category of "Dependents/Unclassified." For instance, during the period 1971–1975, of the total number of immigrants to the United States who declared an occupation, nearly 88 percent were highly skilled professionals.

Table 4.1. Skill Composition by Percentage of Total of Indian Labor Outflow to North America

Occupation	1971–75		1976–79		1980–85	
	US	Canada	US	Canada	US	Canada
Professional & Technical	43.4	11.1	26.9	3.5	15.7	2.8
Executive, Administrative, & Managerial	2.1	1.3	4.7	0.7	5.2	0.7
Clerical & Sales	2.7	5.5	4.2	2.6	3.7	1.5
Service	1.1	1.3	1.0	0.6	2.2	0.7
Farming & Allied	0.3	4.9	1.7	1.3	2.7	3.7
Skilled Workers	2.2	14.0	3.3	3.2	2.9	2.4
Dependents/Unclassified	48.2	57.8	58.2	75.7	67.6	69.4
Total (in numbers)	72,912	42,632	76,561	30,271	98,179	32,657

Studies on this subject have noted the nonavailability of the occupational distribution of immigrants to the United Kingdom. The categories used by Patra and Kapur are based on Nayyar's seminal study on migration and remittances. The category "professional and technical" includes scientists, engineers, doctors, lawyers, architects, teachers, and others with professional expertise or technical qualifications. "Skilled workers" includes workers engaged in production, craft, repair, and operation in the United States and those employed in mining, oil and gas, processing, machining, assembly, repair, construction, transport, and material handling in Canada. See Michael Debabrata Patra and Munish Kapur, "Indian Worker Remittances: A User's Lament about Balance of Payment Compilation," Sixteenth meeting of the IMF Committee on Balance of Payments Statistics, Washington, DC, December 1–5, 2003, BOPCOM-03/20; and Nayyar, *Migration, Remittances and Capital Flows*, 18.

Source: Patra and Kapur, "Indian Worker Remittances."

To put it more into context, during the 1970s, India contributed approximately 19.5 percent of the total number of highly skilled professionals admitted into the United States from around the world—a figure that is quite impressive if we take into account the fact that India's share of the total immigration to the United States in the 1970s amounted to less than 3.8 percent.[46] This steady immigration soon became a source of concern for the Indian government, prompting calls from different quarters to stop the "brain drain."

While not drawing similar governmental attention, a different kind of migration was also taking place at the same time. A rapidly increasing group of unskilled and semiskilled laborers (mostly from the South Indian state of Kerala) were moving to the Middle East to fulfill the demand for labor created in the petroleum-rich economies of the various emirates (table 4.2).

The differences between the two groups of migrants are noticeable. The migration of one group was seen as a drain of national resources and a matter of concern, but the government actually encouraged the migration to the Gulf, seeing it as a means to stem growing levels of unemployment. While the professional migrants to the West had the choice of giving up their Indian citizenship to acquire the citizenship of their host countries (a choice that was exercised by a growing number), the migrants to the Gulf worked without that option. While the migrants to the West were accompanied (or gradually followed) by their immediate families, the Gulf migrants were primarily male laborers who were

Table 4.2.   Skill Composition of Indian Immigrants to the Middle East by Percentage of Total

Occupation	1984	1986
Unskilled Workers	43.0	40.1
Construction	41.7	34.6
Farms and Households	1.3	5.5
Skilled Workers	41.8	47.0
Construction	22.3	21.5
Other	19.5	25.5
White-Collar Workers	3.6	6.5
High-Skilled Workers	3.2	5.2
Medical	1.3	1.0
Technical and Supervisory	1.9	4.2
Other	8.4	1.2
Total (in Numbers)	205,922	113,649

Source: Patra and Kapur, "Indian Worker Remittances."

generally separated from their families for the duration of their contracts. Scholars studying patterns of migration from South Asia have rightly noted this stark contrast between the two groups of migrants. Although it is vital to not lose sight of these differences, I would argue that it is far more important to focus on what was common to the two groups.

Taken together, the skilled professionals and the semiskilled and unskilled laborers were the first significant migration from postindependence India. Unlike the communities hailed as Indians abroad in the early twentieth century, whose relationship to India had been a source of contention in the aftermath of independence, the new migrants were citizens of the "sovereign, socialist, secular, democratic republic of India." Even when they chose to acquire new citizenships,

Table 4.3. Estimated Composition of Remittances to India by Origin in Millions of Rupees

Year	North America	Western Europe	Britain & Australia	Middle East & Other Oil Exporting Countries	Other Developing Countries	Total
1970–71	284	114	223	37	147	805
1971–72	312	194	347	58	207	1,118
1972–73	391	159	275	46	170	1,041
1973–74	432	189	442	74	287	1,424
1974–75	670	349	443	259	481	2,202
1975–76	1,105	502	620	1,316	694	4,327
1976–77	1,651	664	590	2,704	628	6,237
1977–78	1,382	786	1,026	4,868	1,111	9,173
1978–79	1,566	949	1,013	4,813	1,097	9,438
1979–80	2,210	1,192	1,631	7,904	1,784	14,721
1980–81	2,100	1,684	2,548	12,194	2,771	21,297
1981–82	3,355	1,866	2,195	10,975	2,538	20,829
1982–83	3,363	1,828	2,494	13,708	2,915	24,308
1983–84	3,871	2,119	2,460	15,000	3,033	26,483

As this table reveals, the remittances from the migrant workers of the Middle East were the most significant portion of the total inflow of remittances into India. This trend continues through much of the 1980s and the early 1990s. At the time of the introduction of economic liberalization in India, the total inflow of remittances amounted to Rs 36,260 million, of which remittances sent from North America amounted to Rs 8,645 million as against Rs 14,499 million from the Middle East. For details on how these estimates were arrived at, see Deepak Nayyar, *Migration, Remittances and Capital Flows.*

Source: Nayyar, *Migration, Remittances and Capital Flows.*

they were first-generation immigrants in their host countries—immigrants who had close familial ties to India. These ties meant that significant portions of their earnings (far more significant in the case of the Gulf migrants) were being repatriated to India in the form of remittances (see table 4.3).

Notwithstanding the steadily increasing flow of remittances through the 1970s, the Indian state found itself on the verge of severe exchange crises several times during the course of the decade. While encouraging the migrants to continue sending remittances to family members, successive Indian governments focused on attempting to regulate the overall sphere of foreign exchange transactions, including those involving the NRIs. The passage of the Foreign Exchange Regulation Act (FERA) of 1973 was an important part of this larger effort. It included clauses that limited foreign equity ownership in Indian companies; severely restricted transactions in foreign exchange, including those between residents and nonresidents (unless specifically permitted); and imposed strict controls on industrial foreign collaboration and import of technology.[47] To a large extent, the passage of FERA seemed to mark a deliberate attempt by the Indian state to declare both its intentions and its ability to continue the strict regulation of foreign capital that had been the cornerstone of its economic policy since independence.[48] Despite this, however, by the end of the decade, the Indian state faced yet another impending economic crisis—one that it found itself unable resolve without international assistance.

The NRI Portfolio Scheme

By 1980, in the wake of the oil shocks of the previous decade and a drought that severely affected its agricultural output, the Indian economy was on verge of a severe crisis. In the immediate aftermath of its victory in the general elections, the Congress-led government of Indira Gandhi had come to the conclusion that the only way to stave off the crisis was by negotiating for an IMF loan. But loans, especially of the magnitude that the Indian government needed, came with strings attached. More specifically, the Indian government was well aware that in return for the loan that it sought, the IMF would require implementation of a set of policies that were aimed at reducing the barriers to foreign investment and trade. However, given the travailed history of past attempts to negotiate with the IMF, the matter was far from a simple quid pro quo. In the early part of the 1960s, the Indian state faced a growing crisis of food security, relying primarily on food aid from the United States to feed its population. When the Indian government requested a two-year food aid agreement with the United States in 1965, American President Lyndon Johnson used it as an opportunity to demand an opening up of the Indian economy and support (or, at a minimum, neutrality) for the U.S. involvement in Vietnam in return for smoothing the path to loans from the IMF and the World Bank. While Johnson's demands were initially met with great anger, the problems facing the Indian government were compounded by a foreign exchange crisis, with its reserves reaching an all-time low of $500 million, from the high of $1.87 billion barely a decade before. Given this crisis, the Congress government of Indira Gandhi agreed to the conditions imposed by the IMF in return for a $200 million loan. The acceptance of the conditions—primarily devaluing the currency, restraining fiscal spending, freezing wages, and further opening the economy to foreign imports—was in fact more a rhetorical strategy than an actual policy shift. However, once the arrangement with the IMF became public knowledge, the government faced a barrage of public criticism for giving up its sovereign right to stand against imperialist policies in exchange for food aid. Bowing to pressure from across the entire political spectrum, the Indian government abandoned critical components of the reform package and lost the aid pledges of various foreign donors. The devaluation of the Indian rupee failed to turn the economy around, delivering a severe blow to the credibility of Gandhi's government, which then faced a major electoral defeat in 1967.[49]

Given that the main political actors in 1980 were the same ones who had suffered the ramifications of the earlier debacle, it was not surprising that they opted to follow a different path this time around. The Indian government decided to preempt the official request for the loan by adopting a substantial macroeconomic structural adjustment plan as part of its sixth five-year plan program.[50] It was only after announcing this plan that the Indian government asked for and received a $5 billion loan from the IMF. It was, at that time, the largest loan given by the IMF to any developing country. Officially, the IMF loan did not come with any conditions. However, as the deliberations of Gandhi's economic team made very obvious, it was the anticipated demands of the much-needed loan that provided the impetus and the imperative for the new economic policies.[51] Most of the policies focused on easing restrictions on the inflow of foreign capital were presented as part of a strategic restructuring of the Indian economy that the government had decided to undertake on its own volition. It is in this context that we need to situate the announcement of the "NRI portfolio investment scheme," as part of the 1982 budget.[52] The scheme specified that portfolio investment was permitted in the shares of companies registered in the Indian stock exchanges by "non-residents of Indian nationality or origin," as well as by corporate bodies that were at least 60 percent owned by such nonresidents. Insofar as the procedure to purchase these shares was concerned, the corporate bodies had to approach authorized dealers (the nationalized banks) with applications that specified the extent of nonresident Indian ownership and were certified by an "overseas auditor/chartered accountant/certified public accountant." The applications were then to be referred to the Reserve Bank of India (RBI), which would grant permission to the concerned corporate bodies or individuals after scrutinizing the documents.[53]

In February 1983, Swraj Paul, a London-based businessman of Indian origin, started acquiring shares in two major Indian companies under the provisions of the NRI portfolio scheme. The companies were Escorts (founded by H. P. Nanda)[54] and DCM (founded by Lala Shri Ram).[55] While management of both companies was concentrated in the hands of their respective founders' families, the majority stockholder in both cases—in keeping with the dominant pattern at that time—was the Indian state.[56] The story of Escorts is a good case in point. At the time of the Paul controversy, the family of the founder H. P. Nanda held around 15 percent of the total equity capital of Escorts through a private holding company called Harparshad and Co., while the major shareholders were six government-owned financial institutions. Among the latter were two distinct types of institutions. The first category consisted of institutions that primarily acted as investors, such as the Life Insurance Corporation of India (LIC), the General Insurance Company of India (GIC), and the Unit Trust of India (UTI).[57] The second included institutions that had been established by the Indian state to make project finance available to industries. These included the Industrial Development Bank of India (IDBI), the Industrial Finance Corporation of India (IFCI) and the Industrial Credit and Investment Corporation of India (ICICI).

At that juncture, NRI investments in Indian companies were restricted by rules that permitted the purchase of a total of 1 percent of an Indian company's shares. To get around that rule, Paul used a front of thirteen companies registered in the tax haven of the Isle of Man.[58] Within a matter of three months, the buying frenzy undertaken in the name of the thirteen NRI companies more than doubled the stock price of both Indian companies.[59] The situation was perceived as dire by some of the leading industrialists in the country, who, at the urging of Escorts founder H. P. Nanda, decided to intervene at the highest governmental level. A small group that included the grand old man of Indian industry, J. R. D. Tata, even flew to New Delhi to discuss the issue with Finance Minister Pranab Mukherjee.[60] They argued to little avail that the Indian state was reneging on its traditional role as protector of Indian industry and was being blind to the potential danger of unrestrained foreign investment. Although Mukherjee refused to entertain these concerns, and the prime minister refused to even meet with J. R. D. Tata, one of the main moving forces behind the Bombay Plan, the Indian capitalists got a momentary respite due to an internecine struggle taking place within the ruling Congress Party.

In April 1983, Rajiv Gandhi, son of Prime Minister Indira Gandhi and presumptive heir to the leadership of the Congress, made his debut in the Indian parliament by participating in the debate on the finance bill and speaking out on the issue of NRI investments. Going against what was seen as the official policy of his mother's government, he argued that while NRIs ought to be allowed to bring in new technology and set up new industrial units in India, they should be prevented from making attempts that would destabilize well-run existing companies. Reacting to the brewing Escorts-DCM controversy, he stated unequivocally: "The danger of Indian companies being taken over by non-resident Indians is real [and] unless our financial institutions are careful, we will allow foreign agencies through Indians abroad to take over companies which are running well."[61] The possibility of such takeovers, he argued, was very real because the government had not declared a ceiling on total NRI investments. He suggested that while sticking to its policy of limiting individual NRI purchases to 1 percent of the total shares of any company, the Indian government should limit the total NRI holdings in any given company to less than 2 or 3 percent. Such a move would ensure that Indian companies would not have to face the threat of takeovers by NRI consortia.

In response, on May 2, 1983, the finance minister announced that there would be a cap on NRI holdings in India. The extent of shares that NRIs could hold in any Indian company would be limited to 5 percent of the company's total paid-up capital. To ensure that they would not capture management control, the total amount of shares that individual NRIs could hold was capped at 1 percent. He further claimed:

> The government's overall policy towards investment by NRIs has been to encourage such investments, as they can make a durable contribution to the economy in terms of inflows of foreign exchange. Where they involve direct establishment of new industries, they also permit the inflow of technology and management skills. In order to promote such investment flows the regulations governing investment by NRIs in terms of portfolio investment in existing companies, and also direct investment in new companies was liberalized.... *I would like to state categorically that it is certainly not the intention of the policy to permit... speculative takeover of established Indian companies by NRIs...* it is important to prevent any possibility of misuse of the liberalized facility. Accordingly, the government has decided that the liberalised scheme under which investments can be undertaken without RBI's prior permission will operate subject to a ceiling of 5 per cent on the total NRI holding of paid-up equity capital.[62]

Insofar as the Escorts-DCM takeover attempt was concerned, however, this rule applied only to shares that were purchased after May 2, 1983. Soon after the law concerning new ceilings on NRI investments was passed, the Escorts board met to discuss the legality of the purchases made by Paul. The management argued that Paul had not only acquired nearly 10 percent of Escorts shares *after* the government had passed its new laws but also had not sought the permission of the Reserve Bank of India before making the purchase. On both counts, there-fore, the purchases made by Paul's Caparo group of companies violated India's foreign exchange and investment laws. As a first step, the Escorts board passed a resolution setting up a "share scrutiny and transfer committee" that would look into the issue in detail. Exposing the emerging fissures in the hegemonic project that had shaped the postcolonial Indian state, the two board members repre-senting the financial institutions (D. N. Davar of the IFCI and A. Hariharan of the LIC) abstained from voting on the resolution.[63] As the committee swung into action, the dispute between Paul and the Indian industrialists took on the tone of a pitched battle in the media. Paul accused the management of Indian companies of thriving under protectionism and running their businesses like personal fiefdoms. The management of Escorts and DCM responded by claim-ing that "it hardly befitted Paul, who was a British national with a British pass-port to come to India and abuse its industrialists, people who had lived and worked in India."[64]

Within a short time, the Escorts board made it clear that it considered the share purchases made by Paul's company to be illegal and hence would not reg-ister them. In the meanwhile, Escorts had to get the approval of the state financial institutions to raise new project capital and go ahead with a merger with its sister company, Goetze (India) Ltd. In meetings with Finance Minister Pranab Mukherjee, it was made clear to Escorts CEO H. P. Nanda that the government's approval for the new projects was tied to the issue of registering the shares pur-chased by Paul.[65]

Even as the Escorts-DCM controversy continued in a seemingly unabated form, eleven overseas companies incorporated in the Isle of Man were given per-mission by the RBI to buy stocks in one of India's biggest textile companies, Reliance Ltd. In a matter of months, these companies (with names like "Crocodile Ltd." and, revealing perhaps a crystal-gazing ability among its founders, "Fiasco Overseas Ltd.") invested more than Rs. 22.52 crores in buying Reliance shares. As major media outlets in the country began scrutinizing the buying spree, the mat-ter became highly contested in both houses of the Indian parliament, with the opposition members demanding that the government explain the logic of its position on NRI investments in general and its connections to Swraj Paul in particular.[66] Commenting on Paul's flurry of interviews in the Indian media and his professed love for his motherland, Ram Vilas Paswan, an opposition member of parliament from Hazipur, declared sarcastically:

And then there is the matter of Swraj Paul who is in India these days giving us advice on honorable conduct, whose heart is filled with love for the nation, who himself left for foreign shores in 1965–66 and became a foreign citizen. I don't quite know the exact nature of his relationship with the government, but the government did award him [one of our country's highest civilian honors] the "Padma Bhushan." If it had up to the government, it might have even given him a higher honor such as the "Bharat Ratna."[67]

Paswan went on to argue that even a cursory look at the dealings revealed some troubling facts. After Paul's initial request to the RBI to purchase shares in Indian companies had been denied, he had attempted to circumvent the rules by creating a dummy front of thirteen companies. His attempt to garner the majority of shares was quite clearly a takeover attempt. The purchase of shares under those conditions in DCM and Escorts, finally, was a violation of the rules governing NRI investments in India. However, opposition members claimed that even these issues were minor compared with a different aspect of the case. The public records of the Caparo group revealed that none of the thirteen companies were profitable ventures. In fact, eleven of the thirteen overseas companies that were attempting to make huge investments in DCM and Escorts had declared a loss for the financial year 1980–1981.[68] These records raised the all-important question of how the thirteen companies registered in the Isle of Man managed to get the capital needed to purchase shares in the Indian companies.

The government's initial response to this question argued that its policy toward NRI investment was, first and foremost, "a sound and pragmatic" response to the foreign exchange crisis that India faced in the early 1980s. Minister of Finance Pranab Mukherjee pointed out that it was the Indian parliament that approved the "NRI portfolio scheme" in 1982 as a better alternative to borrowing from the IMF.[69] He further stated:

> What is the idea of the scheme? It is to attract foreign exchange and not merely portfolio investment. We are encouraging them to invest in new areas, areas of new technology, new companies, new series of the existing companies, and also existing equity shares. Why are we doing so? I made it abundantly clear at the time of the budget and at the time of the Finance Bill that I would give [the NRI] wide option to invest because I require the money.[70]

In this context, he argued that it really did not make sense to scrutinize the source of the investments. The NRIs investing in India, regardless of their origin, would continue to do so if and only if they found the climate conducive: "If I want to look at the source, nobody is coming to invest [sic]." The minister also claimed that the companies in question had submitted all the relevant details regarding the names of the shareholders and available capital to the RBI "in strictest confidence," and as such, this confidence could not be abused by discussing the information in Parliament.[71] Furthermore, since the RBI had given the companies permission to invest in India only after ensuring that they met the criteria laid out by the government, the entire discussion regarding the legality of the process was moot.

Opponents challenged the government's stand on several grounds, particularly the notion that a severe resource crunch made it impossible to question potential nonresident investors regarding their finances. Responding indignantly to the claim that any discussion of the overseas companies' finances in Parliament would constitute a breach of confidence, Madhu Dandavate declared, "I want to raise the very basic issue: Who is sovereign—the investor in this country… or the Parliament?" If the sovereignty of the Parliament (which symbolized the sovereignty of the nation-state itself) was to be maintained, then under no condition could the pressures that were being applied by overseas investors be allowed to constrain parliamentary debates. Therefore, he argued, while genuine investors should be welcomed into the country, they should be made aware of the fact that parliamentary jurisdiction was not their concern.[72] Picking up on Dandavate's arguments, others emphasized that the inability, as well as the lack of political will, to investigate the source of NRI investments revealed two major loopholes in the government's NRI portfolio scheme.[73] The first concerned the issue of "black money." If the government had no way of tracing the antecedents of foreign capital, it was quite possible for Indian industrialists to smuggle their undeclared wealth out of the country and bring it back in as NRI investments to avoid the wealth tax. The second issue was even more perturbing. If the system of controls for NRI investments was indeed porous, multinational companies could use NRI companies as conduits for clandestine investments. Holding forth on the latter issue, one member claimed that even the 5 percent limit on NRI investment did not really protect Indian industries in a situation where the government had no way to ascertain where the money came from: "In such a situation, if multi-nationals or giant foreign companies through some other names of non-resident Indians, fake names, invest up to five per cent each and in this way, get control of most of the industries in the country, what will happen to our economy? Where will we stand?"[74] While the fear that the NRI scheme could be used by unscrupulous "giant foreign companies" to get around existing controls and attempt to take over Indian industries was expressed by numerous members, a vocal minority gave a different, yet familiar twist to the argument by claiming that regardless of the origin of the investor, the capital that was coming in through the portfolio scheme was "foreign."

Somnath Chatterjee, a leading member of the Communist Party of India (Marxist), argued that to fulfill the conditionalities that had been imposed by the IMF (such as the liberalization of imports and the inflow of foreign capital), the government had brought to the fore a new category, that of "foreign Indian capital." He further claimed that the NRIs who were being targeted by the new scheme, despite their Indian origin, had voluntarily given up their Indian citizenship and as such were "foreigners." This claim immediately resulted in a furor in the parliament, with members interrupting to argue that many NRIs had been forced to give up their citizenship under conditions of duress, and in any case their holding the citizenship of different countries did not necessarily undermine their connection to India.

What makes this particular exchange pertinent is that the issue of NRI investments had been presented as an alternative to being dependent on IMF loans. Even those who opposed the government's handling of the Paul affair prefaced their criticism by proclaiming: "If I have to choose between going and begging before imperialist instruments like the IMF and non-resident investments, I would rather attract non-resident investments."[75] Given the nature of the Indian national movement and the postcolonial Indian nation-state, the identification of the imperial, exploitative character of the IMF, the World Bank, and other international monetary institutions, conduits of "foreign capital," was not in and of itself surprising. What is more intriguing is the manner in which the "non-resident Indian" or "person of Indian origin" was being constructed as a viable alternative source of much-needed foreign exchange and industrial capital. Nonresident Indians, it was argued by the government and its allies, were in a position to invest in the Indian economy and were naturally more inclined to do so. The capital that would come in through them would not be "foreign," as they themselves were Indians, regardless of where they lived and what citizenship they held.

At one level, the logic of this move seems obvious. The Indian government faced an economic crisis around the same time that NRI businessmen around the world began amassing their fortunes. Recognizing the economic potential of this group, the Indian government inaugurated a gradual shifting of the position that had characterized the relationship between the Indian state and the Indian diaspora for nearly three and a half decades since independence by reemphasizing their "Indianness." The instrumentality of this move seems reinforced by the fact that even the most fervent advocates of NRI investments, when pushed to the corner, admitted that ultimately their Indianness did not matter. The best illustration of this point is provided by the responses of the finance minister to repeated demands by the opposition that the government investigate the source of the NRI investments made under the new portfolio scheme:

> Forget about patriotism and other things. These are the monopoly of ours [sic]. But as a prospective investor, you will be guided by profit motive....[76]
>
> You decide whether you want to have this scheme or not. If you have the scheme, then you cannot expect a *foreign* investor to subject himself to your scrutiny. If you want to find the source of each and every money [sic] which is invested, then his reply to you would be that he is not interested in investing in *your* country.[77] (my emphasis)

Regardless of the rhetoric surrounding the NRIs' commitment to India's economic development, the "pragmatic" Indian government conceded that nonresident Indians were still "foreigners," who consequently were driven less by feelings of patriotism than by a "profit motive." As some members of Parliament pointed out, even the latter did not seem to tempt nonresident investments. Despite claims to the contrary by the government and its allies, NRI investments had not really come pouring in to shore up either India's foreign exchange reserves or Indian industries. In the words of Somnath Chatterjee:

> We do not want to stop [NRIs] from investing in these companies. But, what we find is that except one person, really one person, whose name is in the papers these days and who is holding luncheon meetings, dinner meetings, press conferences, hardly we hear [of] any other person taking advantage of this provision. Where are those non-residents of Indian origin?[78]

Given this context, it would be fairly easy to explain the hailing of the new "Indians" as a not very subtle (or, for that matter, effective) ploy by the Indian government to attract foreign investment. Although the crude economic rationale of this move should not be dismissed, I argue that focusing merely on that link precludes us from asking the far more important question of what made this shift possible. What enabled the Government of India to present what was, after all, a rather dramatic shift in policy as a natural way out of an impending economic crisis? Furthermore, while it was the government that put forth the scenario of the NRI as a viable and desirable alternative to seeking loans from institutions such as the IMF, why was it, for the most part, accepted even by those who challenged the efficacy of the NRI portfolio scheme? To answer these questions, we need to refocus our attention on the developments that revealed the changing nature of the global capitalist economy. At one level, these developments did manifest themselves in the changing profile of the Indian diaspora. More importantly, they made obvious the fracturing of the hegemony of the Indian bourgeoisie, which in turn put into question the dominant understanding of the relationship between the nation and the state that had shaped postcolonial India.

III. Fractured Hegemony and the Question of the Nation-State

As we have seen, the hegemony of the bourgeoisie in the postcolonial Indian state was produced in part by the projection of their particular interests as representing the larger interests of the nation—making the success of Indian capitalists seem intrinsic to the progress of the Indian nation. This representation had begun to unravel, and this unraveling was the most visible feature of the Swraj Paul controversy. While discussions regarding the potential abuses of the scheme raged furiously, the one issue on which the government and the opposition seemed to agree was that the NRI portfolio scheme served the very important purpose of highlighting the failures of the Indian capitalist class. For nearly thirty-four years, Indian industrialists had benefited from a system that allowed them to build up their enterprises using public finances. In this system, although nearly 30 percent of the total shares in the top ninety-seven companies were owned by public financial institutions, the management was under the control of promoter families that generally held around 10 percent. In slightly hyperbolic language, a member of parliament declared: "You allow the 4 percent man to control 50 percent investment by the government. Therefore, the government should come out with structural changes in the system. I say that the transfer of shares [in the Escorts case] is not only justifiable but it is also in the larger interest of our country."[79] The system, as members from both sides of the aisle pointed out, had been in place because of the deep, abiding relationship between the industrial houses and the Indian National Congress that could be traced back to the nationalist movement. At that juncture, nationalist leaders had consistently argued that to support the interests of the industrial houses was to ensure the welfare of the common man. Hence, the government, through the various public financial institutions, had been willing to invest up to "85 percent of the paid-up capital" in most of the large industries.[80] However, the Indian industrialists had misused public funds to expand their empires and "create wealth without risking their own money for investment." G. V. Vyas, one of the members of parliament participating in the debate, remarked:

> Gandhiji had told the big monopoly houses that they shouldn't think of themselves as masters, and that they should work as the trustees of the people. In that way they would serve the nation and ensure its development. But they [the monopolists] behaved like masters and used the money as if it was indeed their own. On that matter the Indian government could not control them at all.[81]

What was needed, therefore, was a new system that would enable the government to restructure the existing private sector in the country.

Government representatives argued that such a system was being put in place by the introduction of measures such as the Nonresident Indian Portfolio Scheme. The rationale of this argument was quite simple at one level. The government (and its supporters) accepted that there was some truth to the media reports portraying the Indian capitalists as feudal lords intent on creating business dynasties, whose lifestyles rivaled those of the early maharajahs. The dominance of big business that had characterized postindependence India had led to public finances being used to bankroll the growing empires of Indian capitalists. Swraj Paul's acquisitions were being challenged in court partly because they had been made under the rubric of a policy that was aimed at changing the nature of this alliance. Inviting nonresident industrialists into the country was a way to ensure that the private sector was characterized by greater competition and more productivity. This partial opening up of the economy did not in any way pose a threat to well-managed and established industries in the country.

While casting a different light on the Swraj Paul controversy, members of the opposition fundamentally agreed with the picture of the Indian capitalists presented by the government and its allies. They, too, argued that the Indian bourgeoisie had exploited national resources for their personal gain and no longer deserved to be supported by the state. However, they pointed out that allowing NRI businessmen like Paul free rein was not a solution to the problem. The controversy surrounding the Escorts case was the result of a clash of interests between different groups of capitalists, with neither side necessarily caring about the Indian nation. This was not to say that all NRIs would prove to be as untrustworthy as Swraj Paul and his ilk; the Gulf immigrants who had consistently remitted their earnings to their families had proved that the Indian diaspora was capable of being committed to the country's development. These were the NRIs who needed to be empowered by the Indian state. Members of the opposition further argued that the controversy provided the Indian government a unique opportunity to reevaluate the role of the state in ensuring national progress. It was obvious that the postindependence strategy of supporting the expansion of the private sector through the use of public resources had reached its limit. Despite the government's protestations to the contrary, what was not so obvious was the path to be taken in the future. This question needed more careful deliberation before the government adopted new policies.[82]

As the preceding summary makes obvious, the debates in the Indian parliament were at one level an attempt by the various political parties to obfuscate the true nature of the postcolonial Indian state by making it appear as though the relationship between Indian capitalists and political representatives was an alliance between equals in which the latter had actually been misled by the former. Though such attempts were ultimately unconvincing political theater, the debates that spilled over into the media discussions of the Swraj Paul incident made one aspect of the scenario very clear: even among its political representatives, the Indian bourgeoisie could no longer sustain its claims of representing the interests of the nation at large in the old ways. To understand how this came about, we need to keep in mind that the hegemony of the Indian bourgeoisie—and, for that matter, the coming into being of the independent Indian nation-state—was made possible in the context of a very specific moment in the development of the global capitalist economy. Under the Keynesian system that emerged after the end of World War II, as institutionalized in the Bretton Woods agreement, state actors were able to exert a level of control over the functioning of domestic economies. More specifically, it was considered both legitimate and desirable for states to regulate the flow of foreign capital and to invest in the public sector. In that context, it is not difficult to recognize the much-touted "Nehruvian socialism" as a manifestation of Keynesian capitalism. However, by the late 1970s, the rapid decline in the manufacturing edge of the United States and the collapse of the main elements of the Bretton Woods system announced the passing of the Keynesian model and the beginning of the neoliberal epoch. Under this changed international context, it was no longer possible for states to hold on to the economic strategies that had worked in earlier decades. In other words, a purely national bourgeoisie found it virtually impossible to sustain their hegemony on the grounds that had succeeded in the past. In the Indian case, reflections of the changing global economic conditions could thus be seen not just in the adoption of a major structural adjustment program in 1981 (the so-called homegrown conditionality) and its offshoot, the NRI Portfolio Scheme, but also in the questioning of the legitimacy of the Indian capitalist class by its own political representatives. What made the latter even easier was that the very same economic conditions that heralded the demise of the Keynesian system also enabled the emergence of a very specific kind of Indian diaspora, with undeniably close familial ties to the motherland. It was the presence of this group, the nonresident Indians, that made it possible for the Indian government to present its portfolio scheme to an overwhelmingly positive initial response. This occurred despite the fact that this scheme marked a major departure from postindependence policy concerning not only foreign investment in the Indian economy but also the Indian state's relationship to the Indian diaspora.

From the mid-1970s onward, the figure of the NRI began to draw greater attention in political and public deliberations regarding the issue of Indians abroad. While the migration of professionals to the West was seen as a cause of concern for the Indian state, the movement of unskilled laborers to the Gulf states provided a study in contrast. Using the argument that the temporary migration of a group that was largely unemployed in India would be beneficial to Indian society at large, various Indian governments worked to facilitate this process.[83] While there has been a lot of scholarly work underscoring the importance of the informal remittances that started flowing into India as a result of these waves of immigration, I would argue that it is a slightly different phenomenon that makes this period so crucial for understanding the changing relationship between India and Indians abroad. I refer here to the blurring of the boundaries between the categories used to distinguish earlier Indian immigrants from the newer waves. Increasingly, in official documents as well as in public, the category NRI—a somewhat amorphous term used initially to describe Indian citizens who did not reside in India—became the shorthand way of referring to the Indian diaspora at large.[84] The interchangeable usage of categories like "Nonresident Indian" and "Person of Indian Origin" is important because it enabled the blurring of distinctions based on rules of citizenship that had been in place since Indian independence, making possible the constitution of the Indian diaspora as a unified social group, with a deep and abiding connection to the Indian nation-state. A related effect of this conflation was the projection from the experiences of a very specific section of NRIs (the Gulf immigrants), leading to the somewhat grandiose and factually unsustainable claim that the Indian diaspora as a whole, partly because of its familial connections, was committed to the general well-being of India. As such, the Indian diaspora was seen as occupying a terrain that was not necessarily "foreign." Consequently, the proposal of the NRI Portfolio Scheme by Indira Gandhi's government was at least initially considered a perfectly logical move to deal with the economic crisis facing the country. It was under the aegis of this scheme that Swraj Paul attempted to build his industrial holdings in India. Paul, in many ways, was an ambiguous figure. Given his abiding familial ties to India (he was born and raised in India, with close family members still holding Indian citizenship at the time of the controversy), it is possible to see him as an insider attempting to challenge the dominant factions of the Indian bourgeoisie. At the same time, he appeared to be a functional part of both a narrowly defined British bourgeoisie (given his citizenship and stockholding in Great Britain) and a broader, newly emerging international capitalist class (given that his mobility rested on the across-the-board dismantling of state control over foreign investments). In setting out these possibilities, the point here is not to arrive at a definitive understanding of which type of bourgeoisie Paul represented. In fact, it was the very ambiguity of this figure that engendered the debates about the nature of the state and its relationship to the nation, making obvious the fracturing of the hegemony of the Indian bourgeoisie.

As these debates raged in (and outside) the Indian parliament, the matter of Escorts versus Swraj Paul and the government of India slowly made its way through the Indian court system. Although the management of Escorts won an important court battle when the Bombay High Court upheld its right to disavow Paul's share acquisitions, the government appealed the judgment to the Supreme Court of India. Even as the case was being heard in the Supreme Court, the assassination of Indira Gandhi on October 31, 1984, led to a sudden change in the political leadership of the country. Rajiv Gandhi, despite his lack of political experience, was chosen by the Congress Working Committee to lead the party in the parliamentary elections. The Congress swept back to power with an overwhelming majority, and Rajiv Gandhi took over as the new Indian prime minister. At his urging, the management of Escorts and Swraj Paul arrived at an out-of-court settlement that involved a buyback of the shares that Paul had purchased. The matter came to an end with neither party claiming a moral or material victory.

In terms of its immediate effects on the relationship between the Indian nation-state and the Indian diaspora, the Swraj Paul controversy seemed to be somewhat of a nonevent. Despite the initial support of the Indian government, Paul—the symbolic diasporic figure—was ultimately unsuccessful in his attempts to become an active participant in the Indian economy. The resolution of the controversy, moreover, maintained a demarcation of the domestic from the foreign, with Paul definitely falling into the latter category. Despite its tepid end, the curious case of Swraj Paul marked an extremely important moment, for it highlighted the particular trajectory of the global capitalist economy, which in turn called into question the hegemony of the Indian bourgeoisie. These developments made both possible and imperative a redefinition of the boundaries of the Indian nation and what constituted national interest. This controversy had significant long-term effects in the sense that it reopened questions regarding the Indian nation and the Indian state that had been treated as settled since the final phase of the Indian national movement. It made obvious the undermining of bourgeois hegemony in postcolonial India, the shifting of India's relationship to its diaspora beyond the terrain of citizenship where it had been lodged since independence, and the reopening of the debates on the kind of state needed to ensure national progress. It was in the context of these unsettled questions that the Indian state faced what came to be seen as the biggest economic crisis in its postindependence history in 1991.

5

From Indians Abroad to the Global Indian

[We] have inherited an economy in deep crisis.... The room for manoeuvre, to
live on borrowed money or time does not exist any more. Any further
postponement of macro-economic adjustment, long-overdue, would mean
that the balance of payments situation, now exceedingly difficult, would
become unmanageable and inflation, already high would exceed the limits of
tolerance....

—*Manmohan Singh, Finance Minister of India, Lok Sabha Debates,*
July 1991

I have always been conscious of the need for India to be sensitive to the hopes,
aspirations and concerns of its vast diaspora. *It is like a parental charge....* It is
with this perspective that we set up a High Level Committee... to examine all
matters relating to the interaction of the community with India.... [My]
government had accepted the Committee's recommendation to permit dual
citizenship for Persons of Indian Origin living in certain countries.

—*Atal Bihari Vajpayee, Prime Minister of India, Inaugural address,*
January 2003

In July 1991, Manmohan Singh, finance minister of the Congress-led government, unveiled what was arguably the most controversial budget in the history of
postcolonial India. Presented in the midst of a major economic crisis, the budget
proposed an ambitious program of neoliberal restructuring. This program, the
government claimed, was absolutely essential to "preserve our economic independence and restore the health of our economy."[1] Holding forth on the proposed economic liberalization program, Prime Minister P. V. Narasimha Rao
declared that contrary to public perception, the reforms were not being initiated
because of pressure from the International Monetary Fund (IMF).[2] In fact, his
government, like all postindependence regimes, remained committed to "rapid

107

industrialization." However, the nature of the global economy had changed, and his government realized that India needed to choose a "different path" to be competitive in a global economy. The different path envisaged by the reformers consisted of three main components: deliberately withdrawing the state from the "nonproductive" public sector, inviting foreign direct investment, and ensuring a greater involvement of nonresident Indians (NRIs) in the Indian economy by offering them greater incentives and opening up new sectors for their investment. While the new economic policy as a whole became a source of intense controversy, the proposed involvement of the NRIs seemed to draw particular ire from opponents. The reason for their reaction is not hard to understand. Reading the signs of an impending economic crisis, nervous NRI investors had been among the first to withdraw their money from India, contributing to a greater loss of confidence in the Indian economy and leading the country to "the edge of a precipice."[3] Echoing themes from earlier debates about the Indian diaspora, opponents of the proposed liberalization program were quick to claim that this act was merely the latest manifestation of a pattern of upholding personal interests at the cost of greater national interests that typified NRIs in general. Although the government and its allies were quick to challenge the opposition's contentions, even they could not deny the charge that NRI withdrawals in the early part of 1991 had precipitated the economic crisis. Despite this seeming betrayal, they argued that it was essential to establish institutional mechanisms that would restore the confidence of the NRIs in the Indian economy, encourage them to participate in India's development, and enable the government to be more responsive to the needs of the Indian diaspora at large.

Just over a decade after the official liberalization of the Indian economy, Prime Minister Atal Bihari Vajpayee—the leader of the BJP-led coalition government—inaugurated the first Pravasi Bharatiya Divas (Day of the Indians Abroad). In his inaugural address, the prime minister acknowledged the Indian state's "parental obligations" toward the Indian diaspora while declaring that India had finally taken its place on the global stage. This was in part due to the "courage, persistence and enterprise" of persons of Indian origin who had "changed the world's perception of Indians, and hence of India." Indians abroad had proved their loyalty not only in their "tireless championing of [India's] cause" whenever "India faced a threat to its security or territorial integrity" but also in their "projecting the truth about India to the world in a credible and effective manner." In recognition of this role, the prime minister declared that his government would introduce the necessary legislation to permit dual citizenship for Indians abroad in certain countries.[4] Fifty years after Jawaharlal Nehru's ultimatum to the Indians abroad to choose either Indian citizenship or the citizenship of their host countries, the Indian government was officially acknowledging that, despite setting up homes in "countries, near and far," despite being "citizens of their adopted countries," the 20 million members of the Pravasi Bharatiya community were truly *Indians* abroad.

As just noted, even a decade prior to the celebration the first Pravasi Bharatiya Divas, the figure of the Indian abroad (whether described as an NRI, a nonresident Indian, or a PIO, a person of Indian origin) and the relationship of this subject to the Indian nation and state was the subject of intense criticism in public and political discourse. This criticism, furthermore, fit well within the rubric of the postcolonial Indian state's official policy toward the Indian diaspora. However, over the course of a strikingly short period of time, the Indian state discarded its decades-old set of policies, moving from a disavowal of its obligations toward the transnational Indian nation to the production of a domestic abroad, signaled by events such as the annual celebration of Pravasi Bharatiya Divas, the establishment of a Ministry of Overseas Indian Affairs, and the passage of legislation permitting dual citizenship. To make sense of this dramatic turnaround, this chapter focuses on analyzing the political struggles that characterized a specific time period—the period that marked the official introduction of the neoliberal restructuring of the Indian economy and set the stage for the production of the Indian domestic abroad. The chapter begins with a brief examination of the political instability and looming balance of payments crisis that provided the visible backdrop for the introduction of economic liberalization in India. I highlight the three main features of the "different path" envisaged by the reforms program: disinvestment from the public sector, a greater openness to foreign capital, and the initiation of a more institutionalized relationship with NRIs. I argue that, taken together, these policies seemed to signify an overt rejection of the socioeconomic agenda that had shaped the postcolonial Indian state. Their imposition and adoption, in other words, symbolized a deep crisis of the hegemony of the Indian bourgeoisie.

As we saw in the last chapter, the hegemony of the Indian bourgeoisie was established in the context of both a particular moment in the development of global capitalism (i.e., the onset of Keynesianism) and the historical experience of the struggles against colonialism. This in turn produced a state that justified its policies in terms of protecting the domestic economy from foreign exploitation and steering the productive forces of the nation to promote the welfare of the people. However, with the institution of neoliberal reforms, the state had officially started the process of dismantling safeguards put in place for this purpose. Furthermore, it was actually inviting foreign investors who could potentially exploit the Indian economy, challenging the very constitutive basis of postcolonial India. In other words, the restructuring of the economy along neoliberal lines marked at a very obvious level the undermining of the raison d'être of the postcolonial Indian state. Despite this, and notwithstanding the intense debates on the subject, neoliberal reforms were not only accepted by the Indian parliament of the day but also sustained and developed by successive Indian governments in the coming years.[5] Given this context, it becomes obvious that to make sense of the crisis engendered by neoliberal restructuring, we need to address two crucial and related questions: first, what were the conditions that made possible the adoption of a set of policies that seemed to go against the commonly held understandings of the reasons for the very existence of the state, and second, what was it that allowed these policies to be justified and sustained over the decades that followed? This chapter addresses these questions by situating the debates surrounding structural reforms within the broader question of the unraveling and remaking of bourgeois hegemony.

The aftermath of the Swraj Paul incident witnessed a series of internecine struggles within the ranks of the Indian bourgeoisie. The result of these struggles was a temporary sidelining of the more traditional industrial houses represented by the venerable Federation of Indian Chambers of Commerce and Industry (FICCI) and the emergence of a new dominant faction of the bourgeoisie represented by what came to be known as the Confederation of Indian Industries (CII). This chapter contends that it was this newly dominant faction of the Indian bourgeoisie, which had, since the mid-1980s, favored and pushed for a more open economy, that paved the way for the adoption of neoliberal reforms in 1991.[6] However, given their negation of the foundational socioeconomic agenda of the postcolonial Indian state, these policies did mark a significant crisis of legitimacy for the Indian bourgeoisie. The task faced by its dominant faction at this juncture was not merely convincing legislators about the necessity of adopting a certain set of economic policies. Rather, it was a larger one of making the connections between their interests (in this case, liberalizing the Indian economy) and the nation's interests appear seamless and natural. I argue that it was this challenge that made imperative the hailing of the diaspora by the Indian state as a natural and *essential* part of India's future. I make this argument by focusing not so much on the more obvious economic rationale (that of NRIs as a source of the much needed and desired remittances and foreign direct investment) but on the production of what Aihwa Ong calls the "new valorized subject."[7] If economic liberalization was not to be seen as an instrumental and calculated attempt by factions of the bourgeoisie to maintain and perpetuate their privileged status, if it was to be sustainable over a longer period of time, then what was needed was a way to make it seem like an essential step in the path of national progress. To put it differently, what was needed was a subject who could plausibly embody national aspirations, the potential for India to succeed in the global economy. In the context of the neoliberal restructuring of the state, then, the rearticulation of bourgeois hegemony made essential a diasporic reimagining of the nation. This chapter concludes with a discussion of how these two ongoing, simultaneous processes have resulted in the production of the Indian domestic abroad, centered on the new subject, "the global Indian."

I. "The Edge of the Precipice"

In March 1991, in a noticeable departure from tradition, Finance Minister Yashwant Sinha presented an abridged "interim budget" to the Indian Parliament.[8] Pointing to the deteriorating economic conditions, Sinha claimed that the new government (which came to power in November 1990) had inherited a crisis of epic proportions, which was the result of consistent "shortcomings in the macro-management of the economy in the past."[9] It was obvious, he stated, that "neither the government nor the economy can live beyond its means for long." Drastic measures and a complete restructuring of the economy were needed. This, how-ever, was a task that had been overlooked because of the political instability that had characterized India in the late 1980s.

As discussed in the previous chapter, the Swraj Paul controversy had come to an anticlimactic end with the agreement brokered by the new government that came to power after Indira Gandhi's assassination in October 1984. The immedi-ate aftermath, however, was far from pleasant for those factions of the Indian bourgeoisie who had aligned themselves against Paul. While some did represent the brokered agreement with Paul as a victory, the unraveling of bourgeois hege-mony became even more apparent with the increasing visibility of various inter-necine struggles. I will return to this point later in this section. For now, it suffices to note that despite the playing out of these struggles, during his five-year term as prime minister, Rajiv Gandhi and his allies succeeded to a large extent in push-ing to the background the intensely contested questions regarding the boundar-ies of the Indian nation and the role of the state that had been brought to the fore by the debates surrounding the NRI portfolio scheme.[10] However, the fact that these questions were simmering just below the surface was brought home toward the end of Rajiv Gandhi's term when General Sitiveni Rabuka came to power in Fiji as a result of a military coup.[11] Rabuka claimed that the coup had become necessary to prevent the Indian community in Fiji, which was nearly half the total population of the islands, from gaining complete control of the state. Arguing that his government was committed to protecting the rights of the Fijians (whom he differentiated from the descendants of the indentured laborers from India), Rabuka instituted a series of measures, including a new constitution sanctioning discrimination against Fijians of Indian origin. The story of the coup that served to legitimize discrimination against the PIO led to a huge public outcry in India. While expressing the Indian state's "distress," K. Natwar Singh, the foreign minister in Rajiv Gandhi's cabinet, declared, "What is happening in Fiji has distinct and unacceptable racial overtones."[12] In many ways, the rhetoric used by various public officials in India was fairly similar to the arguments made by postcolonial Indian governments dealing with the issue of discrimination against the PIO in Burma, Ceylon, South Africa, and East Africa. The government deplored the racism inherent in such practices, claimed that discrimination against the PIO was part of a larger problem of human rights violations, and expressed its concerns in multilateral fora like the Commonwealth and the United Nations.[13] However, what was different in this instance was that the Indian foreign minister seemed to indicate that the Indian state had a duty to protect the rights of the PIO around the world and, moreover, did so in the context of discussing India's growing naval might.[14] The constant reiteration of India's "strength," combined with the invocation of its duties toward "Indians abroad" was construed as so threatening by the Fijian authorities that they closed down the Indian embassy in Suva. While the question of Fijian Indians remained unsettled, a conjuncture of events that included the advent of coalition politics in India and Rabuka's ceding of power to a civilian government tempered the political exchanges between the two countries. This resolution, however, did not put a stop to the ongoing discussions regarding the Indian nation-state's relationship to the Indian diaspora—a discussion that got a further fillip when, within a matter of two years, the figure of the NRI began to loom large in the Indian political imaginary once again.

The background for this reemergence was in part the turbulence that characterized Indian politics at the beginning of a new decade. After serving a full five-year term (1984–1989), the Rajiv Gandhi-led Congress (I) suffered an ignominious defeat at the polls. However, given that none of the other political parties had won enough parliamentary seats to form the government, the only way out of the political impasse was the formation of loose-knit alliances that could stake their claim to power. The era of coalition governments inaugurated by the swearing in of V. P. Singh's National Front in December 1989 proved to be highly unstable for India. Within two years (from December 1989 to July 1991), the machinations of various political parties caused the collapse of two coalition governments—the first was led by the National Front and the second by Chandra Shekhar's Samajwadi Janata Party (SJP)—and the coming to power of a new Congress government led by P. V. Narasimha Rao.[15]

Even in the middle of these political machinations, the signs of an impending economic crisis were hard to miss. Within a relatively short period of twelve months, India had requested and received two major loans from the IMF.[16] As briefly mentioned earlier, Yashwant Sinha (the finance minister during the brief tenure of the Chandra Shekhar government) warned Parliament of the inherent dangers of the situation during the presentation of the interim budget, claiming that the government needed more time to present a comprehensive plan to deal with a crisis of this magnitude. However, before Sinha could present a completed budget, the vagaries of coalition politics in India led to the collapse of the ruling alliance and the emergence of yet another government.

Citing among other reasons "the nervousness of non-resident Indian investors who were taking large sums of money out of the country," the new Congress-led government of Prime Minister P. V. Narasimha Rao devalued the Indian rupee almost immediately after coming to power.[17] This measure immediately drew intense (and critical) public attention because it marked only the third time in India's postindependence history that its currency had been devalued.[18] But the more important source of the controversy was the general perception that the devaluation had been carried out under the dictation of the IMF. When called on by Parliament to defend his government's action, Finance Minister Manmohan Singh began by asserting that the country was facing a grave economic crisis caused in part by a loss of confidence among investors regarding the stability of the Indian currency and the ability of India's banking institutions to stave off a potential "default situation." While accepting that India's balance of payments had been weak for a number of years, he argued that as long as the Congress had been in power (until November 1989), "there was no question of a lack of confidence in our currency." The crisis began when the other parties came to power and "made a statement to the world that 'we have inherited an empty treasury.'" With the increasing speculation about India's balance of payments crisis, it had become impossible to sustain the value of the Indian currency. It was under these conditions and not "at the behest of the IMF" that he, in consultation with the prime minister and other cabinet colleagues, had decided to fix a new exchange rate. This, he argued, would increase the profitability of Indian exports, discourage the import of nonessential goods, stem capital flight, and improve India's balance of payments situation. While the opposition challenged all these claims, pointing especially to the devaluation of 1966 as an exemplar of why such measures would not really help the Indian economy, the real controversy arose less than a week later, after the presentation of the annual budget of 1991.

The Reforms Budget

Echoing his predecessor, Finance Minister Manmohan Singh began by claiming that his government had "inherited an economy that was in deep crisis...due to the combined impact of the political instability [after November 1989], the accentuation of fiscal imbalances and the Gulf crisis."[19] This crisis had been further exacerbated by the sharp decline in capital inflows, caused mainly by the sudden withdrawal of nonresident deposits in the early part of 1991, leading India to the "edge of a precipice."[20] The only way to stave off a potential fall, to "preserve our economic independence and restore the health of our economy," Singh argued, was through a program of "macro-level adjustment." Making very clear what this program would entail, he stated:

The thrust of the reform process would be to increase the efficiency and international competitiveness of industrial production, to utilize for this purpose foreign investment and foreign technology to a much greater degree than we have done in the past, to increase the productivity of investment, to ensure that India's financial sector is rapidly modernized, and to improve the performance of the public sector, so that the key sectors of our economy are enabled to attain an adequate technological and competitive edge in a fast changing global economy.[21]

Despite the similarity in the rhetoric of economic independence, what the plan proposed was not merely an adjustment but a reversal of the Nehruvian vision as embodied in the Industrial Plan of 1956.

Addressing the issue of the public sector, Singh claimed that his government was committed to continuing the Nehruvian tradition of emphasizing the importance of the planning process but that this process needed to become "more sensitive to the needs of a dynamic economy." Setting aside oratorical flights of fancy, what this actually meant was the inauguration of an era of privatization. In that sense, the commitment to the planning process was largely in the realm of rhetoric. The import substitution that had been the hallmark of postindependence governments, while understandable as a political strategy, had generally been "indiscriminate" and "inefficient." In this process, the public sector, which had been envisaged by the founders of independent India as a "vibrant, modern, competitive" element "capable of generating large surpluses," had ended up "an absorber of national savings without adequate returns." So, rather than continuing on a path that had led to "overt centralization and bureaucratization," the government intended to "expand the scope and the area of operation of market forces." The first step in this process would entail a review and eventual trimming by 20 percent of the Indian state's portfolio of public sector investments. Furthermore, "chronically sick" public enterprises would be turned over to the Board of Industrial and Financial Reconstruction (BIFR), which would attempt to rehabilitate those enterprises and make them profitable. As a final step, if the BIFR so recommended, sick industries would be closed down.

Claiming that after decades of planned industrialization it was important to provide access to "capital, technology and markets," Singh also announced the liberalization of the policy regime that governed foreign investment. The measures he proposed included the prompt approval of direct foreign investment in high-priority industries, raising the limit of foreign equity participation to 51 percent. The rationale for this move, he explained, was to ensure that critical industries would have the finances required to import capital goods during the investment stage. Since the "high-priority industries" were geared toward export production, the payment of dividends to foreign investors would eventually be matched by export earnings. At the level of state institutions, the budget proposed a "special board" that would negotiate with multinational corporations and approve foreign direct investment in "selected areas." By taking these steps, the government claimed that it was exposing India's industrial sector "to competition from abroad in a phased manner" and making possible renewed attention to the issues of "cost, efficiency and quality." However, the goal of "attracting substantial investment" was not to be limited to multinational companies.

Calling attention once again to the figure of the NRI, the budget first and foremost proposed a "comprehensive review of policies and procedures bearing on non-resident Indian investments" to ensure that there were no impediments in the path of those who might want to set up new ventures in their motherland. New sectors like infrastructure, housing, and real estate development were to be opened up to NRI investments. Moreover, for the first time, the government proposed establishing a new office to coordinate interactions between the Indian state and NRIs: the Chief Commissioner of Non-Resident Indians. As a more immediate step, however, Singh announced two schemes meant to expedite the inflow of foreign exchange into the country. The first was the announcement of "India Development Bonds," issued by the State Bank of India. These bonds were to be denominated in U.S. dollars and made available for purchase by NRIs and the overseas corporate bodies they controlled. There was to be no ceiling for investments in the bonds, which had a maturity of five years, after which both the face value and the nontaxable interest earned on the bonds were fully repatriable with exchange rate protection. Furthermore, the scheme allowed for the "gifting" of such bonds to resident Indians, who were entitled to similar exemptions from income tax.[22] As mentioned earlier, in the months preceding the foreign exchange crisis (especially in the first few of the year), NRIs were among the first to withdraw their deposits from Indian banks, leading to the incendiary claim that it was their action that precipitated the crisis. While the budget remained studiedly silent on the latter aspect, it did present the decrease in NRI remittances as a real problem facing the country. As a remedy, the second scheme proposed that all foreign exchange remittances into the country from NRIs would be subject to neither scrutiny (under the Foreign Exchange Regulation Act) nor the gift tax that usually applied to such transactions. Knowing that these proposals would draw the ire of the opposition, Singh emphasized that they were essential to rebuild the confidence of nonresident Indians in the Indian economy and that at least the second one would be time-bound, with the immunity given to remittances lapsing after November 30, 1991.

At this juncture, it is crucial to reiterate a point made in the previous chapter. Despite constant references to NRIs in the budget, the group that was being hailed was not limited to those who would technically fit into that category. Although the term "nonresident Indian" was initially meant to describe Indians who lived overseas but held on to their Indian citizenship, in both political and popular discourse it had become a shorthand referring to the Indian diaspora as a whole. This is not to deny that there were still substantial differences in the institutional links between the Indian nation-state and sections of the diaspora. What made the budget of 1991 important is that it was the first legislative attempt since the NRI Portfolio Scheme, discussed in the previous chapter, to collapse those distinctions. Referring to the "NRIs of foreign nationality" in his budget speech, Manmohan Singh made it obvious that they, too, would be able to invest in the newly opened sectors of the Indian economy.[23]

The minister announced these measures as part of the "determined action" undertaken by the government to meet the "grave economic crisis" facing the country. While acknowledging that some of the reforms might point to a path that was different from the one chosen by the founders of modern India, he argued that fundamentally the new government remained committed to the same goals and would not "renege on our nation's firm and irrevocable commitment to the pursuit of equity and social justice." The attempts to read into the reforms some kind of continuity with earlier policies, however, were bound to run into some major obstacles. The proposals put forth in the budget—especially those concerning disinvestment and a greater reliance on foreign capital—seemingly struck at the very heart of the socioeconomic agenda that had shaped the postcolonial Indian state. How, then, do we make sense of what appears to be a paradoxical situation? To understand both the need to read some continuity in reforms and the conditions that made their introduction possible, it is essential to look beyond the supposed moment of the economic crisis.

As we saw in the two previous chapters, the establishment of the hegemony of the Indian bourgeoisie meant that postcolonial India would be characterized by state practices that emphasized citizenship as the marker of national belonging, the nationalization (i.e., state control) of key sectors in industry and banking, and the strict regulation and limited inflow of foreign capital. These practices made sense in the context of the prevailing developments in the global capitalist economy and the historical experiences of an anticolonial struggle. Over the more than four decades of independent India's existence, the hegemony of the national bourgeoisie, admittedly, had been challenged time and again. For instance, moments of economic crises such as those in 1949 and 1966, when the Indian state was forced to devalue its currency in the aftermath of wars with neighboring Pakistan, did get translated into a crisis of legitimacy for the ruling class. However, under the more supportive conditions of a Keynesian-oriented global economic order, these crises could be largely weathered. But the Keynesianism of the early post–World War II decades, connected to the maintenance of the American manufacturing edge, was itself essentially unsustainable in the long run. As this system gave way to the neoliberal phase of capitalist developments on a global scale, it became increasingly harder for factions of the bourgeoisie across different national contexts to push for an agenda promoting policies like capital controls and state involvement in the industrial sector. In this context, it becomes possible to understand not only why Swraj Paul became a cause célèbre but also how his intervention in the realm of Indian industry high-lighted the unraveling of bourgeois hegemony. The analysis of the debates sur-rounding Paul's takeover attempt in the last chapter clearly revealed that by the 1980s, any legitimacy accrued by members of the Indian bourgeoisie as represen-tatives of a larger national cause was slowly, but surely, being undermined. The image of the Indian industrialist that had once been promoted by leaders of the Indian National Congress—as a genuine partner of the nationalist movement, one who put national interests above narrow self-interests—had begun to fray. Gradually taking its place was a picture of a breed that had become entrenched in ill-earned privilege, that depended on familial ties to accrue influence, and that was fundamentally opposed to professional innovation and growth. In the immediate aftermath of the Paul crisis, this latter image gained further ground as stories of infighting among FICCI members became public.

Since its inception in 1927, FICCI had been the institutional flagship of the Indian bourgeoisie, in many ways the embodiment of its claims to represent the interests of the nation at large. Its relationship with the Congress and the nation-alist movement was such that speaking at its fourth annual session, Gandhi declared, "I cannot forget the services rendered by the commercial class, but I want you to make Congress [sic] your own and we would willingly surrender the reins to you... [since] the work can be better done by you."[24] As we saw in the last chapter, in the years leading up to Indian independence, the FICCI leader-ship did take up Gandhi's invitation in a manner that allowed it to present the Indian bourgeoisie variously as an equal partner of the Indian National Congress and as the economic arm of the nationalist movement.[25] Although there were undoubtedly differences among the members of the association on fundamen-tally important issues, including the nature and extent of support for Congress actions during the anticolonial struggle, the institution itself accrued strong nationalist credentials.[26] Despite a major falling out among its most prominent members in the 1960s, these credentials carried FICCI through the first three decades of Indian independence.[27] However, by the mid-1980s, the internecine struggle among the members of the Indian bourgeoisie, already witnessed dur-ing the Swraj Paul controversy, took the form of a well-publicized struggle for control over FICCI. Recognizing the potential for conflict among its members, the founders of FICCI had attempted to create an elaborate set of informal rules to allow appointment of officeholders through consultation and consensus. This complex system, which took account of factors such as familial connections, seniority, and regional affiliation, provided a more or less functioning institutional foundation for FICCI for three decades, until the consensus among the major business houses finally broke down. What started as a conflict between familial factions over the election of the managing committee in 1981 became an all-out war between groups that aligned themselves along regional lines. By 1986, FICCI itself became the biggest casualty of this war, with one of the factions, the Bombay caucus, officially tendering its resignation from the association.[28] The feuding within the ranks of the Indian bourgeoisie, however, continued unabated, with the breakaway section joining the almost moribund Associated Chambers of Commerce and Industry (ASSOCHAM)—a group that had been created in 1920 to represent the interests of British capital—with the express aim of reorganizing it to challenge FICCI's political clout. It was a testament to the success of this group that within two years, FICCI and ASSOCHAM became involved in a very messy and public battle to acquire control of the Joint Business Councils (JBCs) that had been created as a result of bilateral agreements between the Indian state and its major trading partners.[29] Although that particular battle came to an end when the Indian government forced the two associations to sign a Memorandum of Understanding agreeing to joint representation on the JBCs, neither FICCI nor ASSOCHAM gave up on their larger battle, ensuring a continuing undermining of their public credibility.[30]

The conflicts that characterized the relationships between members of the various business associations in India at this juncture were certainly shaped by the rise to power of individuals like R. P. Goenka (the vice president of the united FICCI before its split), H. S. Singhania (the leader of the Bombay Caucus), and L. M. Thapar (the first president of the reorganized ASSOCHAM, a school friend of Prime Minister Rajiv Gandhi), to name but a few of the protagonists. However, focusing merely on the peccadilloes of prominent individuals occludes the larger changes that were taking place in the landscape of Indian industry. Although industry in India was still largely dominated by the handful of family-based conglomerates that had long historical roots, the picture was undergoing a gradual transformation by the 1980s. For the first time in postindependence Indian history, technologically advanced segments of industry—large, medium, or small-scale—began emerging as visible actors.[31] Differentiating themselves from the older, traditional ranks of the Indian bourgeoisie, this new group played up their connections to the modern segment of sunrise industries, presenting themselves not as inheritors of familial legacies, but rather a professionally trained cadre of entrepreneurs who were committed to technological innovation and economic growth. While supporting the Bombay caucus as it broke away from FICCI, entrepreneurs within this faction ultimately did not join ASSOCHAM (the association of choice for the larger industrial families), but rather the Association of Indian Engineering Industry (AIEI). Created in 1972 as a hybrid of two organizations that represented foreign and Indian engineering companies, the AIEI had over the decade of its existence garnered a reputation as a professionally organized institution that was free from the kind of factionalism characterizing FICCI.

With the influx of new blood, the AIEI (renamed the "Confederation of Engineering Industry" in 1986, and later "Confederation of Indian Industry" in 1992) deliberately set out to present itself as the face of a modern, progressive industrial sector. As Stanley Kochanek points out, at an institutional level, the organization was aided not only by the extent of its coffers (it was the richest business association at the time) but also by a well-trained, highly professional secretariat led by its much-lauded secretary-general Tarun Das, a growing network of overseas contacts, and a decentralized system of national, state, zone, and local organizations that allowed a varied and involved membership.[32] Most importantly, there was a one-year limit for officeholders and a strong prohibition of any kind of electoral canvassing. The AIEI/CII made no bones about the fact that its governing philosophy favored "de-regulation, de-control and de-licensing" in all areas and that it was willing to work in partnership with the Indian government to push for favorable policies.[33] On all counts, the organization very deliberately and clearly set itself up as distinct from the old "family business-model" embodied by FICCI. That it had succeeded in doing so became obvious when the young Prime Minister Rajiv Gandhi not only appeared as the main speaker at the organization's annual convention in 1985 but also invited its members to travel as part of the official Indian contingent to the Soviet Union.[34] Within a short period of time, government officials were reported as praising AIEI/CII as "dynamic, efficient and forward-looking yuppies" who could deliver the goods, as compared with FICCI and ASSOCHAM, which were viewed as "aging dowagers whose best days were behind them."[35] Using their growing visibility and credibility with government officials to their advantage, the new breed of yuppie entrepreneurs made their desire for changes in economic policy quite clear. As part of a well-thought-out campaign, the AIEI/CII released a theme paper in April 1991 calling for the opening up of Indian markets. They followed it up by holding meetings with academics, journalists, influential bureaucrats, and parliamentarians from both sides of the aisle to build what they called a "national consensus on economic issues."[36] It was this "quiet revolution" in Indian industry, as Jorgen Pederson argues persuasively, that set the stage for economic liberalization on a scale, and in a way, that had not yet been witnessed in India.[37]

The budget of 1991, it should be recalled, was not a radical break from the past in the sense of introducing policies that were fundamentally different from what had been tried before. If anything, it attempted to bring together economic policies that various governments through the 1980s had attempted to institute. What was different, however, was the manner in which the proponents of liberalization framed this moment. Finance Minister Manmohan Singh concluded his budget presentation with a ringing claim that despite the pain involved in any adjustment program, the structural reforms were but a step in the direction of enabling modern India to fulfill its potential and, in fact, would herald its emergence as a major economic power:

> I do not minimize the difficulties that lie ahead on the long and arduous journey on which we have embarked. But as Victor Hugo one said: "no power on earth can stop an idea whose time has come." I suggest to this august House that the emergence of India as a major economic power in the world happens to be one such idea. Let the whole world hear it loud and clear. India is now wide awake. We shall prevail. We shall overcome.

This assurance, however, did not carry much weight with the opposition, which immediately began to challenge the legitimacy of the budget proposals by accusing the government of lacking "self-respect," of buckling under the pressure of international agencies, of mortgaging India's "economic sovereignty," and of "selling out" to the foreigner yet again.[38]

II. "Continuity with Change"

Countering the optimistic overtones of Singh's speech, members of the opposition argued that all the budget would accomplish was to declare to the world that "there was no strength in the Indian economy" and that India had been reduced to the status of a "beggar country."[39] They further pointed out that the situation was not helped by the government's conflicting claims about the nature of the economic crisis. On the one hand, members of the cabinet had been blaming the various non-Congress parties in power between November 1989 and July 1991 for the loss of confidence among investors that precipitated the foreign exchange crisis. On the other, they were arguing that the deeper structural problems of the economy necessitated a large-scale adjustment program. While the government's attempts to blame the non-Congress parties for the economic crisis were quickly dismissed, the latter claim became the pivot on which an extremely contentious debate revolved. As the opposition saw it, by declaring that the state not only needed to withdraw from the public sector but also had to welcome foreign capital, the government was effectively pronouncing the failure of the policies followed since independence and, by extension, the failure of the postcolonial Indian nation-state itself.

Taking on the claim that the public sector had proved to be not just unprofitable but a drain on national resources, opposition members argued that "earning profits [was] never the sole objective of the public sector."[40] In fact, public sector units (PSUs) had been set up specifically in areas that despite being capital-intensive, did not guarantee high returns. These units were meant to have "pioneered the entry into new areas of industrialization, opened up backward regions, provided the engine for technological development, and generally set the tone for industrialization in this country"—tasks that even the current Congress Prime Minister P. V. Narasimha Rao acknowledged they had fulfilled.[41] This was not to say that all PSUs were being run well or that there was no need to any reforms at all. But to blame them for the country's economic ills just did not make sense. The Nehruvian model that the Indian nation-state had followed since independence had emphasized public-sector industries because of a commitment to a specific vision of social justice and economic development. It was this commitment that was being "overturned" by the new "budget philosophy."[42] Blaming the public sector served the more insidious purpose of generating support for the government's larger project of liberalizing the Indian economy, broadening the scope of the private sector, and inviting in foreign capital through the multinational corporations (MNCs) and, of course, the NRIs.

As part of its program of gradually relaxing the controls on the entry of foreign capital, the government had announced that subsidiaries of multinational corporations would be allowed to have up to 51 percent and, in cases where production would be completely geared toward exports, even 100 percent of foreign equity capital in their companies. In his budget speech, Manmohan Singh had made the argument that such investments would not only improve India's balance of payments situation but also actually serve to make the Indian private sector more open and efficient. In turn, he had claimed, this increased efficiency would eventually be beneficial to the Indian public at large. The opposition, however, presented a different picture. Inviting multinational companies to be a part of the Indian economy, they argued, would be disastrous in the long run. To begin with, it would not necessarily lead to any improvements in India's balance of payments situation, since the Indian government was providing these companies tremendous tax incentives, as well as the right to repatriate their profits. However, what was far more dangerous was the distinct possibility that this move would ultimately lead to an undermining of India's economic sovereignty in the sense of enabling "foreigners" to be in a position of power vis-à-vis the Indian nation-state. As a member pointed out: "Where do we want foreign capital? We want this only in such sectors where we are deficient, where they will bring in technology....What does it mean? We will only have them in those areas that are considered to be crucial. Will they not be in a position to dictate to us after they enter here?"[43] This question resonated deeply across the political spectrum, for it implicitly alluded to the precolonial period in Indian history when foreign traders had been granted special rights by Indian rulers. During the course of several debates on the structural reforms, other members made the connection more explicit. While granting trading rights to the British and French East India Companies in the seventeenth and eighteenth centuries, Indian rulers had unwittingly paved the way for the eventual colonization of India. By overlooking this historical experience, the opposition argued that the present Indian government was leading India down a dangerous path.[44] It was precisely to deflect this line of criticism that the government had emphasized that the foreign capital infusion needed to revitalize the Indian economy would not just come from "foreigners." It would come from "Indians," the NRIs, who despite not residing in India or, for that matter, having Indian citizenship would play a crucial role in shoring up India's foreign exchange reserves in the short run as well as in the long-term restructuring of the Indian economy. The government and its allies further contended that it was to encourage such a partnership that they had put in place schemes whereby NRIs (and Overseas Corporate Bodies, of which they were a part) could buy India Development Bonds and, for a limited period, remit foreign exchange without any fear of legal scrutiny. The measures claimed by the government to be necessary trust-building incentives, however, were challenged by the opposition in terms that echoed the debates surrounding the NRI Portfolio Scheme of 1983.

The schemes presented by the government rested on the relaxation of the regulatory mechanisms that had been put in place by the Foreign Exchange Regulation Act (FERA) of 1973. Opposition members argued that rather than guaranteeing an inflow of foreign exchange, removing these controls could potentially have deleterious effects on the Indian economy. The main concern these members expressed was that the government's schemes would make it easier for unscrupulous businessmen—both resident and nonresident—to launder their "black money." Given that the government was repeatedly assuring NRIs that it would not scrutinize the source of their remittances or their investments, it was quite possible for "people having unaccounted money to transfer that money abroad and get back the same money under some fictitious NRI's name into the country," making seemingly legitimate investments in sectors such as housing that would have high returns.[45] What made the proposal even more problematic was that there was no need to create a fictitious NRI to serve as a front. There was, as CPI(M) member Geeta Mukherjee contended, "a group among [the NRIs]—the Indian businessmen who thrive in American and European markets and also in some tax-free haven," whose resources were mostly "Indian black money laundered through Swiss banks."[46] These NRIs, the opposition argued, would be more than willing partners in any attempts to exploit the many loopholes in the government's schemes. Some members did pointedly claim that they were only speaking of a "particular kind" of NRI and, in doing so, were attempting to temper the high expectations from the social group at large. However, despite these qualifications, underlying much of the criticism of the government's attempts to overcome the foreign exchange crisis was a general distrust of the figure of the nonresident Indian.

Opposition members were also quick to point out that the role played by NRIs in the months leading up to July 1991 was hardly reflective of a deep, abiding patriotism. If anything, NRIs had precipitated the international loss of confidence in the Indian economy by hastily withdrawing their deposits from Indian banks at the first sign of trouble. Given this context, the government's faith in NRIs seemed to be quite baseless. Giving voice to the general skepticism about nonresident Indians, Indrajit Gupta asked: "You expect these people, who have gone out of the country, who left the country in order to make more money abroad, that they will suddenly become patriotic…because of your appeal to them?"[47] He went on to argue that even the government seemed to realize that the appeal to patriotism would not really work and had instead provided numerous incentives in the budget to attract NRI investments. The fact that the budget included extraordinary measures, such as the temporary relaxation of FERA, proved that NRIs were at best unreliable partners who would be willing to invest in India only if provided with guaranteed high returns. Even with these measures in place, there seemed to be no guarantee that the NRIs would be "bringing their money…or even part of it" back into India.[48] Another variant of this argument emphasized that the Indian government was treating as saviors a group of people who had left the country after fully exploiting the available resources and was doing so in a way that undermined the contribution of the "poorest of the poor": NRIs "have studied in government colleges where they were funded by the poor people's money in this country. On every student, Rs 1.5 lakh has been paid by the poorest of the poor of this country. You are putting them at a higher plane making all Indians as second-class citizens to them."[49] It was not just the central government that drew the ire of the opposition on this score. They claimed that the example set by the government was being followed by even state legislators and bureaucrats, who tended to greet visiting NRIs as though "Lord Vishnu had arrived," despite the fact that they were "the people who had left the country and had no interest in it."[50] Even those supporting the budget argued that it had ended up giving a message to the world that only "NRIs money and IMF loan [sic] can save India: otherwise the Indian nation will be in peril." Unfortunately, this was a message that not only overlooked the ability and the willingness of Indians to sacrifice for the cause of the Indian nation but also undermined the "prestige, dignity and pride" of "mother India."[51]

What these discussions make obvious is that, despite the attempts of the Indian government and its allies to present the nonresident Indians as a group that had a deep and abiding connection to the motherland and as such a natural partner in the process of restructuring India, the logic of this move remained dubious and highly contested. The proposals presented by the government—be they about disinvestments in sick industries, a greater openness to foreign direct investment, or the setting up of institutional mechanisms to attract NRI investors—were harshly attacked by the opposition as an "erasure of India's economic sovereignty."

However, even as they attacked these measures, none of the members who stood up to oppose the budget could claim to be surprised by either the extent of the economic crisis or the nature of the proposed solution.[52] The critical balance of payments situation had been brought to the attention of the Indian parliament several months before the budget. Economists in India and abroad had been warning about the threat posed by the dangerously low levels of foreign exchange in the early months of 1991. Even before Prime Minister Rao approached the IMF in July 1991, the two previous non-Congress governments had asked for and been approved for emergency loans from the international institution. The point I am making here is that the political elite of the country had been aware not only of the deepening economic crisis but also of the IMF's gradually increasing involvement in the Indian economy. In this context, were the debates surrounding the budget proposals mere political theater?

The opposition's main charge was that the neoliberal restructuring of the Indian economy represented a break from the "Nehruvian socialism" that, despite minor diversions in the 1980s, had been followed by all postindependence governments.[53] In other words, the most serious problem with the budget was that it embodied a break from continuity. Even while talking in the terms of "macrolevel adjustments" and lasting "structural reforms," the government and its allies made a studied effort to counter this charge. As discussed earlier in the chapter, virtually all the measures proposed in the budget were reversals of the policies put in place after Indian independence. Even while acknowledging this aspect of the reforms, the supporters of the budget presented them as the continuation of a pragmatic policy of safeguarding India's economic sovereignty—a policy that had guided all Indian governments since 1947. They further argued that as proponents of economic liberalization, they did not contemplate or advocate a "complete break from the past."[54] India remained committed to the ideas of a mixed economy at the domestic level and nonalignment at the international level. It could no longer, however, "continue to follow the same pattern of economic development for all times to come."[55] The measures that had been instituted to define the scope of the state after independence, especially in terms of its role in industrial development, had been essential to deal with the legacy of colonialism, but the changing global situation demanded bold steps.[56] Referring to the collapse of the Soviet Union, a supporter of the budget declared that history had shown conclusively that "unless you believe in free trade and the free flow of ideas…the results would be disastrous."[57] In attempting to streamline the "administrative management of public sector undertakings," while encouraging the private sector, the government was bringing this new historical lesson to bear on the shaping of modern India.[58] To fulfill its potential in a changing world, India needed to change. But this was a change that would take place even as the state remained committed to the ideals of nonalignment and democratic socialism that had been put in place by Jawaharlal Nehru. The economic liberalization program thus, asserted Prime Minister Rao, would be the manifestation of "continuity with change." Despite the skepticism and ridicule of the opposition, the government and its allies clung to this theme in all the discussions of the liberalization program and what it meant for India.[59] What was the logic of this seemingly paradoxical claim? Why was it so important for the Indian government to emphasize the notion of continuity even while asserting the disastrous results of past policies? Answering these questions requires going back to the argument that I have made in the two previous chapters.

As many scholars have noted, the process of imagining India had begun long before political independence was attained.[60] Given that the questioning of British rule in India began to a large extent from a mounting dissatisfaction over the material conditions in the country, it is not surprising that "imagining India" entailed questioning the relationship between the nation, the state, and the economy.[61] Explanations of the impoverishment of the Indian nation rested on a particular rendering of the economic history of India—a rendering in which the colonial state was an exploitative agent, focused on draining the riches of the nation. Moreover, unlike other exploitative rulers in Indian history, the British colonial state was not concerned with using some of the wealth they drained from India to improve the lot of the Indian people. Rather, its goal was to use the resources of the Indian nation to serve the interests of metropolitan capital.[62] It was in the context of its inability and lack of desire to provide for the development of the nation that the failure of the British colonial state became most apparent. The successful establishment of bourgeois hegemony during the final stages of the anticolonial struggle therefore rested on the ability to articulate a particular vision of the postcolonial Indian state. This vision, as we saw in the last two chapters, emphasized the ability of the state to cut down existing exploitative economic relations and steer the productive forces of the nation in a way that promoted the welfare of the people. Over the first few decades of independence, successive Indian governments reinscribed this particular vision not only by attempting to exercise strict control over foreign intervention in the domestic economy but also by staging highly publicized struggles with giant multinationals.[63] While there were moments of acute crisis, such as the one engendered by the IMF loan and currency devaluation of 1966, these were presented as temporary setbacks that were quickly overcome. In 1981, for instance, while embarking on a large-scale economic restructuring program that was an essential prerequisite for the much-needed IMF loan, Indira Gandhi's government presented it as an indigenous economic initiative that was in no way connected to the demands of a foreign institution. The adoption of the structural adjustment policies as part of the annual budget prior to receiving the loan allowed the ruling elites to hold on to a patina of sovereignty.[64] By 1991, however, those options were a distant memory. Given the changed conditions of the global capitalist economy, with Keynesianism replaced by neoliberal principles, the immediacy of the balance of payments crisis, and the public role of the IMF, it seemed less plausible (despite the support of the now-dominant faction of the Indian bourgeoisie) to insist that the structural reforms were homegrown or that the Indian state had successively staved off foreign intervention in domestic economic matters. Given this context, while it was obvious that the reforms would be passed by the Indian parliament, the opposition's charges and the government's insistence on a paradoxical framing of the budget begin to make sense.

The opposition argued that by renouncing decades of Nehruvian policies that had emphasized the concept of *swadeshi* (self-reliance), the government had declared its abject surrender to the IMF and "foreign capitalists," and in doing so had set India on a dangerous path. As CPI(M) member N. K. Chatterjee declared in graphic terms: "Today, [the] IMF just opens the door. They impose the IMF's conditions. They want India to open its womb to foreign capital. They want to take us back to pre-1947 days....This budget is the return of imperial capital with much more vigour than the past."[65] The state envisioned by the framers of the Bombay Plan and the leaders of the Indian national movement had been the kind necessary to make a "structural break from the past," wherein the past was understood specifically in terms of the experience of colonialism. The economic liberalization program, it was argued, was an overt attempt to restructure the post-colonial Indian state, and it was not just a change, but a regressive measure that undermined all the institutions and practices that had protected the resources of the Indian nation from the dangers of foreign exploitation. Since this charge was aimed at the raison d'être of the Indian state, it was impossible for the reformers to ignore. Hence, the government and its supporters emphasized the larger continuity that underlay the changes to be wrought by the liberalization program.[66] However, economic reforms in India did not rest on a mere reiteration of continuity. Where the structural break envisaged in the Bombay Plan was enabled by a particular understanding of the relationship between the nation and the state, the restructuring proposed in the 1991 budget was to be facilitated by a rearticulation of this very relationship. Occupying the center stage in this process, making possible a shift in the discursive terrain, was the new valorized subject, "the global Indian"—a subject position that was best embodied by the NRI.

III.   Re-forming India

As discussed in the preceding sections, the government proposals aimed at facilitating NRI investments were attacked on the grounds of their inherent weaknesses as well as on the assumption that NRIs would respond to the initiatives.

Regardless of the accuracy of the portrayal, the opposition gave voice to the sentiment that NRIs had "abandoned India for their own and their family's benefit" and consequently could not be trusted to help India overcome the economic crisis.[67] In responding to these arguments, the supporters of the government, once again echoing past discussions pertaining to the Indian diaspora in and outside the Indian parliament, claimed that while NRIs might have left India for economic reasons, that did not in any way constitute abandonment. If anything, it was the fault of successive governments that had failed to provide employment to even those with higher education. Referring to the opposition's comments on NRIs, one member remarked:

> [They were] asking, why are our doctors going away? Why are our engineers going away? [They do] not know perhaps that our doctors were here and our engineers were here without any employment.... Why are these NRIs compelled to go to foreign countries and work there? Had they been provided with jobs and other facilities here, do you think anybody will leave this country [sic]?[68]

The same member went on to claim that despite having been driven out of the country due to economic necessity, "NRIs were trying to come home and invest all their money here, in their motherland."[69] Without going into the causes of emigration, the finance minister argued in the same vein that the proposals presented in the budget were suggested by NRIs themselves who wanted to contribute to their motherland. In making this claim about concerned and willing subjects, he reiterated to a largely skeptical audience that despite their actions prior to the economic crisis, NRIs were desirous of contributing to India's development and were, in fact, an integral element of the restructuring that would take place in the coming years. However, this claim still glossed over the question of why this was so. As already mentioned, the social category of the NRI was not limited to those who held Indian citizenship; it had been broadened to include all those who could claim Indian origin. The existence of this somewhat loose, all-encompassing category was obvious in the budget speech, when Manmohan Singh referred to the "NRIs who were foreign nationals." If the category NRI included those claiming a *foreign nationality*, then their presumed connection to the modern Indian nation-state was obviously not based on a notion of citizenship. What was it, then, that not only made them *Indians* but also made it so critical for the Indian state to recognize them as such? In other words, what was at stake in the hailing of the Indians abroad? The answer to this question can be found by taking another look at the debates surrounding the structural reform of the Indian state.

As seen earlier in this chapter, the government position on the question of economic liberalization was seen as a mark of a country that had become so weak that it no longer could hold its own in the international arena. In fact, popular discourse surrounding the initiation of liberalization held that the foreign exchange reserves had been so low that the Indian finance minister had to approach the IMF with a begging bowl.[70] This charge was considered so damaging that it prompted offers of resignation from Manmohan Singh (especially in the aftermath of rumors that accused him of complicity with the IMF) and a special appearance by Prime Minister Narasimha Rao in the Parliament to offer a categorical denial. During the course of the debates, Congress party members continued to contest the notion that the budget was dictated by the IMF by pointing out specific issues that went against the general perception of IMF conditionalities.[71] In the case of the specific NRI clauses, they argued that those measures had been proposed by various NRI groups that had wanted to help their motherland, and while the danger of money laundering was very real, the existing regulatory mechanisms would keep it under control. Furthermore, the schemes that had been put in place were temporary, a short-term measure to tide India over its current balance of payments situation. However, to ensure that the country never faced a similar crisis in the future, what was needed was a macro-level structural adjustment, which was what the budget was proposing. Rather than depending on loans from international institutions or, for that matter, building foreign exchange reserves through remittances from PIO, what the country needed was more foreign investment. Unfortunately, a deep-rooted suspicion of foreign involvement in the Indian economy had made it very difficult for the Indian state to adopt policies that might lead to such investments. Insofar as the question of why state practices had been directed toward strict control of foreign investments, the reformers provided an extremely interesting answer.

Articulating a theme that would become almost a mantra for the supporters of liberalization, Manmohan Singh declared in his budget speech: "After four decades of planning for industrialization, we have now reached a stage of development where we should welcome, rather than fear foreign investment. *Our entrepreneurs are second to none. Our industry has come of age*" (my emphasis).[72] The not so subtle argument underlying Singh's claim was that the Indian state had focused on planned industrial development partly out of fear that Indian industry and Indian entrepreneurs could not face the challenge of foreign investment; neither was ready for open competition. While this fear and need for protection might have made sense in the immediate aftermath of independence, it was a phase that India had outgrown "after four decades of planning for industrialization." India was now at a stage where its entrepreneurs could compete with anyone in the world. All that was needed was to acknowledge this by embracing the liberalization program. But something was preventing sections of the Indian population (by that, of course, they meant the opponents of the

restructuring) from taking that all-important step. Prefacing his explanation of
the cause of this hesitancy with an expression of puzzlement as to why foreign
investment in India was dwindling at a time when it seemed to be steadily increasing in other developing countries like Korea and Malaysia, Prime Minister
Narasimha Rao declared:

> All these countries are having a galloping increase in foreign investment.
> The only thing I cannot understand is why it should be that in India, it
> should come down so easily, and why we should be squeamish about invit-
> ing foreign investment. *What else is the reason except an inferiority com-
> plex?* We seem to feel inferior to others who are coming in or whom we are
> inviting. [my emphasis][73]

What was preventing India from taking its place on the global stage, causing it to
fall behind in the path of development, was nothing but a deeply rooted "inferiority complex"—a feeling that "we" were inferior to those that we might invite.
But as Rao went on to argue, there was no need for Indians to hold on to this
inferiority complex. "*We have successfully competed with others and will be able to
compete in the future also*." At any rate, it was incumbent upon the Indian state to
"formulate a policy not on the basis of an inferiority complex but on the basis of
a certain national confidence."[74]

In an extremely important move, the supporters of economic liberalization
shifted the discursive terrain by arguing that state practices geared toward the
regulation of foreign investment stemmed not so much from the experiences of
colonialism as from a lack of belief in the self—the ingrained notion that India
could not compete in the global arena. But that was unwarranted; India was not
only capable of taking on the best in the world but also had succeeded in doing
so in the past. However, the reformers were well aware that mere assertion of success in a global economy would go only so far. Proof of this success was needed,
and Indians abroad provided this proof. It is in this context that it becomes possible for us to make sense of the hailing of the NRI and the reiteration of their
connection to the motherland.

As discussed in the previous chapter, postindependence migration from India
was essentially two broadly defined groups whose journeys were distinct from
earlier colonial movements of people and also when compared with each other.
I have already mentioned the important role of the low-skilled migrants to the
Middle East in enabling a unified discourse surrounding the Indian diaspora in
the 1980s. I now turn to the other group, whose migration from the mid-1960s
onward was seen as part of the brain drain from Third World countries. These
white-collar workers and students pursuing higher degrees in science and technology took advantage of the gradual relaxation of visa regulations in the

developed world (especially the 1965 amendment to the Immigration and Nationality Act in the United States) to move westward. Particularly in the past decade and a half, the experiences of this relatively new immigrant population have been the subject of intense discussions that have highlighted the inherent contestations waged on terrains of nation, class, gender, and generations. However, the dominant discourse embraced by the Indian state surrounding this diaspora is characterized by a distinct triumphalism. Chidanand Rajghatta's celebratory retelling of the success of "India's Silicon Gurus" is a telling illustration of this point.[75]

In Rajghatta's narrative, in the steady trickle of immigration during the 1970s, a number of Indian technology workers (commonly referred to as "techies") began to emerge as entrepreneurial figures in the Silicon Valley of the United States.[76] Emboldened by the success of pioneers like Narendra Singh Kapany (who arrived in the United States as a student from India and set up the first Indian-owned fiber-optics industry in 1960) and Amar Bose (the founder of the Bose Corporation, who despite being half-German was appropriated by the Indian immigrant community as a cult hero), a small group of Indian entrepreneurs helped "jump-start Digital America," while "becoming bold enough to name companies after themselves." Among them were:

> Farouk Arjani, a young Parsi entrepreneur from Bombay [who, in 1973] founded Artec International, a pioneer in word processing....Thampy Thomas, a Keralite who had studied in BITS, Pilani, left National Semiconductor to found Elxsi, among the earliest Silicon Valley ventures to make mainframe computers....In 1978, Sirjang Lal Tandon founded Tandon Computers, one of the earliest suppliers of disc drives to the personal computer industry. Early in the 1980s, Suhas Patil and Umang Gupta, both IIT alumni, respectively founded Patil Systems (which would later become Cirrus Logic) and Gupta Technologies (which would later become Centura Software Corporation). Kanwal Rekhi, another IITian...co-founded (with Inder Mohan Singh and Naveen Jain), the networking company Excelan in 1984.[77]

The acronyms that Rajghatta uses in his litany of names highlight what he saw as common to this generation of Indian immigrants. Thampy was from BITS, the Birla Institute of Technology and Science; Patil, Gupta, and Rakhi were all alumni of IIT, the Indian Institute of Technology. Educated in some of the best engineering schools in India, these immigrants had moved to the West and, despite numerous setbacks, had made their mark in Silicon Valley within a matter of decades.[78] It was these narratives that the reformers turned to in making their argument that India had proven it could succeed in the global economy.

In documenting the tales of NRI success in science and technology, what was highlighted was not only the training the entrepreneurs received in India but also the fact that they had succeeded despite the manifold challenges that they faced. As such, the NRI businessman embodied the new type of Indian entrepreneur— no longer just members of storied business families that were tied to the Indian National Congress, but individuals who through their own merit and professional skills had become successful in cutting-edge industries, while competing on a global playing field.[79] Hailing the NRI as part of the Indian nation thus served a dual purpose for the supporters of economic liberalization. First, they could now make the argument that the Indian nation no longer needed to be protected by the Indian state in quite the same way as envisaged by the leaders of the nationalist movement. As embodied by the NRI, India had shown its ability to hold its own and succeed in a global economy. Second, in reorienting state practices and dismantling the safeguards that had been put in place to protect the nation from the possibility of foreign exploitation, the Indian government was neither giving in to the demands of the IMF nor declaring the failure of the post-colonial Indian nation-state. To the contrary, it was acknowledging that Indian entrepreneurs were "second to none" and that India "had come of age." These triumphal claims, of course, were being made at a time when the Indian state, by all accounts, was facing the worst economic crisis in its history.

IV. The Global Indian and the Making of a "Domestic Abroad"

In her analysis of the Indian state's interactions with the Indian diaspora, Marie Lall notes in a critical tone that, despite the rhetoric surrounding NRIs during the liberalization debates, not much changed in the post-1991 period.[80] As proof of her contention, she points to the fact that despite the initial enthusiasm among the Indian diaspora in the wake of the government's promises to facilitate and open up new sectors for investment (seen especially in their subscription to the India Development Bonds), their actual involvement in the Indian economy has been minimal, with the NRI share of total Foreign Direct Investment plateauing at 5 percent. Lall sees this "lack of involvement" as not only evidence of a failure of the Indian state but also evidence that the "basic relationship between the NRIs and the Indian government" remains unchanged since 1947. In her argument, the hailing of the NRI as a national subject was an attempt by the Indian state to attract investments from a community that it had ostracized.[81] However, "despite the removal of some obstacles," this attempt was not backed by structural changes. The NRIs found that they were "still [expected] to put up with the petty hassles of the Indian bureaucracy, besides having limited rights on residency periods, they are still expected to build new industry and new technology and know-how despite having limited property and importing rights."[82] Consequently, NRIs have held back from investing in India, a fact that highlights yet another "missed opportunity" for the Indian nation-state.[83] Lall's claims about the trajectory of NRI investments in India are unquestionably true. However, in emphasizing an impoverished version of an "economic rationale" argument—wherein state actions are explained and evaluated purely in terms of the ability to harness investments—Lall's analysis not only overlooks the intrinsic connections between the political and economic realms but also misses the logic behind the Indian state's social empowerment of the NRI as a newly valorized subject.

Even as the supporters of liberalization in India asserted that NRIs had both the resources and desire to come to the aid of the country in its time of need, they sounded a cautionary note about the dangers of relying too much on such aid. While chastising members of the opposition who had "cast aspersions on Non-residents," Finance Minister Manmohan Singh made a point of assuring the House that his government was not "giving any undue facilities to Non-Resident Indians." They knew well that "neither the non-resident Indians abroad, nor the IMF, nor the world community can solve our problems... [only] we can find solutions to those problems."[84] This was not to deny that the balance of payments issue had made it imperative for India to find new options to deal with the crisis. Given that NRIs had the resources and India needed foreign exchange, it made sense for the government to "explore this particular thing."[85] However, neither Singh nor his supporters had many illusions about how much (and under what conditions) NRIs would be willing to "assist" India. In that time period, it would have been hard for the reformers to overlook the panic-stricken withdrawal of NRI accounts prior to the 1991 crisis. This suspicion of NRI commitment was also obvious in the emphasis the government placed on time-bound, high-return schemes as part of its special incentives to attract NRI investment. It is, of course, implausible to deny the existence of an economic rationale in the Indian state's hailing of NRIs as "*Indians* abroad." Given the balance of payments situation in 1991, such a claim would hardly make sense.[86] What I am arguing here is the need to understand that rationale in a richer, more historically and politically contextualized manner. Far from being "economic" in the impoverished, technical sense of the word, the crisis that made structural adjustment imperative struck at the very heart of the bourgeois hegemony that shaped postcolonial India. In this context, the figure of the NRI served a far more important purpose than just a potential source of foreign exchange. The diasporic reimagining of the nation was an essential element of the neoliberal restructuring of the state. Without the former, the latter would have been understood as the abject surrender of hard-won sovereignty and an open declaration of the failure of the postcolonial project. To the extent that economic liberalization could be legitimized in India, it rested on the figure of the PIO/NRI—now, the "*Indian* abroad."[87]

The hailing of the PIO/NRIs as part of a larger Indian nation has continued in and through different sites in the years that have followed.[88] Successive Indian governments persisted with the liberalization program, despite the stated opposition of some to the process in 1991, and continued the official valorizing of the NRI/PIO, setting the stage for the production of the Indian domestic abroad.[89] However, despite steadily increasing remittances, given the negligible investments by NRIs and demands for more rapid restructuring from foreign investors, the ruling elite continued to face charges that they had undermined the nation's self-esteem and reduced India to the status of a beggar nation that could no longer refuse the demands of foreigners. It was not surprising, therefore, that successive administrations felt pressure to hold a "demonstration" that could prove India could still hold its own in the global arena.[90] It is in this context that it is possible for us to catch a glimpse of how the political and economic dimensions of the domestic abroad can help shape the contours of security policy as well.

On May 11, 1998, the BJP-led Indian government announced that "at 1545 hours, India conducted three underground nuclear tests in the Pokhran range."[91] This was followed by two more tests on May 13, at which time the government announced the successful completion of the planned series. The 1998 tests were conducted by a government that was well aware of the consequences of "going nuclear." After all, the Rao government, which had attempted to carry out tests in 1995 and 1996, had been warned what it could expect if it exercised its nuclear option: increased tension in the subcontinent, moral condemnation by the international community, and economic sanctions from the developed world.[92] The nuclear tests were carried out despite knowledge of the consequences because, insofar as the Indian state was concerned, what was at stake was much more fundamental.[93] Given my argument about the crisis engendered by economic liberalization, it makes sense that even the opposition parties initially greeted the tests with warm approval. If anything, the strong condemnation voiced by the nuclear powers served to reinforce this support. Conducting nuclear tests in the face of opposition from the great powers was one way of demonstrating that India could still chart its own course—appearing to maintain certain Nehruvian traditions even while turning back on the "old methods."[94] As Prime Minister Vajpayee asserted in his address to the Indian parliament: "These tests are a continuation of the policies set into motion, that put this country on the path of self-reliance and independence of thought and action.... This crucial decision to opt for self reliance was taken by us when we rejected the Cold War paradigm and chose the more difficult path of non-alignment."[95] In the immediate aftermath of the tests, the dominant view was that the tests had in some manner stemmed the "subversion of national interests." As an article noted, "After years of worrying about economic problems and foreign pressure [Indian] voters suddenly feel virile."[96] In the parliamentary discussions of the nuclear tests, opposition members who challenged the government's rationale for the tests still claimed that they were an expression of sovereignty—an expression that could be questioned only by Indians themselves and not by any outside power. If any attempts were made to punish India for this exercise of sovereignty, the opposition parties would stand by the government.[97] As one parliamentarian claimed, the actual conduct of the nuclear tests was "a tribute to the country, a tremendous tribute to our scientists and a tremendous tribute to Shri Jawaharlal Nehru, Shrimati Indira Gandhi, Shri Rajiv Gandhi, Shri Narasimha Rao, Shri Inder Kumar Gujral and all the other Prime Ministers who said, 'Go ahead with this programme.'"[98] Even a critic of the BJP, writing in the widely respected Leftist journal *Economic and Political Weekly*, started his analysis with the claim that the "dramatic assertion of the sovereign status and rights of India, after the dreary years of their denigration by the ruling elite as outdated notions in the era of globalization, certainly deserves accolades."[99]

As the rhetoric both inside and outside the Indian parliament made clear, the nuclear tests were seen and celebrated as a reassertion of Indian sovereignty at a time when it seemed most questionable because of the nearly decade-long economic liberalization program. In that sense, the connection of security policies to the economic dimension of the domestic abroad seems quite obvious. But what about the political dimension? Even as most of the developed countries imposed economic sanctions on India, the government declared that the Indian nation was strong enough to withstand the sanctions, for among its subjects were the NRIs who would stand by a "Resurgent India." The Resurgent India Bonds issued in the immediate aftermath of the tests were oversubscribed by PIO/NRIs and brought $4.5 billion into the Indian state's treasury, in some way giving credence to the government's claim.[100] Explaining the reaction of NRIs to the nuclear tests, one commentator declared in overwrought terms:

> The sound of the bomb revived Indian civilization, which has been in intensive care unit for centuries.... [The nuclear tests] made [NRIs] shed their shame in associating with India, which to them was a failed civilization.... After that, the NRIs, who used to abuse India, began admiring India. From then on gradually national self-confidence grew.[101]

Without overemphasizing the irony of highlighting a nuclear blast as a mode to revive anything, let alone a "failed civilization," it should be noted that the period after the nuclear tests saw an intensification in the production of the Indian domestic abroad. The PIO/NRIs, it was argued, had come to the rescue of the motherland, as was their duty, and it was now essential for the Indian state to recognize and acknowledge its responsibilities toward the Indians abroad. Accordingly, in August 2000, the BJP government announced the establishment of the High Level Committee on the Indian Diaspora, which would be given carte blanche to engage with all sections of the Indian diaspora and recommend to the government a "broad but flexible policy framework" to facilitate the involvement of the diaspora in India's development while making it possible for the Indian government to be more receptive to their needs.[102] After meeting with representatives of various diaspora groups (especially those related to the umbrella organization Global Organization of People of Indian Origin, known by its acronym GOPIO)[103] and carefully perusing the policies adopted by other countries toward their diasporas,[104] the High Level Committee presented its final report to the Indian government in December 2001. Among its recommendations were a PIO card scheme that would institute a visa-free regime for people of Indian origin, the establishment of Pravasi Bharatiya Samman awards to recognize the achievements and contributions of Indians abroad, and the celebration of the Pravasi Bharatiya Diwas (Day of the Indians Abroad) that would highlight "the pride of the motherland" in the successes of "her children abroad," who now numbered more than 20 million (table 5.1).

Following the recommendations of the High Level Committee, the Indian government offered PIO cards for sale (initially priced at $1,000 and later reduced to $250) in its various embassies, published the first list of Pravasi Bharatiya Samman awards, and announced that they would be handed to the honorees at the celebration of the first-ever Pravasi Bharatiya Diwas (PBD) on January 9, 2003.[105]

Jointly hosted by the Indian government and FICCI at a cost of approximately $49 million, these celebrations marked a definitive moment in the production of the Indian domestic abroad in two ways.[106] The more obvious way was Prime Minister Vajpayee's declaration that in view of Indians abroad having achieved the required "delicate balance" between affirming their loyalty to their country of adoption and their motherland, the Indian government would introduce legislation permitting dual citizenship during the forthcoming session of the Indian parliament. Less obvious, but equally important, was the articulation of a theme that had been implicit since 1991. Welcoming 2,000 delegates to the three-day celebration, Prime Minister Vajpayee declared that the gathering was actually a homecoming of the children of Mother India, who, despite adopting the citizenship of other countries, had not lost their "common identity"—their Indianness. As to what that Indianness meant, he pointed to the "success of every category of [Indian] emigrants all around the world."[107] Indians abroad, he claimed, had reached "the pinnacle in so many diverse fields of human endeavor" because of "their dedication to their chosen professions" and willingness to overcome "trials

Table 5.1.   The "Indians Abroad" at a Glance (December 2001)

Country	Persons of Indian Origin	Nonresident Indians	Total
Australia	160,000	30,000	190,000
Canada	700,000	150,000	850,000
Fiji	336,579	250	336,829
Guyana	395,250	100	395,350
Kuwait	1,000	294,000	295,000
Malaysia*	1,600,000	15,000	1,665,000
Mauritius	704,640	11,116	715,756
Myanmar*	2,500,000	2,000	2,902,000
Oman	1,000	311,000	312,000
Qatar	1,000	130,000	131,000
Reunion Islands	220,000	55	220,055
Saudi Arabia		1,500,000	1,500,000
Singapore	217,000	90,000	307,000
South Africa			1,000,000
Trinidad & Tobago	500,000	600	500,600
UAE	50,000	900,000	950,000
UK			1,200,000
USA			1,678,000
Yemen	100,000	900	100,900

This list is excerpted from the more exhaustive list of the overseas Indian populations of 134 countries compiled in the report.

* The total figure in the case of Myanmar and Malaysia also includes the population deemed as stateless and thus legally outside the categories of PIO and NRI.

Source: Report of the High-Level Committee on the Indian Diaspora (2001).

and tribulations." This in turn could be traced to the "indomitable spirit" that characterized India and Indianness.[108]

The question of what constituted India and Indianness dominated the discussions surrounding the PBD celebrations. To mark this momentous occasion, the popular Indian weekly *India Today* published a special issue commemorating "The Global Indian," who was "Doing Us Proud."[109] In his editorial, the well-known journalist Aroon Purie claimed that one did not need the Indian government to tell the world that there was a 20-million-strong Indian diaspora. Through a "quiet, gradual, but relentless" migration, Indians had effected what he called "a reverse colonization." Despite arriving in places such as Fiji as indentured labor during the colonial period, Indians had overcome insurmountable odds, and "today, their children are presidents, prime ministers, senators, tycoons and Nobel prize winners." Echoing a theme that framed the Pravasi Bharatiya celebrations, Purie declared:

> Persons of Indian Origin are impossible to typecast.... They come in all shapes and sizes, fit all descriptions. What links the astronaut on our cover with the Punjabi sheep farmers in New Zealand?[110] What connects white-collar techies in Silicon Valley to the Indians who seem to have a monopoly on 24-hours stores in Britain—or the Patels who so dominate the US motel industry that motels are often referred to as "Potels"? *It is the will to succeed.*

In other words, what made them "Indians" was the "indomitable will"—the spirit of enterprise that was intrinsic to India. Wherever they went, regardless of the passport they carried, this spirit characterized all Indians. As Purie concluded quite seriously, "You can take an Indian out of India, but you cannot take India out of an Indian."

Nearly four decades before the celebration of the first Pravasi Bharatiya Divas, the Indian Parliament had been the site of fervent debates surrounding the fate of certain PIO groups. In discussing the plight of PIO in East Africa during the early 1960s, the issue of what constituted the "spirit of India" and whether it was embodied by the Indian diaspora was raised by several members. During the course of those debates, supporters of the government's policy of noninterference in what it characterized as the "internal affairs" of the newly independent African states argued that the PIO in East Africa did not deserve the protection of the Indian nation-state precisely because in their "pursuit of wealth," they had become "completely devoid of [everything] that free India stood for."[111] At that juncture, "India" stood for certain principles—to fight against colonization, to challenge all forms of exploitative socioeconomic relations—that were best embodied in the concept of *swadeshi* (self-reliance), and "Indianness" was understood in terms of an identification with those principles. But in the restructured India, *swadeshi* itself had been redefined in ways that stretched the limits of credulity. Holding forth on his government's understanding of the concept, Finance Minister Yashwant Sinha declared during a presentation at the Harvard Club, "*Swadeshi* is pro-globalization because it is pro-Indian without being anti-foreign. And that is the important message from India: you can be pro your own country without being anti any other country. Therefore, *swadeshi* is the best means of globalization."[112] As Vajpayee had claimed in his inaugural address during the first PBD celebrations, Indians abroad had over the years achieved the delicate balance of being part of their adopted country while retaining their loyalty to their motherland. Consequently, he declared that his government would introduce the Dual Citizenship (Amendment) Bill in parliament. In December 2003, making a final, decisive break from the Nehruvian policy that had delineated postcolonial India's relationship with the diaspora, the parliament unanimously passed the bill that granted the right of overseas Indian citizenship to PIOs from sixteen countries.[113] Although dual citizens could not participate in electoral politics (in the sense of either voting or running for political office) or, for that matter, even accept government jobs, they would be guaranteed certain other rights available to Indian citizens—both resident and nonresident.[114] They could, for instance, travel to India without a visa, stay in the country without having to register their presence with the police, invest in agriculture and industry, acquire land and property in India, and enroll their children in Indian educational institutions. A revision to this bill in 2005 extended the possibility of overseas Indian citizenship on these terms to all PIOs who either had been or were eligible to become Indian citizens at the "commencement of the Indian constitution" (January 26, 1950), as long as their host countries permitted dual citizenship.[115] In practice, the purpose of the amendments to the Citizenship Act was a straightforward one. Even though the categories of NRI and PIO had increasingly been used interchangeably in official and public discourse, Indian citizens who did not reside in India (and were, thus, the official NRIs) had certain rights that noncitizens, even if they were of Indian origin, did not. By creating the new legal category of "Overseas Citizen of India," the Indian state was consciously extending to all persons of Indian origin the same rights that had been granted to nonresident Indians in "financial, economic and educational fields."[116] The rhetorical blurring of the two categories and the extension of the boundaries of the nation had now been officially institutionalized. *Swadeshi* had indeed gone global, and with the production of the domestic abroad, so had India and the Indian.

V. Coming Full Circle

In January 2004, more than 2,500 delegates from sixty-one countries gathered in New Delhi to celebrate the second annual Pravasi Bharatiya Divas. Welcoming the delegates, Prime Minister Atal Bihari Vajpayee declared that he still carried with him the "memory and the melody" of the *jugalbandi* ("duet") that had been performed by two of India's best known musicians—Pandit Ravi Shankar and Ustad Bismillah Khan—during the inauguration of the first Pravasi Bharatiya Divas. According to Vajpayee, what made the event so memorable was not only the music created by the artists but also the fact that the performance served as a "pointed metaphor" for the relationship between India and Indians abroad: "It reminded us that Pravasi Bharatiya Divas itself is a celebration of the *jugalbandi* between the 22-million-strong Indian Diaspora and your motherland, between the Bharatvasis (those residing in India) and the Bharatvanshis (those hailing from India)."[117] It was this *jugalbandi*, he declared, that had brought closer to reality the dream of a "Shining India"—"an India that had resolved to regain her past glory, and indeed surpass it, an India that would be a major economic powerhouse and a major contributor to humanity's all-sided evolution to a higher level."[118] While India had made progress in the realms of both diplomacy and the economy, the Pravasi Bharatiyas (Indians abroad) had continued to serve as India's best ambassadors overseas by embodying "hard work, competence, integrity and loyalty to their host countries" and succeeding in their chosen fields. In Vajpayee's terms, it was these combined efforts—from resident Indians and Indians abroad—that ensured that despite being held during cold Delhi winters, the Pravasi Bharatiya Divas would always symbolize "spring time for India."

Vajpayee's claims of the impending emergence of a "Shining India" set the tone for the rest of the conference. Speaker after speaker pointed out that the Indian economy had registered an 8.4 percent growth in the last quarter, that the Indian state's coffers were "overflowing with more that $100 million in foreign exchange," that inflation was under control, that Indian corporations were emerging as "global players with impressive investments overseas and acquisitions abroad," and that India was being perceived around the world as a growing information technology (IT) power and one of the most desirable destinations for multinational corporations like Microsoft and Intel.[119] As Minister for External Affairs Yashwant Sinha put it, "Slowly, but steadily 'Brand India' was making its presence felt." There was a "feel good factor" evident in all discussions regarding India, and this factor had acquired a "special glitter" because of the innumerable achievements, "both individual and collective," of the Indians abroad. Bound to India by the "magical umbilical cord of history, culture, tradition, social and historical ties," Indians abroad constituted the group that was most exultant about India's success.[120] This was obvious in the comments of some prominent NRIs and PIO recounted by Prime Minister Vajpayee in his address: "There was no better time to be an Indian or to be in India."[121] However, what the Indian state wanted to emphasize in celebrating the second Pravasi Bharatiya Divas was that Indians abroad were an intrinsic part of India's journey to a bright future. Through their achievements, they had not only burnished India's image abroad but also inspired Indians to "strive harder, to be bold and adventurous in the quest for a better life."

Acknowledging the historical debt owed by the Indian nation-state to the Indians abroad, the Citizenship Amendment Act granting dual nationality had been passed unanimously by the Parliament. But spokespersons for the Indian state were quick to point out that this was just the beginning of a long process of institutionalizing India's relationship with its diaspora. In addition to existing tax breaks and investment opportunities, Vajpayee announced plans to subsidize higher education for the children of NRIs and measures to engage more closely with second- and third-generation emigrants, the "youth of the diaspora," who needed to be "exposed to the land of their forefathers in order for them to see, understand and comprehend their Indianness." In addition, he announced the establishment of the Pravasi Bharatiya Kendra (Center for Indians Abroad), an institute with a seed grant of Rs 25 crores that would "serve the multifarious needs of the diasporic community."[122]

Throughout the three-day event, the organizers were at pains to point out that the feting of the Indian diaspora extended across the entire political spectrum. They highlighted the fact that opposition members—ranging from the leader of the opposition, Sonia Gandhi, who hosted a luncheon for the delegates, to functionaries of the Communist parties and regional parties like the AIADMK—were involved in the celebration of the Pravasi Bharatiya Divas, if not in its actual planning.[123] However, the speeches of the various delegates and the presentations at the panels made it obvious that the celebration of the Indian diaspora converged remarkably well with a triumphant recounting of the successes of the Bharatiya Janata Party (BJP)-led National Democratic Alliance (NDA), which had been in power since 1999. The constant reiteration of the successes of the administration in its diplomatic endeavors and its management of the economy and the lauding of Vajpayee as a visionary leader seemed a bit excessive (even considering that the Pravasi Bharatiya Divas was a state-sponsored celebration) until placed in the context of a reelection campaign.[124]

In 2004, with political pundits and opinion polls across party lines predicting an easy victory, the BJP-led government decided to offer its resignation to the president and call for early general elections. In this context, the Pravasi Bharatiya Divas was an important occasion for the BJP to trumpet its successes while drawing attention to the fact that it had been at the forefront of forging links among members of the "global Indian family." As the party claimed, the "Shining India" that formed the centerpiece of its reelection manifesto could not be built without the active involvement of the Bharatvanshis ("those hailing from India"). The Pravasi Bharatiya Divas was declared a triumph, and the BJP-led coalition was perceived as having set off on what was to be a victorious campaign.[125]

In May 2004, India went to the polls. In a result that took political pundits, the ruling party, and the opposition by surprise, the BJP and its allies suffered a stunning defeat. In the most symbolically potent moment of the elections, Chandrababu Naidu, the chief minister of the southern state of Andhra Pradesh, the self-proclaimed CEO of "Andhra Pradesh, Inc.," the man feted by the World Bank and Microsoft as the figure embodying the new liberalized India, and one of the most dependable allies of the BJP, conceded the defeat of his Telugu Desam Party (TDP). The Congress, now led by Sonia Gandhi, the widow of

Jawaharlal Nehru's grandson, emerged with 145 seats as the biggest party in a hung parliament and eventually formed the government with support of its allies and the Left under the banner of the "United Progressive Alliance."[126] In the aftermath of the BJP's defeat, commentators across the political spectrum acknowledged that the election results were a resounding rejection of the liberalization policies that the government had pursued intensely. The "feel good" factor and the 8.4 percent growth rate that speakers at the second Pravsi Bharatiya Divas had flaunted had obviously not trickled down to the masses, who made their voices heard on election day.

As the new prime minister, Manmohan Singh, took office, he acknowledged the rationale of the Congress Party's electoral triumph by declaring that his government would slow the pace of economic liberalization and give it a "human face" by embracing a "common minimum program" (CMP) that would focus on improving the lot of India's billion-plus population. While promising to scrutinize the manner in which "disinvestment" had been carried out, Singh made it clear that his government would not turn away from liberalization per se. Like the BJP, the new Congress-led government (regardless of the popular mandate) believed that India's future lay in continuing its economic reforms and building bridges with the global Indian family. In May 2004, in one of its early announcements, the new government made it clear that it would continue with the tradition of celebrating Pravasi Bharatiya Divas that had been established by the BJP-led government. It would, in fact, go one step further and establish a Ministry of Overseas Indian Affairs responsible for "overseeing and implementing policies for India's engagement" with the diaspora.[127] In the twilight of the Nehruvian project, ironies abounded in the postcolonial Indian nation-state: the Congress, which had introduced economic liberalization in 1991, came back to power with an antiliberalization mandate; Manmohan Singh, a man who did not even run for election, was nominated to the post of prime minister; Singh, the person most closely associated with the liberalization program, took over as prime minister with a promise to slow down and "humanize" economic reforms; and a ministry that had once been an important part of the colonial state apparatus was reincarnated to propel the institutionalization of the Indian state's relationship with Indians abroad.[128] Regardless of the political party in power, the project of producing the domestic abroad was not one that could be abandoned. As Singh had once promised in his earlier incarnation as finance minister, it was indeed the era of "continuity with change."

Conclusion

At Davos on Thursday night, the high and mighty had a choice of events: a speech by U.N. Secretary General Kofi Annan or the popular annual jazz dinner... [but] about 700 participants at this year's World Economic Forum gabfest opted for another venue at the Central Sporthotel in Davoz Platz. The event? India's Republic Day celebration cocktail. There they were, the important and influential from former US Presidential candidate John Kerry to PC master Michael Dell to the chief executives of Citicorp and UBS. Panitchpakdi Supachai, the former World Trade Organization Chief was amazed. "Just five years ago, the India reception attracted 50, maybe 60 people. But look at it now! India is doing so well now, it doesn't need our help."

—*Manjeet Kripalani, "Selling India Inc. at Davos,"* BusinessWeek, *January 30, 2006*

In Davos, the Indians threw the best parties, laid on the most stimulating discussions, and were generally impossible to overlook.... But this year, the shine is off.... There are two obvious signs of this change in Davos.... This year, the Indian parties so far have been conspicuously empty.... More seriously, [at a] breakfast about India that featured an all-star cast of speakers... [instead] of the self-confident message of the past three years... the tone was a lot more muted.... For now, India is no longer everywhere, at least at Davos.

—*Peter Gumbel, "India Loses Its Davos Sparkle,"* Time.com, *January 29, 2009*

In January 2006, as participants in the World Economic Forum checked into their hotel rooms, they were greeted by the sight of gift baskets that included iPods and pashmina stoles, which were described as "a gift from the Himalayas to keep you warm in the Alps."[1] The less poetic truth of the matter was that the gifts had been delivered to the participants at the behest of the Indian delegation, which proudly claimed to represent not only a country but also a brand, "India

Inc."[2] Backed by a $5 million budget, the 150-strong delegation, which included three cabinet ministers and forty-one chief executives, came to Davos with a plan that was summed up by the campaign slogan, "India everywhere."[3] From art exhibits to gala receptions, from special sessions to informal gatherings, from billboards on street corners to advertisements on buses that promoted the "fastest-growing free market democracy," India did appear to be everywhere. As one commentator observed on the first day of the meeting, "there were few places one could go...without seeing, hearing, drinking or tasting something Indian."[4] The omnipresence of what the delegates referred to as "India Inc." at Davos was, of course, no accident. It was the result of a carefully orchestrated campaign that was "completely steered" by the Confederation of Indian Industry (CII).[5] And its goal was a simple one: to "give India a voice."[6] Less euphemistically, the campaign was meant to "showcase the arrival of the global Indian entrepreneur" and India as a preferred destination for foreign investment.[7] And if reactions during and immediately after the meeting were any indicators, the goals were well on the way to being attained. As forum organizers marveled at the unprecedented expansiveness of the advertising blitzkrieg, high-powered delegates flocked to India Inc. events, and several foreign delegations even seemed willing to work out informal trade agreements.[8] Moreover, what seemed to underscore the campaign's success was the fact that its message ostensibly resonated beyond Davos.

In an issue published a few months after the World Economic Forum meeting, *Time* magazine picked up the mantra of "India Inc." to declare that far from being the slumbering elephant of the past, India had arrived as the next global economic superpower. Just in case one did not want to read the featured articles themselves, the magazine's cover image was an excellent clue to the way the editorial team understood India Inc. The cover portrayed a young woman in traditional South Indian dance costume and jewelry, with a headset. Although the image itself was somewhat ham-handed in presenting the not too novel notion of a land in which modernity and tradition coexisted, the small article on the cover model was somewhat more interesting.[9] Self-consciously discussing the cover, the article reveals that the young woman was not a professional model. However, she was uniquely qualified to represent the main story, "the globalization of India," for she was "Indian, but grew up in Nigeria," and "live[d] in California." She was, to put it simply, the global Indian or, as the article's title claimed, "the face of India."

In prose that could justifiably be mistaken as part of a press release by the CII or the Indian government, the main story in the issue began by noting that not many Americans would be surprised to "find that their dentist or lawyer is of Indian origin, or shocked to hear how vital Indians have been to California's high-tech industry." It was evident that in "ways big and small, Indians are changing the world," and this was happening because "India itself was being transformed."[10] To drive home the point about the new global India, the magazine drafted literary and media celebrities of Indian origin, like the director Mira Nair, to write about specific transformative personal experiences. But just in case the reader was still wondering about the exact nature of India's transformation, the online edition of the magazine included an important feature. Originally part of the magazine's Asian edition, the feature was an article about Ratan Tata, the CEO of the Tata group of industries.[11]

Situated firmly in the hagiographical tradition, the article showcased the scion of the Tata family not only because of his corporate successes but also because those successes were the result of a change that was emblematic of India's own metamorphosis. The Tata group, as the article reminds us, was founded by J. N. Tata, a man who was a "nationalist, driven by the idea of a strong, self-reliant India." However, "after independence in 1947, the group came to symbolize all that was bad about India." After initially losing their airline and insurance businesses to nationalization, the Tatas were shielded from outside competition, and their companies became "bloated and calcified" under the restrictive bureaucracy of the "license raj" unleashed by the "Congress party socialists." In Ratan Tata's own words, the corporation was in a rut because the people involved "were not driving [themselves] hard enough in a protected environment." All of that, however, changed in 1991. As the Indian state embraced neoliberal restructuring, Ratan Tata took over as the new chairman and instituted his own reforms, "overhauling the firm's culture." In the decade and a half that followed, he oversaw a series of measures, including shedding half of Tata Steel's 78,000 workers, which lowered costs and boosted productivity. This "streamlining and consolidation" have borne visible fruits, with prestigious new international acquisitions (including Britain's Tetley Tea and South Korea's Daewoo commercial vehicles), an annual revenue of $21.7 billion (seven times what it was in 1991), and an impressive market value of $39.9 billion (fourteen times what it was in 2000). These successes, the article notes, are primarily due to the vision of a man whose lifestyle is simple despite his immense wealth, a man whose self-confidence is matched only by his understanding of the needs of a modern economy, a man who knew it was time to change the company's relationship with the employees "from patriarchal to practical." Ratan Tata, the tycoon of modest appetites, was remarkable not just because of his phenomenal business successes, but because he embodied the spirit of the age, the spirit of the new Indian entrepreneur, the spirit of the new global India.

Reports such as these—singing the praises of new Indian entrepreneurs, while presenting them as symbols of the transformed and powerful India—were certainly not limited to occasional issues of *Time* magazine. In the first decade of the new century, it looked as though the equation between neoliberal restructuring, a vibrant successful India, the new Indian entrepreneur, and the diasporic yet rooted "global Indian" had been established in ways that seemingly made sense. Year after year, the same themes could be found in the speeches made by various state officials and business leaders during the celebration of Pravasi Bharatiya Divas (Day of the Indians Abroad), instituted as an annual event. Regardless of the venue (the event shifted from New Delhi to Mumbai to Hyderabad to Chennai) or the political party in power, the celebrations, much like the campaign at Davos, underscored a straightforward claim made by the ruling class: India was everywhere, because the global Indian was everywhere; by embracing its global stature, India was self-confidently staking its position as a force to be reckoned with in the international system. Given the apparently robust economic figures and optimism that surrounded India's projections for growth, these claims did, at some level, seem plausible. However, even as the rearticulation of bourgeois hegemony seemed to be proceeding successfully, there were a few troubling signs that suggested less than sturdy foundations.

"All That Is Solid Melts into Air..."

In the years following the celebration of the first Pravasi Bharatiya Divas, the Indian stock market drew quite a bit of global attention.[12] Considered a certain bet, the Indian markets had seen an inflow of $30 billion from foreign institutional investors like Fidelity and JPMorgan Chase in less than three years.[13] The stock market index, the Sensex, had nearly tripled in the same period. However, by May 2006, "for investors, the fun had stopped." The Sensex dropped by nearly 30 percent, with one plunge of 10 percent unfolding during a two-hour period. Despite attempts to explain the mayhem as temporary growing pains that would be offset by the prospects of long-term profits, it seemed as though a note of caution had begun sneaking into the laudatory hailing of India Inc., the global India.[14] After the collapse in mid-2006, it did appear as though the Indian markets were back on track. In the next twelve months, there were signs of a rally, none as promising as the response to the news of an initial public offering by Reliance Power, a company operated by Anil Ambani, who, like Ratan Tata, was seen as a symbol of successful global Indian entrepreneurship. Expecting huge profits once the company officially started trading, eager investors ensured that the shares were oversubscribed seventy-three times within days of its being offered.[15] However, on February 11, 2008—the launch day, when Reliance Power shares were supposed to double their value—investors lost an estimated $121 million, as the stock crashed, "taking the Bombay Stock Exchange's Sensex index with it."[16] Dragged down by Reliance, within the span of a single day the market had dropped nearly 8 percent. As investors scrambled to find convincing explanations of what had gone wrong, the country's finance minister attempted to reassure them the debacle was not a portent of things to come and that, unlike the "economies of some developed countries, which are facing some stress," the Indian economy was sound. There was, as he put it, "no reason to allow the worries of the Western world to overwhelm us."[17] Unfortunately for the minister, the material reality of the global economic meltdown, which at that time was only in its embryonic stages, could not be denied by mere rhetoric. In a single week in October, the Sensex dropped more than 16 percent, requiring the Reserve Bank of India to intervene twice, cut its cash reserves by 1 percent, and inject nearly $13 billion into the financial system. As foreign investors continued taking money out of the country, new statistics revealed an economy that was slowing down.[18] Even more worrisome was the likelihood that the fastest growing sectors—information technology (IT) and business process outsourcing (BPO)/knowledge process outsourcing (KPO)—which had earned nearly $8.4 billion in export revenues the year before (nearly three times what it earned in 2003–2004), would be the most seriously affected by the global financial crisis.[19] When it became impossible to continue making claims about the insulation of the Indian economy from the global crisis, Indian policy makers did admit that profits in the IT sector would be adversely affected. However, they kept reiterating the generally accepted notion of the intrinsic strength of the IT sector, which supposedly stemmed from the structural reform of the economy, as well as the post-1991 professionalization of Indian business. The IT sector, they argued, was well equipped to weather the stormy seas of the global economy and remain the bedrock of the nation's economic growth. However, even that notion had to be reassessed within a year of the Reliance fiasco.

On the morning of January 7, 2009, B. Ramalinga Raju, the chairman of Satyam Computer Services, India's fourth-largest IT company, sent a mea culpa letter to his board and the Securities and Exchange Board of India. In the letter, Raju claimed that he had "inflated the amount of cash on the balance sheet...by nearly $1 billion, incurred a liability of $253 million on funds arranged by him personally, and overstated [the] September 2008 quarterly revenues by 76% and profits by 97%." Satyam, the company he had cofounded more than two decades earlier, ironically enough was named for the Sanskrit word for "truth."[20] The letter, which ended with an apology and a resignation, sent shock waves beyond the Satyam boardroom and company headquarters. The Sensex index dropped 7.3 percent, while Satyam stocks fell nearly 80 percent. Goldman Sachs dropped its recommendations on Satyam, while JPMorgan Chase warned that earnings per share might actually be 80 percent less than what was reported.[21] The implications of the scandal, however, went beyond its immediate effect on Satyam employees and shareholders. Realizing the potential damage to India's reputation as a leader in the industry and a reliable provider of IT services, representatives of the Indian IT sector and Indian industry at large went on the offensive to paint the Satyam case as an exception, the proverbial bad apple. To make this argument, they began by focusing on the peccadilloes of the founder and chairman, in particular, the fact that his company—despite representing the most modern and developed sector of the Indian economy—was very much run in the old way, building on political patronage and funding family-run projects.[22] Newspaper and magazine articles pointed out that Raju, who had spent nearly a decade in the United States, had returned to India to cofound the company with his two brothers. Even when the company went public, its management was primarily in the hands of the Raju family. In fact, as late as December 2008, Raju had attempted to use company funds to help his sons by buying the two infrastructure companies that they ran for a total of $1.6 billion. When the foreign investors who held nearly 47 percent of Satyam stock responded by dumping the company's NASDAQ-traded American depository receipts (ADR), causing a nearly 50 percent drop in a day's trading, Raju backed off from his decision.[23] However, the newly minted critics claimed that the incident should have served to underscore the fact that Satyam's business model was still settled within the anachronistic patriarchal framework that had permeated the old Indian economy. In addition, it was pointed out that there had been early warning signs about other problems peculiar to Satyam. In September 2008, for instance, the World Bank had banned the company, after it was revealed that Satyam employees had hacked into its system to access sensitive information. In the months that followed, Satyam had also managed to get embroiled in litigation with a former client that had filed a case against the company for intellectual fraud and forgery. All of this, it was argued, showed why the debacle at Satyam was not something that should make investors rethink the strength of the Indian IT sector.[24]

Notwithstanding these valiant attempts, the Satyam scandal could not simply be wished away or explained as a peculiar exception. The reasons were quite straightforward. Satyam was not a small-time, pop-up enterprise: it was India's fourth-largest IT company, a crown jewel of its IT sector, with supposedly 53,000 employees and offices across the world. Among its clients were Nestlé, the world's largest food company; General Electric; Telstra, Australia's largest telephone company; and ArcelorMittal, the world's largest steel manufacturer. Before his precipitous fall, its chairman and founder had been much feted for his many accomplishments by political elites both in India and abroad.[25] The board of Satyam had some of the biggest names in the Indian corporate world. The numbers on employment and profits had been "verified" over the years by a well-established auditing firm (PricewaterhouseCoopers). Satyam had been constantly held up as a shining model of the new India Inc. and rewarded by state actors across the political spectrum. The claim that Satyam's downfall was the result of corporate malfeasance perpetrated by a single man, who apparently had managed to hoodwink one and all, thus stretched credulity. If anything, the revelations about the functioning of Satyam cast the spotlight (understandably unwelcome, insofar as the Indian ruling class were concerned) on the deep ties that bound the Indian corporate elites and the political system. As more and more information about Raju's ties to other corporate titans and the ruling Congress Party became public, and it became known that other Indian IT companies such as Wipro (the third largest in the country) had also been banned by the World Bank for questionable business practices, there appeared to be a corresponding increase in reports about the decreasing confidence of foreign investors in the Indian market. Magazines and newspapers that had once painted a picture of the unstoppable India Inc. now began to sound notes of caution, not only about the state of the Indian IT sector and the general levels of corporate governance in the country but also about the prospects of India's economic growth.[26] It was under these gathering clouds that the Indian delegation made its annual pilgrimage to the World Economic Forum at Davos.

As participants and observers were quick to note, unlike past years, the buzz surrounding the Indian delegation was virtually nonexistent. The large gatherings at cocktail receptions, the huge audiences at sessions devoted to the Indian economy, the celebratory aura that surrounded all India-centric events—in fact, everything that the cheerleaders of India Inc. had crowed about for three years— were no longer to be seen. India was barely a blip on the radar this year at Davos, let alone anywhere else, and the reasons were not just growing concerns about the state of corporate governance in the country. Given the meltdown of financial markets and the looming crisis of capitalism, the focus of the global elite who gathered annually at Davos was a very simple one: to somehow figure out ways to ensure their very survival. In that context, the fact that India remained a peripheral player in the global economy was a far more significant factor than the ability of the Indian delegation to throw the best parties in town.

In the first decade of this new century, the Indian elites presented a rosy picture of a nation-state that had finally developed the self-confidence to accept its global position and responsibilities. With its stellar gross domestic product (GDP) growth rates above 9 percent per year, its edge in information technology, its massive and growing educated workforce, and its booming exports, especially in outsourcing, India, they claimed, had arrived on the global stage. Given the increase in foreign direct investment (FDI) and foreign investment in the Indian stock market, their main audience concurred. However, these facts about the Indian economy are what can best be termed contingent truths. Even if one took the economic statistics provided by the Indian government at face value, the growth of the Indian economy was very much tied to the developments of capitalism on a global scale. The increase in foreign investments in India took place during a period when financial markets across the world (and especially in the United States) seemed to have finally defied the laws of gravity (or at least the law of value), achieving stratospheric heights. Indian exports grew, especially in the IT-based outsourcing sector, at a time when the Fortune 500 companies that were their main clients reported substantial profits. As the IT sector grew, so did employment opportunities for the much-lauded educated workforce—India's "demographic advantage." So long as these trends continued, it was possible for the ruling elites in India to brush aside inconvenient facts like the actual decrease in per-capita agricultural output (despite the continuing dependence of a substantial part of the population on agriculture), growing levels of rural poverty, and the subsistence of more than half the population on less than $1.50 a day, and for them to continue to reassert India's status as, if not an actual economic superpower, at least a potential one.[27] Those assertions, much like the profits of Lehman, Merrill-Lynch, Citigroup, Bernard L. Madoff Investment Securities LLC, or Satyam, had a tenuous grip on reality. Seemingly plausible, seemingly credible, they were, as closer looks revealed, quite hollow. The juxtaposition of the epigraphs about Davos thus reveals not so much a picture of a once great economic powerhouse brought to its knees, but rather the hollowness of the grandiose claims of India everywhere.

As the financial markets began to unravel in the last two years, the Indian bourgeoisie and its political representatives first attempted to assure investors that the Indian economy would not be affected.[28] When it became apparent that such claims were unsustainable, they tried to argue that the effects would be minimal. However, much like all the other claims about India Inc., these, too, do not bear up to close scrutiny. Even at the most obvious level, projections of India's GDP growth have been based on expectations of continued growth in exports. However, as the most recent figures released by the Indian government indicate, exports have actually declined by 28 percent, continuing a trend of successive declines throughout 2009.[29] Given that one of the most visible export-earning sectors of the Indian economy, the IT sector—one in which India could credibly claim to be a global leader—has already suffered several reverses, it is evident that the global economic crisis will have even greater effects. The IT sector, especially the outsourcing industry, has been a boon for the Indian bourgeoisie and political elites not just because of the exponential growth in profits that occurred over a short span of time, but because the employment opportunities provided by these industries buttressed claims that the success was essentially national in character, while global in scope. But as outsourcing loses its sheen and as the industry's global clients take stock of their losses, it is only natural to expect to see massive sectoral layoffs in India.

Unemployment, however, is only one part of the larger picture. Indian society, reflecting global trends, continues to be characterized by extremely high levels of inequality. In March 2008, *Forbes* published its annual list of the world's richest men. Of the top ten, four were Indian.[30] Even more interesting was the fact that

India ranked as the country with the largest number of billionaires in the world. As the magazine noted approvingly, the cumulative worth of these fifty-three individuals was an astonishing $335 billion, which amounted to 31 percent of India's GDP.[31] More than any statistics released by the Indian government, these figures put India's stellar growth in the proper perspective.

What, one might wonder, do these developments have to do with the production of the domestic abroad? This book has argued that the production of the domestic abroad—the concurrent diasporic reimagining of the nation and neoliberal restructuring of the state—makes sense only in the context of the rearticulation of bourgeois hegemony. In the Indian case, the hegemony of the Indian bourgeoisie, which was initially established in the context of anticolonial struggle, laid the foundations for a very specific understanding of the boundaries of the nation and the extent of the authority of the state. It was this understanding that framed the policies of the Indian state toward the Indian diaspora in the aftermath of independence. However, as the previous chapters make clear, the conditions under which bourgeois hegemony was possible were peculiar to a particular stage of the development of capitalism on a global scale. The change in these conditions, combined with the change in the broader demographic character of the group counted as Indians abroad, set the stage not only for the fracturing of the hegemony of the Indian bourgeoisie but also for the necessity of its rearticulation. It is in this context that one can understand the dramatic shift in the Indian state's attitude and policies toward the Indian diaspora.

The production of the Indian domestic abroad rested on the successful establishment of a particular set of equations: neoliberal restructuring and the opening of the Indian markets, which served the interests of the dominant faction of the Indian bourgeoisie, actually served the interests of the nation at large; the embrace of liberalization was a sign of national self-confidence; the success of the global Indian entrepreneur was the success of the Indian nation-state; the Indian diaspora was best represented in the figure of the global Indian, who, through a clever sleight of hand, also became the global Indian entrepreneur; and the feting of the global Indian, the diasporic Indian, was actually the celebration of India as a global actor whose time had finally arrived. Contrary to the way in which these assertions were presented by the business leaders and political elites, these equations did not, in fact, add up. The global Indian celebrated by the Indian state, for instance, is a stereotypical figure of an entrepreneur who has struggled and triumphed against mighty odds, whose Indianness in fact can be traced to the unwillingness to give up, even under less than salubrious conditions. Undoubtedly, among the 20 million or so in the Indian diaspora, one could find individuals who fit within this rubric. However, contrary to the impression that one might get from perusing the speeches at any of the Pravasi Bharatiya Divas events, the differences in the origins, experiences, and challenges faced by those characterized as the Indians abroad do not exist merely as a rhetorical stepping-stone on the way to a rousing crescendo hailing the global Indian family. Beyond originary moments, geographical locations, generational gaps, and questions of gender and religion, there exist real, material, sociological differences among the various sections of the Indian diaspora. These differences, the acknowledgment of which serves to function purely as a rhetorical flourish before being quickly swept under the rug, not only imply differing interests and relationships to the structures of the Indian state but also show the essential hollowness of the figure of the global Indian. Much like claims of India's economic might and its arrival on the global stage, this hollowness can be camouflaged under the right conditions, but it is fundamentally unsustainable in the long run. The trope of arrival that figures constantly in the Indian ruling elites' description of achievements—real or imagined—is a good indication that even they are aware of the shaky premises of their rearticulated hegemony.

In the two decades since the introduction of neoliberal restructuring, India's arrival on the global stage has been proclaimed innumerable times: in the early 1990s, when restructuring was introduced; in the mid-1990s, when stories of Indian successes in the Silicon Valley became commonplace; in 1998, when the Indian state openly announced its nuclear capabilities with a series of tests carried out in defiance of the wishes of the United States; at the turn of the century, when the Indian government established the High Level Committee on the Indian Diaspora; at the celebrations of the first Pravasi Bharatiya Divas in 2003; at Davos with the "India Everywhere" campaign; in 2009, when *Slumdog Millionaire* swept the Oscars.[32] The list could go on and on. But it is striking that in all this time, in the years that the Indian state has been actively involved in the production of the domestic abroad, India has been in a perpetual state of arriving but has actually never arrived. In holding up the figure of the global Indian as an illustration of India's intrinsic abilities and will to succeed, the bourgeoisie attempted to present neoliberal economic reforms as the panacea to the ills of the nation at large. Instead, the phenomenon of the domestic abroad has served only to underscore the intrinsic and increasingly fragile foundations of bourgeois hegemony in India.

The Domestic Abroad in International Relations

The domestic abroad phenomenon, as made clear in the early chapters of this book, is not peculiar to a particular nation-state. At this point of time in history, a large number of nation-states, including the People's Republic of China, Russia, Turkey, South Korea, the Philippines, Tunisia, Morocco, Jordan, Haiti, the Dominican Republic, Hungary, Portugal, Ecuador, Poland, Italy, and Greece, are actively involved in constituting sections of their diasporas as not just part of a larger deterritorialized nation, but a new constituency that is connected to, and has claims on, the institutional structures of the state. In this context, what makes the production of the Indian domestic abroad interesting is precisely the fact that it is symptomatic of a larger global trend. This is not to deny that to understand the Indian domestic abroad one needs to seriously engage with a very specific complex historical and political landscape that is in some ways unique: the legacy of British colonialism, the nationalist struggles waged against it, the presence of a relatively strong national capitalist class on the eve of independence, and the emergence of a remarkably uneven diaspora of unskilled laborers and technically proficient Silicon Valley multimillionaires. The later chapters of the book indeed are devoted to providing such an engagement. The purpose of this book, however, is not only to provide an explanation of the Indian domestic abroad but also to offer a larger theoretical argument about international relations.

This book argues that the domestic abroad should be understood as the product of the processes through which a national bourgeoisie, in the context of the development of capitalism on a global scale, is compelled to rearticulate and reestablish a seemingly organic connection between its interests and the interests of the nation at large. The point is not to assume that the alignment of social forces or, for that matter, the way in which these processes played out in the Indian case is exactly the same in every context where one sees the production of a domestic abroad. On the contrary, the theoretical framework I propose is predicated on the need to pay close attention to the peculiarities of each historic and geographical context—to the conditions in which specific nationalist movements emerge, the nature of the social forces that shape them, the type of state projects that are enabled and legitimized at particular historical junctures, and the ways in which these reflect and affect the development of capitalism on a global scale.

Within this framework, to make sense of the production of the Mexican domestic abroad, for instance, we would need to address the following interrelated questions: what were the historical conditions and political struggles that produced Mexico as a modern nation-state? What was the alignment of social forces that shaped the authority of the Mexican state and the limits of the Mexican nation? How have these alignments changed over time? Who were the groups constituted as "Mexicans" (both in terms of the imagined community of the Mexican nation and the institutional structures delimiting membership through citizenship clauses), and what are the changes in the nature of the membership within this group, especially when framed within the historical context of migration from Mexico? In what ways do these processes reflect and affect the development of capitalism on a global scale?[33] Similarly, to understand the relationship of the Russian state to the Russians in the near abroad, we would need to analyze the specific historical, political struggles under which the new Russian nation-state emerged. In particular, we would need to focus on the alignment of social forces that enabled the introduction of perestroika, glasnost, and the transition to a capitalist economy. The processes through which the new Russian capitalist class has attempted to position itself as a legitimate ruling class, I would contend, are key to making sense of the centrality of the near abroad for successive Russian governments.[34] In the case of China, Deng Xiaoping's introduction of neoliberal restructuring marked an important moment in the changing relationship between the People's Republic of China (PRC) and the Chinese diaspora. While this moment provides an important segue into the production of the Chinese domestic abroad, any attempt to analyze this phenomenon would have to take into account a number of critical and interconnected factors, such as the complex nationalist struggles surrounding the emergence of modern China in 1949, the larger international political framework that shaped both the nature of the Chinese Communist Party and the Chinese state founded by Mao Zedong, the particular landscape of social classes that enabled a purportedly Communist regime to transition smoothly to "Capitalism with Chinese characteristics," the lengthy history of the Chinese state's often conflicted relationship with its diaspora, and the different moments of China's relationship with its neighbors in Asia, given its history as both an imperial power and an imperial colony.[35]

The preceding paragraph is quite evidently not intended to serve in lieu of an in-depth analysis of the domestic abroad across different contexts. Given the highly contingent nature of the specific historical and political struggles that underlie nation-state projects, it is neither desirable nor plausible to distill a parsimonious formula that enables us to provide a quick and concise analysis of the nature and meaning of this phenomenon across the board. However, a framework that enables us to understand and analyze how the boundaries of the imagined community of the nation and the nature of the state are intrinsically connected to the development of capitalist social relations, at both global and national levels, is the essential first step in understanding and explaining the politics of the domestic abroad. The goal of this book has been to develop such a framework and set the stage for future research by systematically revealing the ways in which it can work to explain some of the most pressing issues in contemporary international relations. But what about the discipline of international relations (IR) itself?

This book sheds new light on a phenomenon that has generally been disregarded by IR scholars. It reveals the manner in which the changing relationship between the nation and the state, negotiated on the terrain of capitalist social relations, can give rise to forms of transnationalism that are not only essentially national in character and scope but also serve to reinforce state authority. While this book was not written with the primary intent of making an intervention in the peculiar, highly specific debates between the various "-isms" of IR, I do not believe that one can overlook the nature and implications of disciplinary ortho- doxies. As seen in chapter 2, the one disciplinary theoretical tradition that this book critically engages with is constructivism. Given the subject matter of the book, the reasons for this are quite obvious: constructivist scholars have been at the forefront of questioning that which has generally been taken for granted in the study of international relations, be it the relationship between nation and state, the identity of nation-state actors, or the relevance of transnationalism as a phenomenon. But despite the critical attention paid by scholars in this tradition to the task of denaturalizing what is taken to be a given in global politics and unraveling the historical roots of international relations, they have strangely enough been silent about the full implications of the peculiar conditions under which their own theoretical tradition emerged within the discipline.

The most commonly accepted narrative about the theoretical development of the discipline and the unfolding of the "great debates" presents the emergence of constructivism as a moment that marked a fundamental challenge to existing international relations traditions—primarily neorealism and neoliberalism— that had arrived at a theoretical impasse. Constructivism (a tradition with roots in social theory), it is argued, arose to provide a novel and necessary alternative to the mainstream, rationalist modes of making sense of the world. While ini- tially occupying a somewhat peripheral position in the discipline, over the past two decades constructivists (or at least certain strands within the tradition) have moved comfortably to the disciplinary mainstream, becoming what Michael Barnett has termed "a success story."[36] In the process of achieving this "success," constructivism, as I have argued elsewhere, has very deliberately carved a space for itself in a way that has essentially ignored questions related to the develop- ment of capitalism on global or national levels.[37] While there have been different variants of this tradition—some more self-consciously critical than others— what has characterized constructivist scholarship as a whole has been a concern with the politics of identity formation and the importance of normative and ideational structures, understood as more significant than (if not completely dis- tinct from) material structures. The problems with these ontological commit- ments, as this book reveals, become obvious when one applies this framework to analyzing contemporary political phenomena like the domestic abroad. For these are not the sort of limitations that can be overcome by merely adding a pinch of capitalism or a dash of class to an existing theoretical medley.[38]

The ignoring of capitalist social relations by a tradition that prides itself on explaining the essentially social character of international politics, however, is not a question of mere oversight. Constructivism, it should be recalled, attained disciplinary recognition in a very specific historical context: at a time when the Soviet Union and the political-theoretical tradition it was deemed to represent had supposedly been consigned to the dustbin of history—at a time, moreover, when the fumes of ever expansive and seemingly triumphant capitalism intoxicated quite a few intellectuals.[39] Recent history, however, has powerfully demonstrated the necessity to return to many questions that were considered to have been settled once and for all. In returning to these questions, international relations will have the opportunity, and may well be compelled, to revisit the hoary categories of theoretical paradigms that are at present regarded as long surpassed.

Appendix

Table A.1.   Political Parties in Power and in the Opposition in India (1947–2004)

August 15, 1947—India becomes independent from British rule.
January 26, 1950—Adoption of the Indian Constitution

Year	Ruling Party/Parties	Prime Minister	Main Opposition
1952–1957	INC (339 Seats)	Jawaharlal Nehru	CP (18); Socialists (12)
1957–1962	INC (359)	Jawaharlal Nehru	CP (27); PSP (18)
1962–1967	INC (366)	Jawaharlal Nehru (June 1962–May 1964); L. B. Shastri (June 1964–Jan. 1966); Indira Gandhi (January 1966–February 1967)	CP (29); Swatantra Party (23); Jan Sangh (13); PSP (13)
1967–1971	INC (278)	Indira Gandhi	Swatantra (42); Jan Sangh (32); DMK (24); CP (21); CPI-M (18)
1971–1977	INC (346)	Indira Gandhi	CPI-M (25); CP (23); DMK (23); Jan Sangh (22)

(*Continued*)

157

Table A.1. Continued

Year	Ruling Party/Parties	Prime Minister	Main Opposition
1977–1980	Janata Party (292)	Morarji Desai (1977–79); Charan Singh (1979–80)	Congress-I (151); CPI-M (21); AIADMK (19)
1980–1984	Congress-I (369)	Indira Gandhi	Janata-S (41); CPI-M (38); Janata Party (18); DMK (16)
1984–1988	Congress-I (409)	Rajiv Gandhi	TDP (30); CPI-M (22)
1989–1991	National Front	V. P. Singh 1989–1990) Chandra Shekhar (1990–1991)	Congress-I CPI-M; BJP
1991–1996	Congress-I	P. V. Narasimha Rao	BJP; CPI-M; Janata Dal
1996–1998	BJP (May 16–June 1, 1996)	A. B. Vajpayee	Congress (I); CPI-M; Janata Dal
	United Front	H. D. Deve Gowda (June 1996–April 1997) I. K. Gujral (April 1997–May 1998)	BJP; Congress-I
1998–1999	BJP (182)	A. B. Vajpayee	INC (139); CPI-M (32); Samajwadi Party (20)
1999–2004	National Democratic Alliance (BJP, TDP, DMK, Janata Dal-U; Shiv Sena)	A. B. Vajpayee	INC; CPI-M; AIADMK; BSP
2004–2009	United Progressive Alliance (INC), with outside support from BSP, Left Front	Manmohan Singh	BJP
2009–	United Progressive Alliance (INC) with outside support from BSP, SP, Janata Dal (Secular), Rashtriya Janata Dal	Manmohan Singh	BJP; CPI (M)

* The Congress (I) was a breakaway faction of the Indian National Congress led by Indira Gandhi. In 1998, the party readopted the moniker "Indian National Congress."

INC – Indian National Congress; CP – Communist Party; PSP – Praja Socialist Party; DMK – Dravida Munnetra Kazhagam; CPI-M – Communist Party of India (Marxist); AIADMK – Anna Dravida Munnetra Kazhagam; BJP – Bharatiya Janata Party; BSP – Bahujan Samaj Party; SP – Samajwadi Party

Table A.2. Estimates of Indian Immigration to the United Kingdom and North America, 1951–2000

Country	1951–60	1961–70	1971–80	1981–90	Total (end of 1990)	Total (end of 1999–2000)*
United Kingdom	NA	125,600	83,040	51,480	260,120	1,200,000
United States	2,120	31,214	172,080	261,841	467,255	1,678,765
Canada	2,802	25,772	79,903	79,304	180,781	850,000

* Report of the High Level Committee on the Indian Diaspora (2001).

Source: Michael Debabrata and Muneesh Kapur, "India's Worker Remittances: A Users' Lament about Balance of Payments Compilation," Sixteenth Meeting of the IMF Committee on Balance of Payments Statistics, Washington, DC, December 1–5, 2003.

Table A.3. Estimates of Indian Immigration to the Middle East, 1975–1999

Country	1975	1979	1983	1987	1991	1999
Bahrain	1,725	26,000	30,000	77,000	100,000	150,000
Iraq	7,500	20,000	50,000	350,000	NA	NA
Kuwait	32,105	65,000	115,000	100,000	88,000	200,000
Libya	1,100	10,000	40,000	25,000	12,000	20,000
Oman	38,500	60,000	100,000	184,000	220,000	450,000
Qatar	27,800	30,000	40,000	50,000	75,000	100,000
Saudi Arabia	34,500	100,000	270,000	380,000	600,000	1,200,000
UAE	10,750	152,000	250,000	225,000	400,000	750,000
Others	NA	68,000	21,000	21,000	10,000	130,000
Total	266,255	501,000	916,000	1,096,000	1,505,000	3,000,000

Source: Report of the High Level Committee on the Indian Diaspora (2001).

Notes

Chapter 1

1. Gregory Rodriguez, "Vicente Fox Blesses the Americanization of Mexico," *Los Angeles Times*, December 10, 2003.

2. At that time, approximately 17 million of that population were located in the United States. David Thelen, "Re-Thinking History and the Nation-State: Mexico and the United States," *Journal of American History* 86, no. 2 (1999): 439–455.

3. Quotation on "*el pochos*" from Earl Shorris, *Latinos*, cited in Yossi Shain, "The Mexican-American Diaspora's Impact on Mexico," *Political Science Quarterly* 114, no. 4 (1999–2000): 677–678.

4. Rodriguez, "Vicente Fox Blesses the Americanization of Mexico."

5. Carlos Gonzalez Gutierrez, "Fostering Identities: Mexico's Relations with Its Diaspora," *Journal of American History* 86, no. 2 (1999): 545–567.

6. As noted on the "Office of the President for Mexicans Abroad" Web site Metropolis International: "Fox's government has revolutionized Mexico's public policies for its citizens abroad in five central ways: 1) Elevating to the cabinet level, an office for assistance to Mexicans abroad and Mexican-Americans; 2) Placing migration at the top of the post-NAFTA U.S.-Mexico bilateral agenda, a place it had never before occupied; 3) Supporting the state-level network of offices for migrant assistance, called Conofam; 4) Eliminating corruption and human rights abuses committed against Mexicans returning to visit, principally along the border; and 5) Maximizing the potential for migration to solve problems of underdevelopment in traditional sending regions, through increased remittances received by individual

families and programs to promote investment in those regions." Juan Hernandez, Omar de la Torre, and Julie M. Weise, "Mexico's New Public Policies for Its Citizens Abroad" at http://www.international.metropolis.net/events/rotterdam/papers/36_ Torre.htm.

7. Rodriguez, "Vicente Fox Blesses the Americanization of Mexico."

8. Juan Hernandez et al., "Mexico's New Public Policies for Its Citizens Abroad."

9. The main streets of New Delhi leading to the fairground where the conference was held (and the fairground itself) were festooned with banners in the color of the Indian national flag, bearing these very words. During the course of informal interviews, various organizers and participants constantly reiterated the notion that the meeting was a "family gathering". For the official stance on this, see p. 1 at http://indiandiaspora.nic.in/ch1.pdf.

10. All the quotations in this paragraph are from L. K. Advani's speech, though the themes he articulated were reiterated by different members of the administration during the course of the conference. See pp. 95–99 at http://indiandiaspora.nic.in/ch6.pdf.

11. "A World of Exiles," *Economist*, January 2, 2003.

12. Ibid.

13. See, for instance, Linda Basch, Nina Glick Schiller, and Cristina Szanton Blanc, *Nations Unbound: Transnational Projects, Postcolonial Predicaments and De-Territorialized Nation-States* (Langhorne, PA: Gordon and Breach, 1994); Yossi Shain, *Marketing the American Creed Abroad: Diasporas in the U.S. and Their Homelands* (Cambridge: Cambridge University Press, 1999); Tony Smith, *Foreign Attachments: The Power of Ethnic Groups in the Making of American Foreign Policy* (Cambridge, MA: Harvard University Press, 2000); Paul Hockenos, *Homeland Calling: Exile Patriotism and the Balkan Wars* (Ithaca, NY: Cornell University Press, 2003).

14. As I show in chapter 2, this can be seen particularly in the discourse of "deterritorialization" and "postnational formations" that frames much of the discussion on diasporas. On the question of diaspora scholarship and novelty, see Robert Smith, "How Durable and New Is Transnational Life? Historical Retrieval through Local Comparison," *Diaspora* 9, no. 2 (2000): 203–234; Latha Varadarajan, "Out of Place: Re-Thinking Diaspora and Empire," *Millennium: Journal of International Studies* 36, no. 2 (2008): 267–293.

15. See, for instance, Robert Smith, "Diasporic Memberships in Historical Perspective: Comparative Insights from the Mexican, Italian and Polish Cases," *International Migration Review* 37, no. 3 (2003): 724–759; Laurie Brand, *Citizens Abroad: Emigrants and the State in the Middle East and North Africa*: (Cambridge: Cambridge University Press, 2006); Myra Waterbury, "The State as Ethnic Activist: Explaining Continuity and Change in Hungarian Diaspora Policies" (PhD diss., New School for Social Research, 2006). For a more recent analysis of the subject from a Foucauldian perspective, see Francesco Ragazzi, "Governing Diasporas," *International Political Sociology* 3, no. 4 (2009): 378–397.

16. Another example would be the attempts made by Fascist Italy to establish connections with the Italian diaspora in the early decades of the twentieth century. See Smith, "Diasporic Memberships in Historical Perspective."

17. Opening up markets to international capital, privatizing the public sector, offering national treatment to foreign companies, eliminating trade barriers, and removing regulatory and institutional restraints from the labor market are all part of neoliberal restructuring. For a succinct discussion of the emergence and spread of this form of restructuring, see David Harvey, *A Brief History of Neoliberalism* (New York: Oxford University Press, 2007).

18. For a brief overview of some of the debates, see *Diaspora: A Journal of Transnational Studies* 1, no. 1 (1991).

19. As Vijay Mishra points out in the *SPAN* special issue on diaspora, the Oxford English Dictionary seems to be frozen in time insofar as its definition of *diaspora* is concerned. It refers only to the dispersion of the Jews that took place more than 4,000 years ago, and even its examples of the usage of the term (bar one) refer to the Jewish experience. See Vijay Mishra, "Introduction," *SPAN* (Diasporas, special double issue) 34–35 (November 1992–May 1993): 1–2. See also Gabriel Sheffer, *Modern Diasporas in International Politics* (London: Croon Helm, 1986); Robin Cohen, *Global Diasporas: An Introduction* (London: UCL Press, 1997).

20. Khachig Tölöyan, "The Nation-State and Its Others: In Lieu of a Preface," *Diaspora: A Journal of Transnational Studies* 1, no. 1 (1991): 3–7.

21. William Safran, "Diasporas in Modern Societies: Myths of Homeland and Returns," *Diaspora: A Journal of Transnational Studies* 1, no. 1 (1991): 83–99.

22. Ibid., 83.

23. Ibid., 84.

24. "A diaspora is defined as the *collective, forced dispersion of a religious and/or ethnic group* precipitated by a disaster, often of a political nature," in G. Chaliand and J.-P. Rageau, *The Penguin Atlas of Diasporas* (New York: Viking Penguin, 1995), xiv.

25. Vijay Mishra, for instance, argues that a comprehensive definition of *diasporas* should account for relatively homogeneous displaced communities brought to serve the empire (slave, contract, indentured, etc.) coexisting with other races/indigenous communities; emerging communities based on free migration and linked to late capitalism; and any group of migrants that sees itself on the periphery of power or excluded from sharing power." See Mishra, "Introduction," *SPAN*. See also Vijay Mishra, "The Diasporic Imaginary: Theorizing the Indian Diaspora," *Textual Practice* 10, no. 3 (1996): 421–427.

26. The word *diaspora* is a derivative of the Greek word for dispersion ("to sow, to scatter"), which was initially used to describe the Greek conquest and settlement of Asia Minor and the Mediterranean. As Cohen points out, the Greek diaspora was established through varied means, including trade, conquest, free migration, and settlement. The dispersion of later diasporas, he argues, however, can be traced to a dominant cause. Based on these historical considerations, he proposes a classification

of various diasporas as "victim," "labor," "imperial," "trading," and "cultural" diasporas. See Cohen, *Global Diasporas*.

27. For a detailed discussion of the "dispersion" of the term/concept diaspora and
its consequences, see Rogers Brubaker, "The 'Diaspora' Diaspora," *Ethnic and Racial
Studies* 28, no. 1 (2005): 1–19.

28. As Brubaker (ibid., 12) puts it, diaspora as a category of practice "does not so
much *describe* the world as seek to *remake* it."

29. Ibid.

30. For a discussion of the concept of "hailing" that is pertinent to its use here, see
Louis Althusser, "Ideology and the State," in *Lenin and Philosophy and Other Essays*,
trans. Ben Brewster (New York: Monthly Review Press, 1971), 171–184.

31. Brand's *Citizens Abroad* is one of the few recent scholarly works that have
addressed the phenomenon that I term the "domestic abroad." It provides an incisive
analysis of the institutional dimensions of the relationship between states and emigrant communities in the case of four Middle Eastern states (Tunisia, Morocco,
Lebanon, and Jordan). For her discussion of the various explanations of this phenomenon, see Brand, *Citizens Abroad*, particularly chapter 1.

32. Brand (*Citizens Abroad*, 17) highlights two aspects of the economic explanations: (1) the employment incentive works in the case of states that realize they cannot provide adequate employment opportunities for their citizens and therefore are
interested in resettling their emigrants in places where they can be gainfully employed,
and (2) states try to cultivate the loyalty of emigrants to maintain a particular level of
remittances. Given the importance placed on the role of remittances in understanding the significance of diasporas in general, I focus here on the second aspect.

33. "A World of Exiles."

34. Cited in Shain, "Mexican-American Diaspora's Impact on Mexico," 668.

35. Ralph Chami, Connel Fullenkamp, and Samir Jahjah, "Are Immigrant Remittance Flows a Source of Capital Development?" IMF Working Paper WP/03/189, 2003.

36. Ibid.

37. On the history of China's relationship with the Chinese diaspora, see Stephen
Fitzgerald, *China and the Overseas Chinese: A Study of Peking's Changing Policy, 1949–
1970* (Cambridge: Cambridge University Press, 1972); Constance Lever-Tracy, David
Fu-Keung Ip, and Noel Tracy, *The Chinese Diaspora and Mainland China: An Emerging
Economic Synergy* (New York: Macmillan, 1996); Aihwa Ong, *Flexible Citizenship: The
Cultural Logics of Transnationality* (Durham, NC: Duke University Press, 1999).

38. Igor Zevelev, *Russia and Its New Diasporas* (Washington, DC: USIP Press,
2001), 4. In terms of the percentage of the total population in these republics, Russians
(or those seen as being of Russian origin) account for the following: Kazakhstan, 37.8
percent; Latvia, 34 percent; Estonia, 30.3 percent; and Ukraine, 22.1 percent. See Pål
Kolstø, "Territorializing Diasporas: The Case of Russians in the Former Soviet
Republics," *Millennium* 28, no. 3 (1999): 607–631.

39. Zevelev, *Russia and Its New Diasporas*, 5. It is indeed noteworthy that Zevelev's work is among those on the subject that almost completely ignore the economic value of the Russian diaspora as a possible reason for the Russian state's interest in them. See also Neil Melvin, *Russians beyond Russia: The Politics of National Identity* (London: Pinter, 1995).

40. Given the differences that exist among the large number of nation-states involved in the production of the domestic abroad, such a claim would indeed be unsustainable.

41. While offering a nuanced critique of the limitations of remittances arguments, even Brand's analysis falls back on a similar assumption. For instance, in pointing out that the initial initiatives toward emigrants by the Tunisian, Moroccan, and Lebanese states seem to have been driven by decolonization, Brand asserts: "None of this is to deny…[the] contention that *economic factors* have played an important role in state institutional development although they seem to have been less of a driving force than one might initially imagine." Clarifying further what she means by "economic factors," Brand goes to explain: "Depending upon period, all four states acknowledged the importance of *expatriate contributions and manifested an interest in maximizing emigrant contributions to the national economy.*" Brand, *Citizens Abroad*, 217, my emphasis.

42. As Robert Smith notes, the main promise of this pact was "peace for prosperity," which translated into certain state practices, including the assumption of a "nationalistic stance towards the outside world, and its interventionist economic actors, especially the United States, powerful transnational corporations and international financial institutions like the IMF and the World Bank." Robert Smith, "Transnational Public Spheres and Changing Practices of Citizenship, Membership and Nation: Comparative Insights from the Mexican and Italian Cases." Paper presented at the International Center for Cooperation and Conflict Resolution (ICCCR) Conference on Transnationalism, May 18, 1998.

43. Shain, "The Mexican-American Diaspora's Impact on Mexico," 671–672.

44. Juan Hernandez, Omar de la Torre, and Julie M. Weise, "Mexico's New Public Policies for Its Citizens Abroad," Paper presented at the Metropolis Conference, Rotterdam, The Netherlands, November 28, 2001.

45. Aihwa Ong notes that with Deng Xiaoping's rise to power, "socialist nationalism was repositioned through a re-engagement with global capitalism." The latest phase of the restructuring of the Chinese economy was officially launched during Deng's 1992 tour of South China, when he called for the "construction of 'a few Hong Kongs' as part of 'one hundred years of market reforms and modernization.'" The influx of investments from overseas Chinese that characterized China's economic miracle largely emerged in the aftermath of 1992. See Aihwa Ong, *Flexible Citizenship*, 37.

46. This argument forms the crux of chapter 5.

47. The relationship between the domestic abroad and neoliberal restructuring is obviously a complex one. In the rest of the book, I provide a more detailed argument regarding the relationship of neoliberal restructuring to this phenomenon.

48. Benedict Anderson, *Imagined Communities: Reflections on the Origin and Spread of Nationalism* (London: Verso, 1991).

49. The "Overseas Citizenship" legislation, passed unanimously by the Indian parliament in March 2003, extends this right to persons of Indian origin living in sixteen countries: Australia, Canada, Finland, France, Greece, Ireland, Israel, Italy, Netherlands, New Zealand, Portugal, Republic of Cyprus, Sweden, Switzerland, United Kingdom, and the United States. As my later discussion of this process will reveal, numerous factors (including the fact that many of the host states in which sections of the Indian diaspora reside are less open to the idea of dual citizenship) are generally presented as reasons for the limited nature of the initiative. This type of dual nationality is, as Rainier Baubock puts it, "symbolic," as it does not guarantee anything other than the right of return. See Rainier Baubock, "Towards a Political Theory of Transnationalism," *International Migration Review* 37, no. 3 (2003): 700–723. For more information on Indian overseas citizenship, see http://www.indiaday.org/government_policy/dual_citizenship.asp.

50. As Brand points out, "Many sending states of the global South have long been characterized by varying degrees of authoritarianism, and hence by the treatment of the 'citizen' as a subject rather than participant." From this standpoint, the move toward a "more open, participatory" system of government helps create the conditions under which citizenship as a concept can acquire a new, perhaps more expansive meaning. See Brand, *Citizens Abroad*, 18.

51. In this sense, the Mexican diaspora is far from being part of a "global" nation. If we were to harness rhetoric to empirical reality, the extent of the Mexican nation would at best be the boundaries of the North American continent.

52. Smith, "Diasporic Memberships in Historical Perspective," 726.

53. Ong, *Flexible Citizenship*, 21. In this tradition, I include Ong's own writings, Robert Smith's writings on diasporic transnationalism, and the work of scholars like Saskia Sassen, who have focused on issues such as the changing meaning of citizenship.

Chapter 2

1. Cited in Myra Waterbury, "The State as Ethnic Activist: Explaining Continuity and Change in Hungarian Diaspora Policies" (PhD diss., New School for Social Research, 2006). Both the tone and the content of Antall's declaration were replicated by Mexican leader Vicente Fox almost a decade later.

2. The discussions of the role of the Hungarian state toward "Hungarians beyond the border" had started taking on an added urgency toward the mid-1980s as the

Soviet Union began withdrawing from Eastern European affairs. However, it was the dramatic events of 1989 that created the conditions for these more rhetorical discussions to coalesce into state policy. For instance, in 1989 the Hungarian government created a College of National Minorities within the Council of Ministers to oversee both internal and external minority affairs, and amended the constitution, adding: "The Republic of Hungary bears responsibility for the fate of Hungarians living outside its borders." For an insightful analysis of this process, see Waterbury, "The State as an Ethnic Activist," esp. chapter 5.

3. It is probably a testament to the successful integration of this tradition within disciplinary hierarchies that there are today different variants within constructivist scholarship. In this book, unless otherwise specified, I use "constructivists" and "constructivism" to refer to the dominant strand within this tradition—a strand also known as "liberal constructivism." Some of the best known scholars within this tradition include Alexander Wendt, Michael Barnett, Peter Katzenstein, Emanuel Adler, and Nina Tannewald.

4. Some exemplars of this scholarship include Kathryn Sikkink, "Human Rights, Principled Issues Networks and Sovereignty in Latin America," *International Organization* 47, no. 3 (1993): 411–441; Thomas Risse-Kappen, ed., *Bringing Transnational Relations Back In: Non-State Actors, Domestic Structures and International Institutions* (Cambridge: Cambridge University Press, 1995); Paul Wapner, "Politics beyond the State: Environmental Activism and World Civic Politics," *World Politics* 47, no. 3 (1995): 311–340; Audie Klotz, *Norms in International Relations: The Struggle against Apartheid* (Ithaca, NY: Cornell University Press, 1995); Martha Finnemore and Kathryn Sikkink, "International Norm Dynamics and Political Change," *International Organization* 52, no. 4 (1998): 887–917; Richard Price, "Reversing the Gun Sights: Transnational Civil Society Targets Landmines," *International Organization* 52, no. 3 (1998): 613–644; Margaret Keck and Kathryn Sikkink, *Activists beyond Borders: Advocacy Networks in International Politics* (Ithaca, NY: Cornell University Press, 1998); Thomas Risse, Stephen Ropp, and Kathryn Sikkink, eds., *The Power of Human Rights: International Norms and Domestic Change* (Cambridge: Cambridge University Press, 1999); and Sanjeev Khagram, James Riker, and Kathryn Sikkink, eds., *Restructuring World Politics: Transnational Social Movements, Networks and Norms* (Minneapolis: University of Minnesota Press, 2002).

5. Sikkink, "Human Rights, Principled Issue Networks and Sovereignty in Latin America," 412; Keck and Sikkink, *Activists beyond Borders*, 1.

6. A comprehensive view of the human rights discourse can be found in Risse, Ropp, and Sikkink, *The Power of Human Rights*.

7. See for instance, Wapner, "Politics beyond the State."

8. On the idea of the emergence and meanings of "women's rights," see Rebecca J. Cook, ed., *Human Rights of Women: National and International Perspectives* (Philadelphia: University of Pennsylvania Press, 1994).

9. An analysis of transnational workers networks (TWN) can be found in Thalia Kidder and Mary McGinn, "In the Wake of NAFTA: Transnational Workers Networks," *Social Policy* 25, no.4 (1995), 14–22.

10. Price's analysis of the International Campaign to Ban Landmines (ICBL) is a good illustration of this point. While Price discusses the role played by the Canadian state in the process, it is mainly to highlight how this involvement helped the transnational alliance gain access to fora that it otherwise could not. See Price, "Reversing the Gun Sights."

11. Richard Price, for instance, defines transnational civil society in terms of "a set of interactions among an imagined community [meant] to shape collective life that are not confined to the territorial and institutional spaces of states." See Price, "Reversing the Gun Sights," 615.

12. As Ronnie Lipschutz points out, the dominance of certain liberal norms, especially those emphasizing the rights of the individual, forms the implicit basis of most of the work on global civil society. See Ronnie D. Lipschutz, "Reconstructing World Politics: The Emergence of Global Civil Society," *Millennium* 21, no. 3 (1992): 389–420.

13. Other IR scholars attempting to explain aspects of diaspora politics have also noted this particular tendency of disciplinary transnationalism scholarship. See, for instance, Fiona B. Adamson and Madeline Demetriou, "Remapping the Boundaries of 'State' and 'National Identity': Incorporating Diasporas into IR Theorizing," *European Journal of International Relations* 13, no. 4 (2007): 489–526; see also Sarah Wayland, "Ethnonationalist Networks and Transnational Opportunities: The Sri Lankan Diaspora," *Review of International Studies* 30 (2004): 405–426.

14. Scholars like Price or Keck and Sikkink do see states as part of the transnational networks, to the extent that the transnational actors involve state institutions in promoting their causes. However, for the most part, the transnationalism literature in IR treats nation-states as entities that are *acted upon* by transnational networks.

15. In an act that both recognized and further solidified Wendt's standing within the discipline, the International Studies Association selected his *Social Theory of International Politics* (Cambridge: Cambridge University Press, 1999) as the "Book of the Decade (1991–2000)."

16. See Alexander Wendt, "Anarchy Is What the States Make of It: The Social Construction of Power Politics," *International Organization* 46 (1992): 391–425; and *Social Theory of International Politics* (Cambridge: Cambridge University Press, 1999), particularly 224–233.

17. For a poststructuralist critique of this understanding of identity, see Maja Zehfuss, "Constructivism and Identity: A Dangerous Liaison," *European Journal of International Relations* 7 (2001): 315–348. See also Himadeep Muppidi, *The Politics of the Global* (Minneapolis: University of Minnesota Press, 2004).

18. For a more sustained explication of this point, see Jim George, *Discourses of Global Politics: A Critical (Re)Introduction to International Relations* (Boulder, CO: Lynne Rienner, 1994).

19. I focus here primarily on the two essays by Peter Katzenstein and the conceptual piece by Ronald Jepperson, Alexander Wendt, and Peter Katzenstein in Peter J. Katzenstein, ed., *The Culture of National Security: Norms and Identity in World Politics* (New York: Columbia University Press, 1996): Peter J. Katzenstein, "Introduction: Alternative Perspectives on National Security," 1–32; Ronald L. Jepperson, Alexander Wendt, and Peter J. Katzenstein, "Norms, Identity and Culture in National Security," 33–78; and Peter J. Katzenstein, "Conclusion: National Security in a Changing World," 498–528. For an expanded version of this line of critique, see Latha Varadarajan, "Constructivism, Identity, and Neoliberal (In)security," *Review of International Studies* 30, no. 3 (2004): 319–341.

20. Katzenstein, The Culture of National Security, 14.

21. Ibid.

22. Ibid., 30, my emphasis.

23. Pasha and Blaney's critique of the transnational networks literature, for instance, focuses precisely on this aspect. They argue that the meshing of transnational networks in the social relations of global capitalism and the neoliberal project creates the possibility of their being characterized as interventions in the Third World, in the sense they are identified as being part of the oppressive existing structures of power. There are also situations wherein embattled states seek new ways to maintain their capacity to deal with associational life by making temporary alliances with particular types of transnational networks. In this context, the relationship between transnational networks and states is far from being simply oppositional. See Mustapha Pasha and David Blaney, "Elusive Paradise: The Promise and Perils of Global Civil Society," *Alternatives* 23, no. 4 (1998), 417–450 .

24. A more recent addition to this literature is Fiona Adamson and Madeline Demetriou's discussion of diasporas in IR. The article provides an excellent survey of the field of diaspora studies, while noting some of the shortcomings in the discipline of IR, particularly the theoretical tradition of constructivism, that have led to a general ignoring of diaspora politics. This intervention, however, situates itself as a self-conscious attempt to revive constructivism by incorporating the study of diasporas into discussions of transnationalism and identity, which is quite different from the argument advanced by this book. See Adamson and Demetriou, "Remapping the Boundaries of 'State' and 'National Identity.'"

25. William Callahan, "Beyond Cosmopolitanism and Nationalism: Diasporic Chinese and Neo-Nationalism in Thailand and China," *International Organization* 57 (2003): 481–518; Yossi Shain and Aharon Barth, "Diasporas in International Relations Theory," *International Organization* 57 (2003): 449–479.

26. Shain and Barth, "Diasporas in International Relations Theory," 451.

27. Shain's long list of publications includes *The Frontier of Loyalty: Political Exiles in the Age of the Nation-State* (New York: Routledge, 1989); "Democrats and Secessionists: U.S. Diasporas as Regime De-Stabilizers," in *International Migration and Security*, ed. Myron Weiner (Boulder, CO: Westview, 1993); "Ethnic Diasporas and U.S. Foreign Policy," *Political Science Quarterly* 109, no. 5 (1994/1995): 811–841;

Marketing the American Creed Abroad: Diasporas in the US and in Their Homeland (New York: Cambridge University Press, 1999); "American Jews and the Construction of Israel's Jewish Identity," *Diaspora* 9, no. 2 (2000): 163–201; "The Role of Diasporas in Conflict Perpetuation or Resolution," *SAIS Review* 22, no. 2 (2002): 115–144.

28. Shain and Barth, "Diasporas in International Relations Theory," 451.

29. Ibid., 458.

30. Ibid., my emphasis.

31. Report of the High Level Committee on the Indian Diaspora (Indian Council of World Affairs: New Delhi, 2001), v.

32. I provide greater elaboration of this point in chapter 5.

33. Shain and Barth, "Diasporas in International Relations Theory," 461.

34. Ibid., 460.

35. The effects of this underlying conception of the state are visible even in the authors' discussion of identity. For instance, while citing William Bloom, the authors talk about the "national identity dynamic" as a resource that is open to appropriation by actors who want to gain control of it to influence policy making.

36. "Given their importance, and their status as a *permanent* feature in the imperfect nation-state system" and "More generally, diasporas are *increasingly* able to promote transnational ties." Shain and Barth, "Diasporas in International Relations Theory," 450, my emphasis.

37. To be fair to Shain and Barth, they do pay some attention to the historical and political landscape in their discussion of the Armenian case. But this remains at a descriptive rather than theoretical level and does not really engage with the question of the state per se.

38. In making the argument about the need to understand transnationalism in a way that takes seriously both the idea of nationalism and the role of the state, this book follows the tradition of interdisciplinary scholarship (particularly dealing with the issues of migration and diasporas) represented by scholars such as Roger Smith, Peggy Leavitt, and Rogers Brubaker.

39. The argument about the historically constituted and dynamic nature of national and state identities has been made by numerous scholars. As my discussion later in this chapter will make obvious, within the discipline of international relations, scholars belonging to various schools of the constructivist tradition have been at the forefront of analyses that focus on the question of identity. While my understanding of identity owes a lot to this scholarship, it fundamentally diverges from them in its emphasis on the constitutive role of structures of global capitalism.

40. In this sense, unlike the transnational advocacy network that Richard Price described, they are actually closer to Anderson's conception of the nation as an imagined community. See Benedict Anderson, *Imagined Communities: Reflections on the Origins and Spread of Nationalism* (London: Verso, 1991).

41. Arjun Appadurai, *Modernity at Large: Cultural Dimensions of Globalization* (Minneapolis: University of Minnesota Press, 1997), 9.

42. Ibid., 4.

43. Ibid., 160–161.

44. Ibid., 64; see also 56–57, 61–63. In his work, Appadurai does this through a series of vignettes such as the experiences of his cosmopolitan family during a visit to the South Indian temple town of Madurai and the quotidian experiences of the sex workers portrayed in Mira Nair's *India Cabaret*.

45. Ibid., 9, 58. Appadurai's introduction is a study in trying to leash in an otherwise celebratory discussion of the role of diasporas. He repeatedly makes the point that his theory of rupture is not teleological and that it does not predetermine the fate of nations and nationalism. He claims, "My approach leaves entirely open the question of where the experiments with modernity that electronic mediation enables might lead in terms of nationalism, violence and social justice….I am more deeply ambivalent about prognosis than any variant of classical modernization theory of which I am aware." However, the clearest expression of his political commitment regarding the question of nations and "post-nations" are in the chapter "Patriotism and Its Futures." I turn to this essay later in the chapter.

46. Ibid., 20.

47. Ibid., 159. In this formulation, one can find echoes of Chatterjee and Bhabha's critique of the postcolonial nation-state.

48. This is evident even in a work that situates itself as a critique of Appadurai's argument. In their analysis of diasporic flows in the premodern Indo-Islamic world and the post-Fordist global information economy (specifically in terms of the participation of the South Indian city of Hyderabad), Christopher Chekuri and Himadeep Muppidi make the provocative claim that the significance of diasporas lies not in their newness, but in the fact that they have always been "constitutive elements of a different global order." In their narrative, it is the territorial nation-state that appears as a fleeting interlude. However, what underlies and sustains their argument (like that of Appadurai's) is a conviction regarding the impending irrelevance of the modern territorial nation-state, along with a pronounced suspicion of the dominant form of nationalism embodied in it. See Christopher Chekuri and Himadeep Muppidi, "Diasporas before and after the Nation," *Interventions* 5, no. 1 (2003): 45–57.

49. In its other, though connected usage, the notion of the "postcolonial" has served as shorthand for the sociopolitical and economic conditions that have emerged as a result of the particular historical experience of colonialism. My delineation of the two main usages of the term "postcolonial" is similar to what Desai refers to as "postcoloniality" (the condition, as it were) and "postcolonial critique" in her study of South Asian diasporic cinema. See Jigna Desai, *Beyond Bollywood: The Cultural Politics of South Asian Diasporic Film* (New York: Routledge, 2003). For a glimpse into the often vituperative debates regarding the meaning and relevance of the category of "postcolonial studies"/"postcolonial critique," see Kwame Anthony Appiah, "Is the Post- in Postmodernism the Post- in Postcolonial?" *Critical Inquiry* 17, no. 2 (1991):

348. See also Arif Dirlik, "The Postcolonial Aura: Third World Criticism in the Age of Global Capitalism," *Critical Inquiry* 20, no. 2 (1994): 328–356.

50. Admittedly, the tradition of postcolonial theorizing linked to Fanon and C. L. R. James is far more celebratory of anticolonial nationalism than the later, more critical scholarship, which tended to emphasize the inherent limitations and violent exclusions of nationalist movements.

51. Paul Gilroy, *The Black Atlantic: Modernity and Double Consciousness* (Cambridge, MA: Harvard University Press, 1993), 3.

52. Ibid., 7.

53. On the concept of territorialization, see particularly Bruce Willems-Braun, "Buried Epistemologies: The Politics of Nature in (Post)colonial British Columbia," *Annals of American Geographers* 87, no. 1 (1997); and Joel Wainwright, *Decolonizing Development: Colonial Power and the Maya* (Hoboken, NJ: Wiley-Blackwell, 2008).

54. This idea is best expressed by Homi Bhabha in his critique of the rhetoric of pure cultures. Culture, Bhabha argues, cannot and should not be understood as a self-contained system of meaning or merely one structured by a relationship between a predetermined "self" and "other." Rather, both the self and the other should be understood as being constituted through their interactions in a "Third Space"—a space of hybridity. Making his point through the use of semiotics, Bhabha shows that the process of interpretation of a statement is not merely contained in a simple communication between the two parties designated in a statement. Even when "I" communicate with "You," the spaces we occupy need to be mobilized through a Third Space, "which represents both the general conditions of language and the specific implication of the utterance in a performative and institutional strategy of which it cannot 'in itself' be conscious." While it is in itself unrepresentable, the Third Space as a conceptual tool enables us to understand that meanings are not fixed: "even the same signs can be appropriated, translated, rehistoricized and read anew." Since the meanings of all cultural enunciations are negotiated in this indeterminate, ambiguous, contradictory space, Bhabha argues that it is possible to understand how claims to cultural purity are untenable, even before one turns to empirical examples of hybridity. See Homi K. Bhabha, "Cultural Diversity and Cultural Difference," in *The Postcolonial Studies Reader*, ed. Bill Ashcroft, Gareth Griffiths, and Helen Tiffin, 206, 208 (New York: Routledge, 1995). See also Homi K. Bhabha, "The Commitment to Theory," *New Formations* 5 (1988): 5–23; and "Signs Taken for Wonders: Questions of Ambivalence and Authority under a Tree outside Delhi, May 1817," *Critical Inquiry* 12 (1985): 144–165.

55. Appadurai, *Modernity at Large*, 169.

56. The propensity to overlook states and the interstate system, engendered by this claim, has been remarked upon by critical constructivist scholars in IR. In the introduction of their edited volume on the question of culture and national security (which is set up as a dialogue between scholars trained in anthropology and political science) Weldes et al. engage specifically with Appadurai's argument that we need to

understand global society in terms of the interactions between various "-scapes" (finance-, techno-, ethno-, media-), rather than between nation-states. In responding to this argument, they add "securityscapes" to this list, "pointing out that organized violence and the elaboration of security cultures are also important facts of translocal life, and that, *depending on local circumstance, often work in ways that entrench the state rather than "deterritorialize" it or disarticulate it from the imagined community of the nation*" (my emphasis). See Jutta Weldes et al., "Introduction," in *Cultures of Insecurity: States, Communities, and the Production of Danger*, ed. Jutta Weldes et al., 8 (Minneapolis: University of Minnesota Press, 1999).

57. Appadurai, *Modernity at Large*, 169, 172.

58. Ibid., 172.

59. Mitchell's analysis of the role of the Vancouver-based Hong Kong diaspora in the contemporary global economy remains one of the most incisive critiques of the general tendency among postcolonial and poststructural theorists to automatically celebrate the inherent resistance to power supposedly embodied by diasporas. See Katharyne Mitchell, "Different Diasporas and the Hype of Hybridity," *Environment and Planning D: Society and Space* 15 (1997): 533–553; see also Mitchell, *Crossing the Neoliberal Line: Pacific Rim Migration and the Metropolis* (Philadelphia: Temple University Press, 2004).

60. To that extent, diasporas, as I have argued elsewhere, continue to play an important role in sustaining imperialism as a system of rule. See Latha Varadarajan, "Out of Place: Re-Thinking Diaspora and Empire," *Millennium: Journal of International Studies* 36, no. 2 (2008): 267–293.

61. See, for instance, Neil Melvin, *Russians beyond Russia: The Politics of National Identity* (London: Pinter, 1995); Igor Zevelev, *Russia and Its New Diasporas* (Washington, DC: USIP Press, 2001); Linda Basch, Nina Glick Schiller, and Cristina Szanton Blanc, *Nations Unbound: Transnational Projects, Postcolonial Predicaments and De-Territorialized Nation-States* (Langhorne, PA: Gordon and Breach, 1994); Wayland, "Ethnonationalist Networks and Transnational Opportunities"; Benedict Anderson, "Long-Distance Nationalism," in *The Spectre of Comparisons: Nationalism, Southeast Asia and the World* (London: Verso, 1998,) 74, n.31; see also Aleksa Djilas, "Fear Thy Neighbor: The Breakup of Yugoslavia," in *Nationalism and Nationalities in the New Europe*, ed. Charles P. Kupchan, 85–106 (Ithaca, NY: Cornell University Press, 1995).

62. While both terms have been generally used to refer to the same phenomenon, it is important to keep in mind Rogers Brubaker's admonishment that "national minorities" in the context of discussions of new forms of nationalism, do not refer to an "ethnodemographic fact." Minority nationalism is a political project and the articulation of specific demands by a group that self-consciously understands itself as belonging to a nation. For a detailed discussion of this issue, especially in the context of the dissolution of the former Eastern bloc, see Rogers Brubaker, *Nationalism Reframed: Nationhood and the National Question in the New Europe* (Cambridge:

Cambridge University Press, 1996). What further sharpened the focus on diasporas was a specific conjuncture of events set in motion by the collapse of the Soviet Union. The replacement of the Soviet Union by a large number of new nation-states, as well as the implosion of former Communist states in Eastern Europe, paved the way for renewed attention to the question of nationalism. While this renewed attention did bring its own set of problems to the table, including a tendency to treat nations and nationalisms as primordial entities that could only be repressed for so long, it cast the spotlight on diasporas in two ways. First, the emergence of new nation-states, such as those in the territories of the former Soviet Union, created overnight diasporas who suddenly became an embodiment of a particular "minority nationalism" and whose cause was readily embraced by their putative homelands. Second, their associations with secessionist movements, as in the Croatian case, were critical to the formation of the new nation-states. As such, diasporas took center stage as important players in the rise and spread of the "ethnic nationalism" (which defined national belonging in terms of lineage) that was challenging the predominant idea of "civic nationalism" (which defines belonging in more legalistic terms, such as citizenship and political participation) and changing the political landscape of Europe. On types of nationalisms, see Charles Kupchan, "Introduction: Nationalism Resurgent," in *Nationalism and Nationalities in the New Europe*, ed. Charles P. Kupchan, 1–14; for an analysis of the most common misconceptions about the nationalism engendered by these events, see Rogers Brubaker, "Myths and Misconceptions in the Study of Nationalism," in *The State of the Nation: Ernest Gellner and the Theory of Nationalism*, ed. John A. Hall, 272–306 (Cambridge: Cambridge University Press, 1998).

63. For details on the creation of this diaspora, see Oivind Foglerud, *Life on the Outside: The Tamil Diaspora and Long-Distance Nationalism* (London: Pluto, 1999).

64. Wayland, "Ethnonationalist Networks and Transnational Opportunities," particularly 418–426.

65. Ibid. More specifically, the Tamil diaspora has a substantial presence in India (particularly, the southern Indian state of Tamil Nadu), Malaysia, Australia, Britain, Germany, Switzerland, France, and Canada.

66. Ibid., 419, 421. For instance, in Toronto, there has been a steady increase in what Wayland terms "Tamil social capital," with the establishment of Tamil-language newspapers (half of which are available free of cost), Tamil-language radio stations that keep up a constant stream of extremely popular phone-in shows, and Tamil cultural, social, and business organizations.

67. Acknowledging the role of this group in maintaining pressure on his government, former Sri Lankan President J. R. Jayawardane declared the Tamil diaspora to be the "world's most powerful minority." Cited in Ibid., 415.

68. On the Kurdish diaspora, see Adamson and Demetriou, "Remapping the Boundaries of 'State' and 'National Identity,'" especially 509–513.

69. In addition, as Adamson and Demetriou ("Remapping the Boundaries of 'State' and 'National Identity'") point out, the Kurdish diaspora has also been

extremely active in publishing material that highlights the plight of the Kurds in Turkey and ensuring the sharing of that material with the Kurdish nationalist movement based in Turkey. This sharing of information has been crucial to the politicization of the diaspora at large.

70. Another illustration of the power of diaspora nationalism can be seen in the Khalistan movement that peaked during the late 1980s. Based on a demand for a separate Sikh homeland (Khalistan), the movement ranged in opposition to the Indian state was largely sustained by the Canada-based Sikh diaspora.

71. Alejandro Portes, Luis E. Guarnizo, and Patricia Landolt, "The Study of Transnationalism: Pitfalls and Promise of an Emergent Research Field," *Ethnic and Racial Studies* 22, no. 2 (1999): 217–237; see also Alejandro Portes, "Conclusion: Towards a New World—The Origins and Effects of Transnational Activities," *Ethnic and Racial Studies* 22, no. 2 (1999): 463–477.

72. Portes et al. took this contention even further to argue that while transnationalism "involves individuals, their networks of social relations, their communities, and broader institutionalized structures such as local and national governments," the "proper unit of analysis" was "individuals and their support networks." See Portes et al., "The Study of Transnationalism," 220.

73. This "long distance nationalism," as Benedict Anderson pithily describes it, is not always aimed at defending "minority" rights or organized around demands for a new nation-state. It can also take on the form of defending the territorial integrity of the putative homeland through the expression of support either for the existing government or for an opposition movement or party based in that homeland. For instance, the Hindu nationalist Bharatiya Janata Party (BJP), which has been in power in India intermittently over the past decade, and its ally, the Vishwa Hindu Parishad (World Hindu Council, VHP), have long been supported by diaspora groups based in the West, such as the Overseas Friends of the BJP and the VHP. As many commentators have noted, the very act that heralded the emergence of the BJP as a major actor in Indian politics—the destruction of the centuries-old Babri mosque in Ayodhya in 1993—would not have been possible but for the large amount of money raised by the VHP among its supporters in the Indian diaspora. Similarly, extreme right-wing nationalist parties, be it in Tudjman's Croatia or Yerevan's Armenia, have found their diasporas to be an invaluable source of support. The point here is not to insist that diasporas are intrinsically and automatically tied to extreme forms of official nationalism, for they do have the potential to be (and have, at various points of time in the past, been) part of progressive political movements. Rather, it is to highlight the fact that the reimagining of the nation is a project that can be embarked upon by actors not just in opposition to, but within the rubric of, existing territorial nation-states. See Anderson, "Long-Distance Nationalism," 58–74. On the role of the Indian diaspora in the Hindutva movement, see the special issue of *Ethnic and Racial Studies* on "Hindutva Movements in the West: Resurgent Hinduism and the Politics of Diaspora," 23, no. 3 (2000), particularly Chetan Bhatt and Parita Mukta, "Hindutva

in the West: Mapping the Antinomies of Diaspora Nationalism," 407–441; A. Rajagopal, "Hindu Nationalism in the US: Changing Configurations of Political Practice," 467–496; Biju Matthew and Vijay Prashad, "The Protean Forms of Yankee Hindutva," 516–534; and Chetan Bhatt, "*Dharmo rakshati rakshitah*: Hindutva Movements in the UK," 559–593. Some studies estimate that in the one-year period leading to the destruction of the Babri mosque, Indians in the United States funneled a minimum of $350,000 to the coffers of the VHP. On this, see Prema Kurien, "Religion, Ethnicity and Politics: Hindu and Muslim Indian Immigrants in the United States," *Ethnic and Racial Studies* 24, no. 2 (2001): 263–293. For a broader temporal perspective on these connections, see Shampa Biswas, "Globalization and the Nation Beyond: The Indian-American Diaspora and the Rethinking of Territory, Citizenship and Democracy," *New Political Science* 27, no. 1 (2005): 43–68.

74. As mentioned in chapter 1, there are, of course, exceptions to this. Rogers Brubaker, for instance, discusses what he calls "homeland nationalisms"—the nationalism of the putative home state of national minorities that is aligned antagonistically to the "nationalizing nationalism" of newly independent or reconfigured nation-states. While the latter frames its claims in terms of furthering the interests of a core nation, the former claims to be acting in the interests of the national minority. See Brubaker, *Nationalism Reframed*, especially the introduction and chapters 3 and 4.

75. The analysis in this section builds on the argument laid out in chapter 1.

76. For an argument that emphasizes the centrality of capitalist expansion for contemporary manifestations of transnationalism, see Portes et al., "The Study of Transnationalism," especially 227–228. On the role of capitalism in engendering the mobility of people and shaping a particular form of transnationalism, see Anderson, "Long-Distance Nationalism," especially 62–64.

77. Robin Cohen, *Global Diasporas: An Introduction* (London: UCL Press, 1997), especially 66–77. Scholars like Niall Ferguson go beyond Cohen's simple analytical category to wax poetic about the character of the emigrants from the British isles, the "heaven-born" graduates of universities like Oxford, who braved hot weather and disease-infested climes to fulfill their imperial duty and govern the colonies. See Niall Ferguson, *Empire: The Rise and Demise of British World Order and the Lessons for Global Power* (New York: Basic Books, 2004), 149; and *Colossus: The Price of America's Empire* (New York: Penguin, 2004), 207, 211.

78. The Irish migration to North America (especially in the aftermath of the potato famine in the mid-nineteenth century) presents a slightly different picture, partly because the Irish were not sent either as indentured laborers or slaves by the British colonial authorities. However, it is not far-fetched to make the argument that the Irish migration was driven by the "underdevelopment" of the Irish economy by British colonial rule.

79. The next chapter provides a greater elaboration of this point.

80. On the early phase of Indian emigration, see Hugh Tinker, *A New System of Slavery: The Export of Indian Labour Overseas, 1830–1920* (London: Oxford University Press, 1974).

81. It should be noted that the emigration acts officially allowed the British Indian state to supply indentured labor to the colonies of other imperial powers as well. On the recruitment system, see M. R. Stenson, *Class, Race and Colonialism in West Malaysia: The Indian Case* (St. Lucia: University of Queensland Press, 1980); K. S. Sandhu, *Indians in Malaya* (Cambridge: Cambridge University Press, 1969); Marina Carter, "Strategies of Labour Mobilization in Colonial India: The Recruitment of Indenture Workers for Mauritius," *Journal of Peasant Studies* 19, nos. 3–4 (1992): 229–245.

82. Varadarajan, "Out of Place." On the systemic nature of the violence, see P. Ramaswamy, "Labour Control and Labour Resistance in Plantations of Colonial Malaya," *Journal of Peasant Studies* 19, nos. 3–4 (1992): 87–105; Rana P. Behal and Prabhu Mohapatra, "Tea and Money versus Human Life: The Rise and Fall of Indenture System in the Assam Tea Plantations, 1840–1908," *Journal of Peasant Studies* 19, nos. 3–4 (1992): 142–172.

83. As historians have pointed out, the trade links between South Asia and other regions of the world like East Africa preceded European colonialism. However, the major trade settlements in the interior parts of these regions were a phenomenon that was peculiar to the late-nineteenth- and early-twentieth-century period. For more details on the nature and extent of this migration, see Hugh Tinker, *The Banyan Tree: Overseas Emigrants from India, Pakistan and Bangladesh* (Oxford: Oxford University Press, 1977).

84. It should be noted that the role played by various South Asian trading communities was not unambiguously one of supporting British rule. British authorities did clash with members of the "mercantile diaspora" on the question of their rights within the empire. However, when this did happen, debates about settler rights were often framed in terms of the nonwhite settlers as wanting to impinge upon the rights of the "natives." This had the unfortunate effect of shoring up an image of the South Asian diaspora as having interests inimical to that of the local population. For more details, see Michael Twaddle, "East African Asians through a Hundred Years," in *South Asians Overseas: Migration and Ethnicity*, ed. C. Clake, C. Peach, and S. Vertovec, 149–163 (Cambridge: Cambridge University Press, 1990). See also Hugh Tinker, *Separate and Unequal: India and the Indians in the British Commonwealth* (London: Hurst, 1976); and Mahmood Mamdani, *Citizen and Subject: Contemporary Africa and the Legacy of Late Colonialism* (Princeton, NJ: Princeton University Press, 1996).

85. Even those like Niall Ferguson who see imperial rule as essentially beneficial for the colonies accept this proposition. See Niall Ferguson, *Empire: The Rise and Demise of British World Order and the Lessons for Global Power* (New York: Basic Books, 2002).

86. A great illustration of the oftentimes absurd means through which the "draining of national wealth" took place is provided by Jawaharlal Nehru: "India had to bear the cost of her own conquest, and then of her transfer (or sale) from the East India Company to the British Crown, for the extension of the British Empire to Burma and elsewhere, for expeditions to Africa, Persia, etc., and for her defence against Indians

themselves. She was not only used as a base for imperial purposes, without any reimbursement for this, but she had further to pay for the training of part of the British Army in England—'capitation' charges these were called. Indeed India was charged for all manner of other expenses incurred by Britain, such as the maintenance of British diplomatic and consular establishments in China and Persia, the entire cost of the telegraph line from England to India, part of the expenses of the British Mediterranean fleet, and even the receptions given to the Sultan of Turkey in London." Jawaharlal Nehru, *The Discovery of India* (New Delhi: Penguin, 2004), 305.

87. It should be noted here that most of the former colonies that opted for some form of a planned economy after independence have embarked upon (to varying degrees) IMF-supervised programs of neoliberal restructuring.

88. These have become what the immigration literature refers to as "sending countries."

89. Varadarajan, "Out of Place."

90. See, for instance, Grace Chang, *Disposable Domestics: Immigrant Women Workers in the Global Economy* (Cambridge, MA: South End, 2000); Bridget Anderson, *Doing the Dirty Work? The Global Politics of Domestic Labour* (London: Zed, 2000).

91. Yossi Shain, for instance, has analyzed the role played by this group in acting to build bridges between the home and host states. See Shain, *Marketing the American Creed Abroad.*

92. The very obvious differences between the United States and the Middle East serve to illustrate this point. As early as the beginning of the twentieth century, the United States was already seen as a "home" for a significant group of diasporas—a land that was made by immigrants. The Europeans, Japanese, Chinese, Hispanics, and Indians, though defined as "alien" to the national self at various points of time in the history of the United States, have also been appropriated (particularly through discourses of multiculturalism) into the national mainstream. The Middle East, however, presents a stark contrast to this picture. Those who migrated to countries like Saudi Arabia, Bahrain, and the United Arab Emirates since the 1970s were primarily unskilled laborers and professional men. Even when accompanied by their families, the migrants have generally never been part of the social fabric in these countries.

93. Peter B. Evans, Dietrich Reuschemeyer, and Theda Skocpol, eds., *Bringing the State Back In* (Cambridge: Cambridge University Press, 1985).

94. As Bob Jessop points out in his elegant critique of this literature, its ultimate effect is the "fetishizing and naturalizing [of] the institutional separation between the economic and the political." See Bob Jessop, "Capitalism and the Capitalist Type of State," in *The Future of the Capitalist State*, 37 (Cambridge, UK: Polity, 2002).

95. "Capital is not a thing, but a social relation." See Karl Marx, "Chapter Thirty-Three: The Modern Theory of Colonisation," in *Capital, Volume One*, at http://www.marxists.org/archive/marx/works/1867-c1/ch33.htm.

96. Antonio Gramsci's well-known account of the development of social forces in Italy helps illustrate these points. In surveying the social landscape of Italy, Gramsci

detected a complex articulation of primary and secondary social forces, such as the urban proletariat of northern Italy, the southern peasantry, the agrarian bourgeoisie, and the urban intellectuals. These classes, however, were not snapshots frozen in time. As Gramsci makes clear, the historical development of the northern proletariat, for instance, was decisive in shaping the terrain of Italian society and politics. To that extent, the significance of this class far exceeded its numbers in sociological terms. More important, Gramsci's analysis reveals the manner in which the nature of Italian politics was shaped by the living struggles between these classes. In that sense, Gramsci saw his own analysis as an endeavor that was a necessary precursor to participating in and ultimately helping shape those struggles.

97. As Perry Anderson points out, "hegemony" appears in different contexts throughout Gramsci's *Prison Notebooks*. Anderson also points out that despite the general tendency to treat "hegemony" as though it were Gramsci's invention, the concept has far deeper roots. Tracing the history of this concept, he illustrates how it shifted from emphasizing the nature of the strategy that needed to be adopted by the working class in its struggle against tsarism (in the 1890s) to explaining the dominance of the bourgeoisie (a move made during the Fourth Congress of the Comintern in 1922). It was this latter position, Anderson argues, that was adopted by Gramsci to explain the structures of bourgeois power in the West. This rendering of the history of the concept is important precisely because it situates Gramsci's work within a particular trajectory of the development of Marxism rather than as marking a break from it. The tendency to treat hegemony as a concept invented by Gramsci, critiqued by Anderson, is one that is connected to another which sees in Gramsci a way to go beyond the limitations of "orthodox" Marxism. Such a tendency can be found even in the small subset of scholarship in the field of International Relations (IR) that is characterized as "neo-Gramscian." See Perry Anderson, "The Antinomies of Antonio Gramsci," *New Left Review*, Special hundredth issue, November–December 1976, 5–78, esp. 15–25; see also Antonio Gramsci, *Selections from the Prison Notebooks*, trans. and ed. Quentin Hoare and Geoffrey Nowell Smith (New York: International Publishers, 1997). For an incisive and illuminating analysis of the academic uses and abuses of Gramsci, see Emanuele Saccarelli, *Gramsci and Trotsky in the Shadow of Stalinism* (New York: Routledge, 2008), particularly chapters 1 and 2. For a collection of essays that lays out the framework of the neo-Gramscian scholarship in IR, see Stephen Gill (ed.), *Gramsci, Historical-Materialism and International Relations* (Cambridge: Cambridge University Press, 1993); see also Mark Rupert, *Producing Hegemony: The Politics of Mass Production and American Global Power* (Cambridge: Cambridge University Press, 1995).

98. As David Harvey puts it, "While the slogan was often advanced in the 1960s that what was good for General Motors was good for the US, [by the 1990s] this had changed...into the slogan that what is good for Wall Street is all that matters." A clue about the reasons behind the changing slogan can be found in an important statistic: in 1982, the profits of finance companies were approximately 5 percent of total corporate profits after tax; by 2007, its had grown 8 times to account for more than 41

percent of total corporate profits. For an incisive analysis of the financialization of the American economy and its implications for the development of capitalism, see Nick Beams, "The World Economic Crisis: A Marxist Analysis," at http://wsws.org/media/nb-lecture-1208.pdf; David Harvey, *A Brief History of Neoliberalism* (New York: Oxford University Press, 2005), 33.

99. These relations do not necessarily operate within the demarcated boundaries of the territorial nation-state. Although it is true that in any given nation-state, the national bourgeoisie exercises hegemony on the basis of its own internal equilibrium, it is also the case that to the extent that the capitalist economy continues to become more global, there is an international equilibrium of forces as well. For example, while the opening up of the Indian economy in 1991 did reflect a change in the internal dynamics of the national bourgeoisie, it was also (and perhaps more fundamentally) the result of external pressures brought about by renegotiation of class equilibrium on an international scale.

100. Antonio Gramsci, "Notes on Italian Politics," in *Selections from the Prison Notebooks*, 57.

101. Ibid.; see especially n.5.

102. For Gramsci, this task in part must be accomplished by means of sacrifices on the part of the ruling class. Indeed, Gramsci's concept of hegemony is developed in contrast to what he calls corporatism—a defense of social interests that is too unyielding and mechanistic. However, as Gramsci points out, there can be no doubt "that such sacrifices and such a compromise cannot touch the essential." In other words, these sacrifices confirm, rather than put into question, the political supremacy of the bourgeoisie. I will return to this point in chapter 4 while discussing the ways in which the Indian bourgeoisie managed the transition to independence. See Antonio Gramsci, "The Modern Prince," in *Selections from the Prison Notebooks*, 161.

103. These are the processes that are grouped under Jessop's conceptual umbrella of "strategic selectivity." This is not to deny the importance of what Poulantzas calls the "institutional materiality" of the state. State institutions are an important aspect of what the state is. But rather than be treated as reified objects that embody a sort of presocial state power and demarcate state capacity, institutions should be understood as being socially embedded and possessing a peculiarly political nature. See Jessop, *The Capitalist State: Marxist Theories and Methods* (New York: New York University Press, 1982); and Poulantzas, *State, Power, Socialism* (London: Verso, 2001), 54.

104. The three moments of relation of forces that Gramsci talks about are the objective structure (understood in terms of the development of material forces of production), the relation of political forces, and the relations of military forces.

105. For Gramsci, an analysis of the concept of hegemony always "required a reconnaissance" of the peculiar terrain of each nation. This is clear, for example, in the attention he pays to the "specific Italian tradition, and the specific development of Italian history" to explain the nature of the "peasant question." See Antonio

Gramsci, "State and Civil Society," in *Selections from the Prison Notebooks*, 238; for a brief account of this consistent thread in Gramsci's writing before and after his arrest, see Saccarelli, *Gramsci and Trotsky in the Shadow of Stalinism*, 226, n.97.

106. Partha Chatterjee, *Nationalist Thought and the Colonial World: A Derivative Discourse?* (Minneapolis: University of Minnesota Press, 1986), 49.

107. Ibid., 40.

108. Jessop, "Capitalism and the Capitalist Type of State," 40.

109. Harvey, A Brief History of Neoliberalism, 1.

110. Ibid., 159–165. As Harvey argues, these policies backed and promoted by the state work toward the redistribution, rather than the generation, of wealth. Whether it is through the privatization of formerly public assets, the commodification of everything from intellectual property to nature, the deregulation of the financial sector that has aided the growth of speculation and predatory credit markets, or the revisions of tax codes to provide even further benefits to the already wealthy, the neoliberal state works even more obviously than before as an agent promoting "accumulation by dispossession."

111. For one of the most enthusiastic statements of the neoliberal position, see Keinichi Ohmae, *The End of the Nation-State: The Rise of Regional Economies* (New York: Free Press, 1995).

112. See, for instance, A. H. Amsden, "Third World Industrialization: 'Global Fordism' or a New Model?" *New Left Review* 182 (1990): 5–31; Peter Evans, "The State as Problem and Solution: Predation, Embedded Autonomy, and Structural Change," in *The Politics of Economic Adjustment: International Constraints, Distributive Conflicts, and the State*, ed. Stephen Haggard and R. R. Kaufman, 139–181 (Princeton, NJ: Princeton University Press, 1992); Robert Wade, "Globalization and Its Limits: Reports of the Death of the National Economy Are Greatly Exaggerated," in *National Diversity and Global Capitalism*, ed. S. Berger and R. Dore, 60–88 (Ithaca, NY: Cornell University Press, 1996).

113. Jim Glassman, "State Power beyond the 'Territorial Trap': The Internationalization of the State," *Political Geography* 18 (1999): 669–696, especially 670.

114. Ibid.

115. The phenomenon of outsourcing testifies to this fact. As corporations (especially in the manufacturing sector) move jobs from one country to the other, citing lower labor costs, what we are witnessing is a race to the bottom, as wages and labor rights give way in the context of maintaining competitiveness in the global economy.

116. While one aspect of this is the increased possibility of a genuine international working-class movement, for our purposes at this juncture, it is the changes at the other end of the sociological spectrum that deserve closer scrutiny. For an insightful analysis of the possibilities of a genuine working-class movement under the current economic conditions, see Nick Beams, "The Crash of 2008 and Its Revolutionary Implications," at http://wsws.org/articles/2009/feb2009/nbe4-f07.shtml.

117. Glassman, "State Power beyond the 'Territorial Trap,'" 673. It is precisely this kind of state apparatus that Harvey calls a "neoliberal state." See Harvey, *A Brief History of Neoliberalism*, 7.

118. Among these measures one can count the actions of the U.S. government, which has pumped billions of dollars in foreign and military aid and the setting up of training institutes for bureaucrats from Third World countries, as well as those of interstate institutions like the IMF and the World Bank, which Robert Cox argues are "symbiotically related to expansive capital." See Robert Cox, "Social Forces, States, and World Orders: Beyond International Relations Theory," *Millennium: Journal of International Studies* 10, no. 2 (1981): 126–155.

119. Glassman's analysis focuses on the ways in which the activities of this technocratic elite, whom he characterizes as a "counter-nationalist intelligentsia," have enabled the restructuring of Third World states in particular. See Glassman, "State Power beyond the 'Territorial Trap,'" 685.

120. Glassman's analysis of the "internationalization of the state" builds on the work of scholars like Leo Panitch and Robert Cox. See, in particular, Robert Cox, *Production, Power and the World Order: Social Forces in the Making of History* (New York: Columbia University Press, 1987); and Leo Panitch, "Globalization and the State," in *Socialist Register*, ed. R. Milliband and L. Panitch, 60–93 (London: Merlin, 1994).

121. Even Harvey, who argues that it "never did make much sense to speak of a distinctively US versus British or French or German or Korean capitalist class," given that the ruling class has never really "confined its operations and defined its loyalties to any one nation-state," accepts the proposition that members of this class continue to attach themselves to, feed off, and nurture specific state apparatuses. See Harvey, *A Brief History of Neoliberalism*, 35–36.

122. The logic of Glassman's argument lends itself to this critique. However, it should be noted that Glassman's argument is far more nuanced than, say, that of William Robinson, who contends that the spread of neoliberal restructuring should be understood as the manifestation of the growing strength of a transnational capitalist class, which in turn has resulted in the emergence of a new structure of authority—the transnational state—into which the nation-state is being absorbed. See William Robinson, "Capitalist Globalization and the Transnationalization of the State," in *Historical Materialism and Globalization*, ed. Mark Rupert and Hazel Smith, 210–229 (London: Routledge, 2002).

123. This should be evident from the fact that in the late 1970s and early 1980s, similar measures were adopted in Argentina, China, the United States, and Great Britain—countries that had quite different political systems. More important, the changing of the guard in all cases did not imply a fundamental repudiation of the principles of neoliberal restructuring.

124. For more details, see chapter 5.

125. The CPI(M) in its guise as the ruling party in West Bengal state provides a great illustration of this point. The party, which ostensibly opposed the neoliberal

reforms in 1991, has in fact embraced similar policies at the state level, going to the extent of expropriating land from peasants for the purpose of establishing special economic zones wherein international conglomerates would be offered cheap land, tax exemptions, and promises of freedom from any labor militancy. As was made obvious by its actions in villages like Singur and Nandigram—where opposition to proposed land expropriation was met with brutal police force, ably assisted by local CPI(M) cadres—the party has been willing to back its policies with violence when needed. For a succinct discussion of neoliberal policies in West Bengal, see Sumit and Tanika Sarkar, "A Place Called Nandigram," in *Nandigram and Beyond*, ed. Gautam Ray (Kolkata: Sangehil, 2008); see also Arun Kumar, "West Bengal Left Front's Pro-Investor Land Grab Results in Deadly Clashes," at http://wsws.org/articles/2007/jan2007/beng-j26.shtml; and Kranti Kumara, "Leading Indian Intellectuals Condemn West Bengal's Stalinist-Led Government," at http://wsws.org/articles/2007/mar2007/beng-m19.shtml.

Chapter 3

1. *Lok Sabha Debates*, Vol. 6, September 2, 1957.

2. N. V. Rajkumar, *Indians outside India: A General Survey* (New Delhi: All India Congress Committee, 1951), 5–6.

3. In the decades that followed, opposition political parties did at various points demand that the Indian state change its policy, on the grounds that not only were Indians abroad an intrinsic part of the Indian nation (regardless of their citizenship) but also their mistreatment was a reflection of India's perceived weakness in the international system. Notwithstanding such demands, the Nehruvian doctrine remained more or less in place for more than four decades after independence. For a detailed time line of the political parties in power and in the opposition in India, see Appendix I.

4. Lanka Sundaram, *Indians Overseas: A Study in Economic Sociology* (Madras: G. A. Natesan, 1933), 4.

5. C. Kondapi, *Indians Overseas: 1838–1949* (New Delhi: Oxford University Press, 1951).

6. The migrant Indian groups lived across the various territories of the British Empire, including (A) Colonies of the Indian system: Ceylon, Malaya; (B) Colonies of the Pacific Ocean: Fiji, New Caledonia; (C) Colonies of the South Indian Ocean: The Union of South Africa and East Africa in general, Mauritius, Reunion; and (D) Colonies of the West Indian system: Foreign—St. Croix, Guadeloupe, Martinique, Cayenne, Surinam; British—Demarara (British Guiana), Trinidad, Jamaica, Grenada, St. Vincent, St. Lucia, St. Kitts, Nevis. Apart from this, considerable numbers of Indian settlers were in British Columbia (Canada), California, Mexico, Cuba, Brazil, Gibraltar, Hong Kong, and New Zealand. See Sundaram, *Indians Overseas*.

7. France had, of course, originally abolished slavery in 1794 during the most radical phase of the French Revolution and in response to revolutionary events in San Domingo. For a detailed discussion, see C. L. R. James, *The Black Jacobins: Toussaint L'Overture and the San Domingo Revolution* (New York: Vintage, 1963).

8. For an extensive account of the early phase of Indian emigration, see Hugh Tinker, *A New System of Slavery: The Export of Indian Labour Overseas, 1830–1920* (London: Oxford University Press, 1974.)

9. Contrary to popular belief, this was not the first time that Indians set foot in South Africa. As early as 1653, Dutch merchants had taken groups of Indians to what was then the Dutch Cape Colony and sold them as slaves. However, this group was unable to maintain a distinct identity. The Indian slaves married slaves from East Asia, the Cape, and other parts of Africa and their progeny came to be classified as "Malays." Report of the High Level Committee on the Indian Diaspora (Indian Council of World Affairs: New Delhi, 2001), 75.

10. Sundaram uses the term "assisted" as a euphemism for the forced indentured labor that formed the major component of early emigrant Indian communities.

11. In 1864, the Government of India consolidated the existing nineteen laws of emigration into a single act—Act XIII—that attempted to provide several safeguards to the laborer, including a requirement that he be taken to a magistrate before being shipped out of the country to ensure that he was being paid adequate compensation.

12. Sundaram, *Indians Overseas*, 12.

13. B. Apparsamy, *Indians of South Africa* (Bombay: Padma, 1943), 16.

14. By 1871, the Office of the Protector, which was initially conceived of as a place where the emigrants could come freely to seek advice and assistance, was transformed into a "department for the levy of fees from the emigrants in addition to the ordinary taxation affixed by the law." See Kondapi, *Indians Overseas*, 14.

15. Sundaram, *Indians Overseas*, 14.

16. The main system used for recruitment was the Kangani system. The Kangani (overseer) was paid a fixed amount to go back to the homeland and recruit new labor. The usual recruitment tactic was to present Malaya as a beautiful place where money was plentiful, life easy, and the caste system a thing of the past. The Kangani was paid more for bringing in the recruited labor and more money for each laborer who showed up for work. See M. R. Stenson, *Class, Race and Colonialism in West Malaysia: The Indian Case* (St. Lucia: University of Queensland Press, 1980). See also K. S. Sandhu, *Indians in Malaya* (Cambridge: Cambridge University Press, 1969); and David James Mearns, *Shiva's Other Children: Religion and Social Identity amongst Overseas Indians* (New Delhi: Sage, 1995).

17. The stoppage of emigration to Natal between 1866 and 1874 was a result of complaints by the returning emigrants about physical abuse by employers, nonpayment of wages and allowances to the time-expired laborers who were waiting to return, and illegal stoppage of payment in case of sickness.

18. See, for instance, the Report of the Committee on Emigration from India to the Crown Colonies and Protectorates (Sanderson Committee Report), June 1910.

19. Quoted in Kondapi, *Indians Overseas*, 19. It should be noted that this commission argued without irony that even though an indenture seemed contrary to British ideals, it was the only way for the government to ensure that the emigrants paid for services that had already been rendered, that is, the fully paid passage to the place of work. Furthermore, the indenture merely recognized in law what was already an established fact—that the emigrant was necessarily "dependant on others for the preservation of his health." Sundaram, *Indians Overseas*, 79–80.

20. The Wragg Commission reported not only the dearth of labor that was causing crops to rot "on the ground" in Natal in 1870 but also the reactions to the Act of 1874 that granted the right to own lands to Indian emigrants in exchange for the commutation of return passage: "The majority of the White Colonies were strongly opposed to the presence of free Indians as rivals in either agricultural and commercial pursuits." See Kondapi, *Indians Overseas*, 21–22.

21. Apparsamy, *Indians of South Africa*, 19.

22. This it did despite the recommendations of the Clayton Commission that indentured labor was necessary for the survival of Natal. See Kondapi, *Indians Overseas*, 25.

23. It must be noted, however, that the emigration committees were generally preceded by numerous other commissions, which made the same recommendations without any direct action resulting from them. For instance, labor emigration to Mauritius was discontinued as a result of the recommendation of the Emigration Committee of 1909. The reason given for this recommendation was the extremely harsh vagrancy regulations in the colony. Any indentured laborer could be arrested and tried before a magistrate for not carrying a police pass or return permission from his employer at any given time. The punishment for this offense was usually hard labor or an extremely high fine, thus ensuring that the immigrant was forced back into indenture. These laws were in existence for more than three decades before the colonial Indian government took any steps to protect the Indian emigrants. In fact, as early as 1874, the Earl of Carnorvon, Secretary of State for the colonies, declared: "I cannot but feel that those provisions are *repugnant in principle to the liberty which an emigrant, like every other class of his Majesty's subjects is entitled,* and that nothing but a clear and unquestionable necessity could justify their maintenance." Quoted in Kondapi, *Indians Overseas*, 15, my emphasis. The "necessity"—cheap labor for the plantations—though often questioned, seemed clear enough to justify inaction on the part of the government of India for the next thirty years.

24. Sundaram, *Indians Overseas*, 165.

25. Ibid., 165–166.

26. Moderate leader Srinivasa Sastri, for instance, opened his statement at the imperial conference of 1921 by declaring, "To us, the Empire stands for equality, for

absolute justice." Cited in Hugh Tinker, *Separate and Unequal* (Vancouver: University of British Columbia Press, 1976), 47.

27. Ibid., 51.

28. Mauritius was the honorable exception to this rule. It became the only colony where Indians enjoyed the same rights and privileges as the local population by the mid-1930s.

29. The word *sepoy* is derived from the Hindi word *sipahi*, denoting a soldier, and was used to describe Indian soldiers in the British colonial army.

30. Sundaram, *Indians Overseas*, 139.

31. Quoted in M. C. Lall, *India's Missed Opportunity: India's Relationship with Non-Resident Indians* (Aldershot, UK: Ashgate, 2001), 81.

32. During the Boer Wars, arguing that "it was the duty of the Indian, as a British subject who hoped for ultimate equality in the Empire, to assist Britain," Gandhi organized a stretcher corps that provided medical assistance to the British Army. See Apparsamy, *Indians of South Africa*, 21.

33. Ibid, 26. The success of the movement was seen in the Relief Act that not only abolished the £3 annual license fee but also validated Indian marriages so long as they were monogamous.

34. As Mrs. Naidu remarked in 1924: "It does not take a very learned student to realize that naturally and meritably East Africa is one of the earliest legitimate territories of the Indian nation going so far back as the first century of the Christian era.... East Africa is therefore the legitimate colony of the surplus of the great Indian nation, whether they went forth to colonize these unknown lands from an economic point of view or to satisfy their desire for venture." Quoted in Charles Heimsath and Surjit Mansingh, *A Diplomatic History of Modern India* (Bombay: Allied Publishers, 1971), 308.

35. India became an independent member of the League and Para-League organizations after World War I, even though the Indian delegation was led by non-Indians until 1929.

36. On Indians in Canada, see Kavita Sharma, *On-going Journey: Indian Migration to Canada* (New Delhi: SAB, 1998).

37. The missions sent by the INC after World War I were Malaya and Ceylon (C. F. Andrews and B. D. Chaturvedi, 1923); Ceylon (M. A. Arulanandam, A. V. Dias, Periasundaram, and L. Muthukrishna, 1923); Kenya (Sarojini Naidu and George Joseph, 1923); Kenya (Sridhar Ganesh Vaze and B. D. Chaturvedi, 1924); Zanzibar (C. F. Andrews, 1934); Ceylon (Jawaharlal Nehru, 1939); and Ceylon (Jawaharlal Nehru, C. Rajagopalachari, A. Aryanayakam, and G. Ramachandran, 1946). See Lall, *India's Missed Opportunity*, 86–87, n.29.

38. The Central Indian Association of Malaya created in 1936 was, for the most part, an urban middle-class organization that was more tied to the mainland Congress Party than to the demands of Malayan labor.

39. Rajkumar, *Indians outside India*, 11.

40. Sundaram, *Indians Overseas*, 126–127.

41. Apparsamy, *Indians of South Africa*, 69.

42. Quoted in Lall, *India's Missed Opportunity*, 83.

43. Apparsamy, *Indians of South Africa*, 76.

44. An On Looker, *The Status of Indians in the Empire* (Lahore: Kitabistan, 1944), 4.

45. This claim had formed the basis of the nationalist demand for independence from British rule. See Gyan Prakash, *Another Reason: Science and the Imagination of Modern India* (Princeton, NJ: Princeton University Press, 1999), 201.

46. At this stage, India was still a British colony, though its independence from British rule was viewed as inevitable. As a stepping-stone to complete independence, the INC and the Muslim League participated in elections that led to the formation of the first provisional Indian government.

47. While there was to be no Indian in the Transvaal Assembly, in deference to the Afrikaner demands, the Indian representatives in both the Natal and Union Assemblies were to be of European descent. See Tinker, *Separate and Unequal*, 294.

48. Especially given that actual military intervention was not a possibility in 1946, the question of whether an independent India would take recourse to overt force to protect overseas Indians remained a rhetorical one.

49. On Looker, *The Status of Indians in the Empire*, 27.

50. Letter from Under-Secretary Arthur Creech-Jones to Jawaharlal Nehru, June 30, 1947. Cited in Tinker, *Separate and Unequal*, 310.

51. Sitaramayya's statement, which forms the first epigraph of this chapter, was far from exceptional. To a large extent, as the chapter shows, it reflected the sentiments of stalwarts of the Indian nationalist movement, at least until official independence was granted.

52. The reasons for this had a lot to do with the fact that the emigrant populations from undivided India were predominantly Hindu and hence not necessarily seen as being connected to the new nation-state of Pakistan. In East Africa, however, the overseas Indian community, which had a strong Muslim component, was increasingly being referred to as "Asians."

53. For a detailed study of the Indian community in Burma, see N. R. Chakravarti, *The Indian Minority in Burma: The Rise and Decline of an Immigrant Community* (London: Oxford University Press, 1971).

54. The author of the offending book was actually a Burmese Muslim. See Tinker, *Separate and Unequal*, 150.

55. The main such group was called *Kala Htoon Thin* (literally, "Bash the Indian") and was organized by Thakin Ba Swe, who later served as the Burmese Prime Minister in 1956–1957.

56. The Indian government placed the total number of Indians who were prevented from returning under this act at 153,000. See Tinker, *Separate and Unequal*, 308.

57. For a detailed history of Indians in Ceylon and their relations with India, see P. Sahadevan, *India and Overseas Indians: The Case of Sri Lanka* (New Delhi: Kalinga, 1995).

58. Cited in E. F. C. Ludowyk, *The Modern History of Ceylon* (London: Weidenfeld and Nicholson, 1966), 164–165.

59. On Looker, *The Status of Indians in the Empire*, 11.

60. Tinker, *Separate and Unequal*, 182.

61. A reminder regarding the terminology: the term "Person of Indian Origin" (PIO) was used both by the Ceylonese and the Indian government to describe the Indian population of Ceylon. This was in part a recognition of the fact that migration from Tamil Nadu (in Southern India) could be dated to at least to the ninth century, a millennium prior to British rule over the Indian subcontinent. As I have already noted, the term PIO came to be used interchangeably with "Indians abroad" and "overseas Indians" by the Indian government to describe the Indian diaspora.

62. For a detailed analysis of the provisions of these acts, see Sahadevan, *India and Overseas Indians*, 125–132.

63. Ibid., 132. Nehru's letter to Senanayake dated July 17, 1949.

64. Ibid.

65. Kondapi, *Indians Overseas*, 419–420.

66. The Chettiars were a caste group from South India who had immigrated to Southeast Asia and Burma in the late nineteenth century and found success as businessmen and moneylenders.

67. Bajpai, the man who had accompanied Srinivasa Sastri to the various imperial conferences, had been appointed the head of the Indian Ministry of External Affairs after independence.

68. As the plantation population of Indian origin became aware of the various citizenship laws, they made some serious attempts to acquire Ceylonese citizenship. In 1958, 237,034 citizenship applications covering 829,619 people were filed with the Ceylonese state. By August 1958, only 24,559 applications covering 96,923 persons were accepted, 196,063 applications covering 696,252 persons were rejected, and the rest were pending. In effect, those who had been refused Ceylonese citizenship were deemed "stateless." See *Lok Sabha Debates*, November 25, 1958.

69. See Lall, *India's Missed Opportunity*, particularly chapter 3 for an elaboration of this argument.

70. Through the first three decades of independence, the Ministry of External Affairs coordinated with various state governments to come up with comprehensive rehabilitation schemes for repatriates from countries like Burma and Ceylon and later Uganda and Kenya. One such scheme is detailed in a statement on Burmese repatriates presented in the lower house of the Parliament. Its provisions include special employment opportunities, business loans, and the grant of land through "Land Colonisation Schemes." See *Lok Sabha Debates*, February 16, 1966.

71. As Sankaran Krishna has argued, the emphasis on the importance of India's "natural boundaries" combined with the trauma of partition—a trauma described by Nehru as the "[breaking] up [of] the body of India"—led to the inscription of a cartographic anxiety into the very genetic code of postcolonial India. This anxiety has, over the decades, taken the form of not only a close official monitoring of all representations of India's body politic in maps but also the occasional delineation of party politics along the themes of who can best protect the territorial integrity of the country. See Sankaran Krishna, "Cartographic Anxiety: Mapping the Body Politic in India," in *Challenging Boundaries: Global Flows, Territorial Identities*, ed. Michael J. Shapiro and Hayward R. Alker, 193–214 (Minneapolis: University of Minnesota Press, 1996).

72. In making this argument, I follow postcolonial scholars who understand territoriality to be a dynamic effect of state practices. See, for instance, Timothy Mitchell, *Colonizing Egypt* (Berkeley: University of California Press, 1991); and Bruce Willems-Braun, "Buried Epistemologies: The Politics of Nature in (Post)colonial British Columbia," *Annals of American Geographers* 87, no. 1 (1997).

73. As Vazira Zamindar notes, the problems posed by the displaced populations after partition gave rise to some especially peculiar debates surrounding the issue of political belonging. There were, for instance, those who argued that Muslims in India should be held as hostages to ensure the well-being of Hindus and Sikhs in the territories of Pakistan. A less frightening idea was proposed by Congress leaders like Sardar Patel, who argued that citizenship should be construed in the broadest possible manner, especially so that Sikhs and Hindus who lived or were stranded in Pakistan would not be treated as aliens in India. And then there were those like H. S. Suhrawardy, the leader of the Bengal Muslim League, who argued that living in Indian territory did not conflict with his being a member of the Pakistani legislature. While these debates did not spill over to the broader question of Indians abroad, Zamindar argues persuasively that they reveal the nebulousness of the relationship between "citizen and state, nation and territory" in the immediate aftermath of partition. See Vazira Fazila-Yacoobali Zamindar, *The Long Partition and the Making of Modern South Asia: Refugees, Boundaries, Histories* (New York: Columbia University Press, 2007), 4–5.

74. "At the commencement of this Constitution (26 January 1950), every person who has his domicile in the territory of India and (a) who was born in the territory of India; or (b) either of whose parents was born in the territory of India; or (c) who has been ordinarily resident in the territory of India for not less than five years immediately preceding such commencement, shall be a citizen of India."

75. This is particularly true if we contextualize the development of these citizenship rules in terms of migrations across the new Indo-Pakistani border. Immediately after independence, the Indian state imposed a "permit" system to regulate the flow of the displaced populations across the borders. While restrictive, this system merely served as a stop-gap measure until the introduction of the new citizenship rules and

the move to a regime of passports that settled the question of belonging on legalistic lines that were not easily negotiable. For a careful study of the legislative practices surrounding citizenship, and their role in the making of Indian and Pakistani nation-states, see Zamindar, *The Long Partition*, especially parts 2 and 3.

76. Prasenjit Duara, *Rescuing History from the Nation: Questioning Narratives of Modern China* (Chicago: University of Chicago Press, 1995), 8.

77. I will expand this argument in the following chapter.

78. For what is arguably the most compelling exposition of this view, see R. C. Dutt, *The Economic History of India*, 2nd ed., vols. 1 and 2 (London: Kegan Paul, Trench, Trubner, 1906).

79. For an elaboration of this argument, see Himadeep Muppidi, *The Politics of the Global* (Minneapolis: University of Minnesota Press, 2004). For an expanded version of this line of critique, see Latha Varadarajan, "Constructivism, Identity, and Neoliberal (In)security," *Review of International Studies* 30, no. 3 (2004): 319–341.

80. Congress Session, Jaipur, December 18–19, 1948. Indian National Congress, *Resolutions on Foreign Policy, 1947–57* (New Delhi: AICC).

81. Even prior to independence, the interim government hosted the Asian Relations Conference in New Delhi (March–April 1947) and followed it by convening the Asian Conference on Indonesia (January 1949), which demanded the end of Dutch colonialism in the region.

82. Itty Abraham, "State, Place, Identity: Two Stories in the Making of a Region," in *Regional Modernities: The Cultural Politics of Development in India*, ed. K. Sivaramakrishnan and Arun Agrawal (Stanford, CA: Stanford University Press, 2003), 404–425.

83. Ibid., 415. As Abraham shows, there were crucial differences between member-states, especially in terms of their attitude toward the United States, the Soviet Union, and the People's Republic of China. The attempt to emphasize their supposedly common goals in the face of these obvious, fundamentally divergent worldviews produced statements that were noteworthy to the extent that they seemed to stretch the limits of diplomatic language. The final communiqué, for instance, consisted of the delicately worded statement that "the subject of Communism in its national and international aspects were generally discussed and the prime ministers made known to each other their respective views on and attitudes towards Communist ideologies" and included the final statements that reaffirmed the "unshakeable determination [of the members] to resist interference in the affairs of their countries by external Communist, anti-Communist or other agencies." Cited in Abraham, "State, Place, Identity," 412.

84. Ibid., 415.

85. *Lok Sabha Debates*, March 16, 1953.

86. *Lok Sabha Debates*, April 9, 1958.

87. Chakravarti, *The Indian Minority in Burma*, 174–187; see also W. S. Desai, *India and Burma* (Bombay: Orient Longmans, 1954), 102–111.

88. Jawaharlal Nehru, *Lok Sabha Debates*, September 2, 1957.

89. *Lok Sabha Debates*, September 10, 1954.

90. Especially given that Nehru had emphasized Asian solidarity and close connections between India and China (embodied in the slogan "*Hindi-Chini Bhai Bhai*," translated as "Indians and Chinese are brothers"), underplaying the potential of a Chinese attack.

91. *Lok Sabha Debates*, vol. 30, April 28, 1964.

92. All India Congress Committee, Indore, September 13–14, 1953. Indian National Congress, *Resolutions on Foreign Policy*. A statement reflecting these principles was also voiced by Deputy Minister of External Affairs Dinesh Singh, more than a decade later on the floor of the Indian Parliament: "Those people of Indian origin who wish to stay in Africa and who have made their home in Africa must identify themselves completely with the people of those countries and with the aspirations of those people." *Lok Sabha Debates*, February 20, 1964.

93. Dinesh Singh, *Lok Sabha Debates*, vol. 42, April 30, 1965.

94. It was a portrayal that the Colonial Office seemed quite ready to buy. See, for instance, the already-mentioned Devonshire Declaration of 1923 that limited the property rights of Indian settlers.

95. Re: Indian Repatriates from the Independent Countries of Africa, *Lok Sabha Debates*, May 4, 1964.

96. Ibid.

97. Ibid. The contrasting picture, according to the opposition, was provided by the Chinese, who despite coming from "two Chinas…say that they are Chinese [when they go abroad] and look after one another." This was partly responsible for the growth in China's influence.

98. Ibid.

99. Dinesh Singh, *Lok Sabha Debates*, vol. 42, April 30, 1965.

100. The British Nationality Act (1949) extended British citizenship to all "British subjects"—those who were born and/or resided in any of the dominions. However, this was limited by the Commonwealth Immigration Act of 1968, which limited entry into the United Kingdom to only those British passport holders who could prove a "continuing relationship" with Britain—by showing documents proving that either one of the parents or the grandparents of the aspiring entrant was born in Britain. This effectively ruled out a significant section of the East African PIO. During this period, the Indian Ministry of External Affairs put pressure on Whitehall to relax its rules to permit the PIO who had claimed British citizenship in the 1950s to enter the United Kingdom.

101. As an opposition member remarked, the mass deportation of Indians was but "one more example of the ugly treatment meted out to citizens of Indian origin because of the general loss of Indian prestige and influence and because of their belief that they could do with Indians what they like with impunity." *Lok Sabha Debates*, vol. 12, February 16, 1968.

Chapter 4

1. *Swadeshi* means "self-reliance"; *swraj* (also spelled *swaraj*) means "self-rule," "independence."

2. The category of nonresident Indian became popular in the political and public lexicon after the passage of the Foreign Exchange Regulation Act (FERA) of 1973 and has since been used interchangeably with categories such as Indians abroad, persons of Indian origin, and more recently, the Indian diaspora. Initially mentioned in the Income Tax Act of 1961, this category was merely meant to refer to the residency clause to determine levels of taxation for Indian citizens. Within the provisions of FERA, the nonresident Indian category was presented as the converse of the resident Indian—that is, someone who did not fulfill the requirements of being a resident Indian. By extending this, the Reserve Bank of India presented its FERA-based definition of NRIs as those Indian citizens who have indicated an indefinite period of stay abroad for employment, business, vocation, or any other purpose; who work abroad on assignments with foreign governments or international/regional agencies such as the United Nations; who have been posted in Indian diplomatic missions abroad; and who have been deputed by the Indian government on temporary assignments abroad. See Reserve Bank of India, *Exchange Control Facilities for Investment by Non-Resident Indians* (New Delhi, 1988), 1–2. It was only after the passage of the Foreign Exchange Management Act (FEMA, 1999), which replaced FERA, that the category of NRI was extended to include foreign citizens of Indian origin. For definitions of this term and its relationship to others such as "persons of Indian origin," see *Handbook for Overseas Indians* (New Delhi: Ministry of Overseas Indian Affairs, 2009).

3. In doing so, my argument engages closely with the analyses of the Indian national movement proffered by Aditya Mukherjee and Partha Chatterjee. Both scholars argue that in its final stages, it was a bourgeois nationalist movement that worked to create an interventionist state and facilitated the "dominance and expansion of capital." Chatterjee's work, in that sense, goes beyond some of the limitations of postcolonial scholarship discussed in the earlier chapters. The difference in the two analyses under consideration is that while Chatterjee sees the dominance of the bourgeoisie as an intrinsic limitation of postcolonial nationalism, Mukherjee presents his argument almost as a defense of the farsightedness of the Indian capitalist class. See Aditya Mukherjee, *Imperialism, Nationalism and the Making of the Indian Capitalist Class, 1920–1947* (New Delhi: Sage, 2002), and Partha Chatterjee, *Nationalist Thought and the Colonial World: A Derivative Discourse?* (Minneapolis: University of Minnesota Press, 1986).

4. Mukherjee argues that Indian capitalists were able to overcome colonial barriers primarily through three methods: first, by investing in new areas such as sugar, cement, paper, iron, and steel; second, by gradually encroaching (even in small measures) on traditional areas of European influence, such as banking, life insurance,

jute, and shipping; and third, through faster growth in economic sectors and geographic regions that were dominated by Indian capital. See Mukherjee, *Imperialism, Nationalism and the Making of the Indian Capitalist Class*, 27.

5. Ibid., 1, emphasis in original.

6. From 1905 onward, the Indian National Congress held what came to be known as the Indian Industrial Conference along with its annual conventions. In 1915, partly at the urging of the leaders of the Indian National Congress, the Indian Merchants Chamber organized the first Indian Commercial Congress. In 1920, the commercial and industrial bodies merged to form the Indian Industrial and Commercial Congress. See Ibid., 35–74.

7. The question of the class character of the Indian National Congress cannot be understood in purely sociological terms. In that sense, it is possible to argue that given its broad-based membership at its height, and given the fact that its leadership did come from different strata of society (albeit most of them were closely connected to the landowner and capitalist classes), the Congress was a mélange of social classes. However, as I pointed out in chapter 2, class is not merely a sociological category. In that sense, the true class character of the INC—its role as the political representatives of the Indian bourgeoisie—can be understood by analyzing the development of its social orientation and political programs. The first part of this chapter focuses on this task.

8. The timing of this publication and the ensuing conflict among sections of the Indian capitalists (with G. D. Birla rebuking Walchand and others for losing sight of their larger cause) is not surprising, given that the period 1933–1936 is considered by historians to be Nehru's "most radical period," when he "was on the verge of becoming a Marxist." See Bipan Chandra, "Jawaharlal Nehru and the Capitalist Class, 1936," in *Nationalism and Colonialism in Modern India* (New Delhi: Orient Longman, 1979), 171–203.

9. The signatories of the manifesto included Naoroji Sakalatwala, Purshotamdas Thakurdas, Chimanlal Setalwad, Pheroz Sethna, Cowasjee Jehangir, Shapurji Billimoria, Homi Mody, Walchand Hirachand, V. N. Chandavarkar, Mathuradas Vissanji, C. L. Mehta, and K. R. P. Shroff. For a full text of the Bombay Manifesto, see the Bombay *Tribune*, May 20, 1936. Letters by individual signatories making the same points were published in the *Times of India* on May 11, May 29, and June 11, 1936.

10. In a similar vein, Nehru declared in his address to the Indian Progressive Group of Bombay that "scientific socialism, or Marxism was the only remedy for the ills of the world." Quoted in the *Times of India*, May 18, 1936. See also Bipan Chandra, "Jawaharlal Nehru and the Capitalist Class," 177, 188.

11. As Gramsci points out, the establishment of bourgeois hegemony is a process that requires occasional sacrifices and compromises on the part of the ruling class. Unlike A. D. Shroff and Walchand Hirachand, G. D. Birla and his associates seemed to be well aware of this fact. See Antonio Gramsci, "The Modern Prince," in *Selections*

from the Prison Notebooks, trans. and ed. Quentin Hoare and Geoffrey Nowell Smith, 161 (New York: International Publishers, 1997).

12. G. D. Birla to Purshotamdas Thakurdas, cited in Bipan Chandra, "Jawaharlal Nehru and the Capitalist Class," 193.

13. Ibid. See also S. Gopal, *Jawaharlal Nehru—A Biography,* vol. 1 (Cambridge, MA: Harvard University Press, 1976), particularly chapters 7 and 8.

14. I should note that while the relationship between Gandhi and Nehru was indeed a very close one, the general explanation about Gandhi's influence carrying the day seems almost too simplistic. It remains a matter of historical record, though, that Nehru did bow down to the Congress right wing at this juncture; he remained at the helm of the INC and eventually gave shape to the final stage of the Indian national movement.

15. To that extent, its characterization as a form of socialism is itself quite a misnomer.

16. In Chatterjee's words: "It was a reconstruction whose specific form was to situate nationalism within the domain of *state ideology.* Given the historical constraints imposed on the Indian bourgeoisie within the colonial social formation, its intellectual-moral leadership could never be firmly established in the domain of civil society. Of historical necessity, its revolution had to be passive. The specific ideological form of the passive revolution in India was an *ètatisme,* explicitly recognizing a central, autonomous and directing role of the state and legitimizing it by a specific nationalist marriage between the ideas of progress and social justice." Chatterjee, *Nationalist Thought and the Colonial World,* 132.

17. Ibid., 49.

18. Mukherjee, *Imperialism, Nationalism and the Making of the Indian Capitalist Class,* 48.

19. For a more detailed discussion of these measures, see the Annual Report of the Federation of Indian Chambers of Commerce and Industry, 1934.

20. For an elaboration of this argument by three of India's foremost industrialists, G. D. Birla, J. R. D. Tata, and Sir Purshotamdas Thakurdas, see *Memorandum Outlining a Plan of Economic Development of India,* parts 1 and 2 (Harmondsworth: Penguin, 1945).

21. Chatterjee, *Nationalist Thought and the Colonial World,* 132, my emphasis.

22. Ibid., 149.

23. Ibid., 149–150.

24. Ibid., 153.

25. Ibid.

26. The Bombay Plan has to a large extent been treated as an exemplary articulation of the truly "national" character of the Indian bourgeoisie, an illustration of their willingness to put aside their own interests for the sake of the larger national cause. Aditya Mukherjee's argument is a perfect example of this tendency. The argument here goes against the grain in framing the Bombay Plan not so much as a

departure from the general tendency of the bourgeoisie to look after its own interests, but rather as a move to preserve and protect those interests. For an argument that provides a similar analysis about the Bombay Plan, see Vivek Chibber, *Locked in Place: State-Building and Late Industrialization in India* (Princeton, NJ: Princeton University Press, 2006), especially chapter 4.

27. Purshotamdas Thakurdas et al., *A Plan for Economic Development of India (Bombay Plan)*, parts 1 and 2 (Harmondsworth: Penguin, 1945), 9.

28. The main signatories to the plan (also known as the "Tata-Birla plan") were Purshotamdas Thakurdas, J. R. D. Tata, G. D. Birla, Ardeshir Dalal, Lala Sri Ram, Kasturbhai Lalbhai, A. D. Shroff, and John Mathai.

29. Mukherjee, *Imperialism, Nationalism and the Making of the Indian Capitalist Class*, 396 (emphasis in original).

30. It helped that, at this juncture, a large number of the banks that were not owned by foreigners were actually owned by Indian industrialists who had close ties to the INC-led nationalist movement. The Punjab National Bank (one of the fourteen banks that were nationalized under the Bank Nationalization Act of 1969), for instance, was founded in 1895 as a "national bank"—a bank with Indian capital, owned, managed, and operated by Indians for Indians—at the insistence of Lala Lajpat Rai, one of the best-known Congress leaders associated with the *Swadeshi* movement. For a brief official history of the bank, see http://pnbsu.com/pnb/history.htm.

31. This said, they expressed their preference for a system wherein the government would raise capital through state-owned financial institutions and then lend it to the privately owned corporations.

32. "Foreign investments in agricultural, mineral and industrial concerns have resulted in foreign control of India's economic and political life…warping and retarding national development." From John Mathai's draft in the Proceedings of the Sixth Session of the National Planning Commission, September 1945, cited in Mukherjee, *Imperialism, Nationalism and the Making of the Indian Capitalist Class*, 401.

33. As early as the mid-1930s, the annual reports of FICCI made obvious a growing sentiment that Indian capitalists were favorably inclined toward an interventionist state. Part of this could be traced to the fear of Bolshevism, which industrialists like G. D. Birla argued could easily take root in India unless the state immediately dealt with the issue of extreme inequity. However, an equally important argument was articulated by FICCI President N. R. Sarkar: "The days of undiluted laissez-faire are gone forever." The example of advanced industrialized countries proved that for capitalism to get a new lease on life, capitalist classes needed state involvement in the economy. See Annual Report of the Federation of Indian Chambers of Commerce and Industry, 1934. See also Mukherjee, "Planning and Public Sector," in *Imperialism, Nationalism and the Making of the Indian Capitalist Class*, 391–432.

34. Chatterjee, *Nationalist Thought and the Colonial World*, 146.

35. Ibid., 139.

36. Ibid., 158.

37. Mukherjee, *Imperialism, Nationalism and the Making of the Indian Capitalist Class*, 71. While Aditya Mukherjee supports the notion that in its final stages, the Indian nationalist movement was characterized by bourgeois hegemony, he makes the somewhat tautological argument that the conflation of particular class interests with larger national interests was possible because of a genuine coalescence of interests. In doing so, he misses the point that the success of any hegemonic project lies precisely in making the conflation of the particular and the general interests appear genuine.

38. Ibid., 48.

39. While a corporatist account might find this move puzzling, Gramsci's analysis of hegemony, as discussed in chapter 2, points us in the right direction by providing a richer account of the consequences of the Indian bourgeoisie's opposition to this particular bill.

40. It should be noted that the Transfer to Public Ownership Act included a clause about the payment of "suitable compensation" to the shareholders.

41. Established in 1935, the Reserve Bank of India had also served as the Central Bank of Burma until its occupation by Japanese troops, and later until April 1947. After the partition of the subcontinent, it served as the Central Bank of Pakistan until June 1948. For a brief sketch of RBI's history, see http://www.rbi.org.in/scripts/brief-history.aspx#.

42. A clue to the smoothness of the transition to nationalization can be found in the fact that on the first board of directors of the RBI were well-known industrialists like B. D. Goenka, Lala Shri Ram, and Purshotamdas Thakurdas, who were all supporters of the Bombay Plan. In the weeks leading up to the nationalization of the RBI, its chairman, C. D. Deshmukh, made no secret of his opposition to the pace at which the Government of India was attempting to take over the institution. However, despite this opposition, Deshmukh was asked—and agreed—to continue serving as the chairman of the board of directors of the newly nationalized RBI. See "Reserve Bank against Nationalization," *Times of India*, March 23, 1948; see also *RBI History*, vol. 1, at http://www.rbi.org.in/scripts/RHvol-1.aspx, esp. chapters 1–3 and 11.

43. While the majority of the board of directors of the Imperial Bank were Europeans, Indian industrialists like B. D. Goenka (who had also served on the board of the RBI) served on the bank's board as well. The Imperial Bank itself was a product of the merger of the three Presidency Banks of Bengal, Bombay, and Madras, along with their seventy branches, in 1921. Until the creation of the RBI in 1935, the Imperial Bank served as a quasi central bank for the Indian government. However, after 1935, its functions were primarily of a commercial nature. When India attained independence, the Imperial Bank had a capital base of Rs. 11.85 crores (including reserves), deposits of Rs. 275.14 crores, advances of Rs. 72.94 crores, a network of 172 branches, and more than 200 suboffices operating around the country, making it the

most important banking institution in the country after the RBI. With nationalization, the RBI acquired the controlling interest in the Imperial Bank. For a brief history of the Imperial Bank, see http://www.statebankofindia.com/user.htm. In 1969, India's third prime minister (and Jawaharlal Nehru's daughter), Indira Gandhi, oversaw the passage of the Bank Nationalization Act, which nationalized fourteen of the largest remaining banks in the country.

44. Both the Life Insurance Corporation of India (LIC) and the General Insurance Corporation of India (GIC) were created as a result of nationalization policies followed by various governments. The former was created in 1956 by Jawaharlal Nehru; the latter was set up as a parent organization for all general insurance companies in the country by Indira Gandhi in 1971. The main "development" financial institutions created by the government were the Industrial Development Bank of India (IDBI), the Industrial Finance Corporation of India (IFCI), and the Industrial Credit and Investment Corporation of India (ICICI).

45. In the case of Escorts and DCM, the government controlled about 52 percent and 45 percent of the total shares, respectively. See H. P. Nanda, *The Days of My Years* (New Delhi: Viking, 1992), 114.

46. Comparable figures for the period 1981–1990 were as follows: 57 percent of the total number of Indian emigrants with declared occupations were highly skilled professionals, accounting for 13.4 percent of total number of such professionals admitted into the United States, at a time when India's share of the total immigration to the United States was around 3.6 percent. See Deepak Nayyar, *Migration, Remittances and Capital Flows* (Delhi: Oxford University Press, 1994), 21–22.

47. For a detailed discussion of the many aspects of this act and a broader discussion of the regulation of foreign investment in India, see Suma Athreye and Sandeep Kapur, "Private Foreign Investment in India: Pain or Panacea?" *World Economy* 24, no. 3 (2001): 399–424, esp. 402–403.

48. The importance of FERA as a statement of the continuing strength of the Indian state to control foreign interventions in its economy becomes even more obvious when one takes into account the debacle of the 1965–1966 economic crisis. For a discussion of this period, see R. Mohan, "Industrial Policy and Control, in *The Indian Economy: Prospects and Problems*, ed. Bimal Jalan, 85–115 (New Delhi: Penguin, 1982).

49. For a more detailed account of this crisis, see Praveen K. Chaudhry, Vijay L. Kelkar, and Vikash Yadav, "The Evolution of 'Homegrown Conditionality' in India-IMF Relations," *Journal of Development Studies* 40, no. 6 (2004): 59–81. For a broader contextualization of this crisis in the history of Indian economic debates, see Francine Frankel, *India's Political Economy: 1947–1977* (Princeton, NJ: Princeton University Press, 1978); I. G. Patel, *Glimpses of Indian Economic Policy: An Insider's View* (Oxford: Oxford University Press, 2002).

50. The logic of the changes proposed in the new five-year plan announced in 1981 was quite simple: by unilaterally adopting the measures the IMF would attach to

its loans prior to officially acquiring such loans, the Indian state could maintain its claim of being sovereign and not bowing to any external pressure. Scholars have characterized the strategy of preempting IMF requirements for a loan as the development of "homegrown conditionalities." For more on this subject, see Chaudhry, Kelkar, and Yadav, "The Evolution of 'Homegrown Conditionality' in India-IMF Relations."

51. Prior to asking for the loan, Indian officials held discussions with representatives of the IMF in a series of unpublicized meetings in New Delhi, Kuwait, and Libreville, Gabon, to make sure that the "homegrown" structural adjustment program met with the fund's approval and would be sufficient to acquire a precautionary loan. For further details on these meetings, see Chaudhry, Kelkar, and Yadav, "The Evolution of 'Homegrown Conditionality' in India-IMF Relations." See also J. M. Boughton, *Silent Revolution: The International Monetary Fund, 1979–1989* (Washington, DC: IMF, 2001).

52. Even prior to this crisis, the Indian government had started considering the idea that the NRIs could be a potential source of investment capital, while making sure that resident Indian businessmen were part of the ongoing deliberations about the conditions under which NRIs should be allowed to invest in India. To explore this possibility, FICCI and the Indian government sent joint delegations to Europe and the United States to hold talks with prominent businessmen of Indian origin. In fact, H. P. Nanda, the CEO of Escorts, was part of two such delegations (both led by commerce secretaries: P. C. Alexander in 1979 and Abid Hussain in 1980) to the United Kingdom that held meetings with a group of NRIs, including Swraj Paul.

53. Details of the scheme presented in the budget were reiterated in parliamentary discussions over the next two years. For a brief description of the scheme, see the statement by Finance Minister Pranab Mukherjee, "Reported Irregularities in Investments by Non-Resident Indians in Reliance Textiles," *Lok Sabha Debates*, December 14, 1983.

54. Escorts was founded by businessman H. P. Nanda in the aftermath of the partition of the Indian subcontinent in 1947.

55. DCM (the Delhi Cloth and General Mills) was one of the oldest companies based in New Delhi, founded by the well-known businessman Lala Shri Ram, who was one of the signatories of the Bombay Plan. After his death in 1970, the company's management passed into the hands of his two sons, Bharat Ram and Charat Ram, who seldom saw eye-to-eye. During the early period of the takeover, the general speculation in the Indian business community was that the share prices were being driven up by familial strife.

56. In 1983, the public financial institutions held 41.57 percent and 52.01 percent of the paid-up equity capital of DCM Ltd. and Escorts Ltd., respectively. Statement by Finance Minister Pranab Mukherjee, *Lok Sabha Debates*, December 2, 1983.

57. UTI was a mutual funds company controlled by the Government of India.

58. Most of these companies did not have paid-up capital of more than £25,000. Paul also borrowed £13 million from Barclays Bank in London that was then transferred to the Punjab National Bank in India to make funds available to his brokers.

59. Escorts shares rose from Rs. 40 in mid-February to Rs. 80 by May. During the same period, the price of DCM shares went up from Rs. 35 to Rs. 66 before finally plateauing at an all-time high of Rs. 90.

60. J. R. D. Tata had been one of the few Indian industrialists who had expressed reservations about the NRI investment scheme from the beginning, pointing out that it could easily be misused not only by NRIs but also by unscrupulous Indian businessmen who could launder their money and get higher returns by taking it out of the country and bringing it back under the cloak of legitimate NRI investment.

61. Cited in H. P. Nanda, *The Days of My Years*, 104.

62. Ibid., 105–107.

63. Ibid., 118.

64. Ibid., 127.

65. Nanda claims in his memoirs that all his meetings with the finance minister during this period ended with the minister accusing him of "scuttling his non-resident portfolio investment scheme." Ibid., 130.

66. To present a comprehensive picture, I have distilled the main issues from debates that took place in the Rajya Sabha and Lok Sabha in August and December 1983.

67. The Bharat Ratna is the highest civilian honor given by the Government of India. See Discussion Re: Reported Investment in Indian Industries and Takeover Bids of Indian Companies by Certain Non-Resident Indians, *Lok Sabha Debates*, August 24, 1983 (translation mine).

68. Madhu Dandavate, Discussion Re: Reported Investment in Indian Industries and Takeover Bids of Indian Companies by Certain Non-Resident Indians, *Lok Sabha Debates*, August 24, 1983.

69. "We don't want to take loans from the IMF and the World Bank. But, we should definitely encourage persons of Indian origin to invest in India's development." V. C. Jain, Discussion Re: Reported Investment in Indian Industries and Takeover Bids of Indian Companies by Certain Non-Resident Indians, *Lok Sabha Debates*, August 24, 1983 (translation mine).

70. Statement by Pranab Mukherjee, Minister of Finance, Discussion Re: Reported Investment in Indian Industries and Takeover Bids of Indian Companies by Certain Non-Resident Indians, *Lok Sabha Debates*, August 24, 1983.

71. Response by Minister of Finance to a question by Madhu Dandavate, *Lok Sabha Debates*, August 26, 1983.

72. Madhu Dandavate, Reported Irregularities in Investments by Non-Resident Indians in Reliance Textiles, *Lok Sabha Debates*, December 14, 1983.

73. Chitta Basu, Reported Irregularities in Investments by Non-Resident Indians in Reliance Textiles, *Lok Sabha Debates*, December 14, 1983.

74. Bhogendra Jha, Discussion Re: Reported Investment in Indian Industries and Takeover Bids of Indian Companies by Certain Non-Resident Indians, *Lok Sabha Debates*, August 24, 1983.

75. K. P. Unnikrishnan, Discussion Re: Reported Investment in Indian Industries and Takeover Bids of Indian Companies by Certain Non-Resident Indians, *Lok Sabha Debates*, August 24, 1983.

76. Pranab Mukherjee, Discussion Re: Reported Investment in Indian Industries and Takeover Bids of Indian Companies by Certain Non-Resident Indians, *Lok Sabha Debates*, August 24, 1983.

77. Pranab Mukherjee, Reported Irregularities in Investments by Non-Resident Indians in Reliance Textiles, *Lok Sabha Debates*, December 14, 1983.

78. Somnath Chatterjee, Reported Irregularities in Investments by Non-Resident Indians in Reliance Textiles, *Lok Sabha Debates*, December 14, 1983.

79. K. Lakappa, Discussion Re: Reported Investment in Indian Industries and Takeover Bids of Indian Companies by Certain Non-Resident Indians, *Lok Sabha Debates*, August 24, 1983 (translation mine).

80. This figure, cited by several members of the parliament during the course of the debates, was a highly stretched approximation. While the stake of the public financial institutions in the top industrial concerns in India ranged from 40 to 60 percent, it was true that the "founder families" controlled the management, despite being the minority shareholders in most concerns.

81. G. V. Vyas (MP, Bhilwada), Discussion Re: Reported Investment in Indian Industries and Takeover Bids of Indian Companies by Certain Non-Resident Indians, *Lok Sabha Debates*, August 24, 1983 (translation mine).

82. These arguments are summarized from the parliamentary debates that took place in 1983 and 1984 on the issue of NRI investments.

83. As is obvious by the parliamentary discussions regarding this issue throughout the late 1970s and 1980s, Indian governments were so eager to encourage this migration that they often overlooked the unscrupulous tactics adopted by recruiting agencies. Without delving too deeply into the question of its social merits, it is safe to point out that this migration did have a positive impact on the Indian economy in general and on that of Kerala in particular.

84. As the current *Handbook for Overseas Indians*, released by the Ministry of Overseas Indian Affairs, makes obvious, the term itself did not have an official definition until the passage of the Foreign Exchange Management Act in 1999. See *Handbook for Overseas Indians* (New Delhi: Ministry of Overseas Indian Affairs, 2009).

Chapter 5

1. Manmohan Singh, General Budget 1991, *Lok Sabha Debates*, July 24, 1991.

2. I have summarized P. V. Narasimha Rao's statements on the question of economic liberalization from speeches he gave during his tenure as the Indian prime minister. For a full text of the speeches, see *P. V. Narasimha Rao: Selected Speeches* (New Delhi: Ministry of Information and Broadcasting, 1995).

3. The notion of India being in a precarious situation, as well as the idea that the withdrawal of deposits by NRIs was in some way a contributing factor, is all-pervasive in public and media discussions from this period. This particular quote is from Manmohan Singh's budget speech.

4. All the quotes in this paragraph are from Prime Minister Vajpayee's inaugural address at the first Pravasi Bharatiya Divas celebrations, January 9, 2003. See http://www.indiaday.org/pbd1/pbd_PM.asp.

5. As has been noted earlier, the political parties that have formed governments in India in the past two decades have included those like the BJP that had vociferously opposed neoliberal restructuring when it was introduced in 1991 but continued with those policies when in power.

6. For a similar argument about the critical role of the "new breed of Indian entrepreneurs," see Jorgen D. Pederson, "Explaining Economic Liberalization in India: State and Society Perspectives," *World Development* 28, no. 2 (2000): 265–282.

7. Aihwa Ong, *Flexible Citizenship: The Cultural Logics of Transnationality* (Durham: Duke University Press, 1999).

8. This presentation was interrupted by the walkout of several prominent members of the opposition who claimed that the postponement of the regular budget was "an abdication of the [minister's] responsibility towards the country" at a time when the "situation was grim" and it had become imperative "to defend the economy." See Interim Budget, *Lok Sabha Debates*, March 4, 1991.

9. The budget deficit of the Central Government reached Rs. 13,000 crores, on 30th November 1990, as a consequence of revenue shortfalls and expenditure overruns. The Wholesale Price Index registered an increase of 8.5 per cent, while the Consumer Price Index rose by 11.9 per cent, during the last eight months of the current financial year. The sharp deterioration in the balance of payments situation led to a rapid depletion of foreign exchange reserves, which dropped to Rs. 3142 crores at the end of November 1990 and this sum was not even sufficient to finance imports for one month. Interim Budget, *Lok Sabha Debates*, March 4, 1991.

10. This was done in part by not putting in place any new measure that might lead to a greater institutionalization of India's relationship with the diaspora. Responding to a question regarding NRI investments in parliament on February 22, 1991, Finance Minister Yashwant Sinha referred to the 1982 provisions as framing the government's policies toward NRIs. While claiming that these policies were being constantly reviewed by the government "in the light of suggestions received from different quarters including NRIs and NRI organizations," Sinha made it clear that NRI investments were too minimal to have any impact on the Indian economy. See Written Answers to Question Re. Investment by NRIs, *Lok Sabha Debates*, February 22, 1991.

11. In April 1987, a left-of-center government under Timoti Bavadra came to power with the declaration that it would end discrimination against Indians. Within a matter of months, this government was overthrown in a military coup led by

General Sitaveni Rabuka. Though the general ceded power to civilian authorities, he remained the power behind the throne until he became the premier of Fiji in 1992.

12. Speech by K. Natwar Singh at the 42nd Session (16th Plenary meeting) of the United Nations General Assembly, September 29, 1987, http://www.un.int/india/ind186.htm.

13. In this case, India's representations actually led to the suspension of Fiji's Commonwealth membership.

14. For more details see, P. Sahadevan, *India and Overseas Indians: The Case of Sri Lanka* (New Delhi: Kalinga, 1997).

15. Chandra Shekhar's tenure as prime minister was even briefer that that of V. P. Singh's. The SJP-led government was in power from 10 November 10, 1990, to June 20, 1991, when it was brought down as a result of a no confidence motion instigated by the Congress. In the meanwhile, the assassination of Rajiv Gandhi by the Liberation Tigers of Tamil Eelam (LTTE) on May 21, 1991, led to a shift in the balance of power within the Congress, with P. V. Narasimha Rao emerging as the new leader of the party.

16. Two IMF loans were drawn during July 1990 and January 1991, amounting to Rs 1,173 crores and Rs 3,334 crores, respectively, by the V. P. Singh government and the Chandra Shekhar government.

17. At one point, nearly $80 million was being withdrawn by NRIs every week. For details on NRIs withdrawals and the 1991 crisis, see "What Price NRI Deposits?" *Business Line*, July 31 2004, at http://www.thehindubusinessline.com/2004/07/31/stories/2004073100071000.htm; see also James Gordon and Poonam Gupta, "Non-Resident Deposits in India: In Search of Return?" *Economic and Political Weekly*, September 11, 2004, 4165–4174.

18. The devaluation of the Indian rupee had occurred immediately after the first two wars with Pakistan in 1949 and 1966, respectively.

19. Manmohan Singh, General Budget 1991, *Lok Sabha Debates*, July 24, 1991.

20. Ibid. In language that was remarkably similar to that used by Yashwant Sinha less than four months prior, he claimed that the "room for manoueuvre [*sic*], to live on borrowed money or time, does not exist any more" and that any "further postponement of macro-adjustment, long-overdue would mean that the balance of payments situation, now exceedingly difficult, would become unmanageable and inflation, already high, would exceed limits of tolerance."

21. Unless otherwise noted, all quotations in this section are from Manmohan Singh's budget speech to the Indian parliament on July 24, 1991.

22. In the sense that while the bonds were available for purchase only by NRIs, they could be (once bought) given as gifts to resident Indians, who would then also be exempt from paying any income tax on the returns from the bonds.

23. See, for instance, his description of the provisions in the budget regarding NRI investments in the housing sector: "At present *NRIs of foreign nationality* are required to obtain specific permission under section 31 of the Foreign Exchange

Regulation Act (FERA) to acquire residential property. It is now proposed to provide general exemption from this provision to such persons."

24. That the "commercial class" did make the "Congress its own" is now a matter of historical record. However, the crux of Gandhi's speech—his faith in the abilities, the commitment, and the interests of the "commercial class"—is quite remarkable in that it makes the need for any scholarly analysis of the relationship between the Indian bourgeoisie and the Congress almost redundant. FICCI presents this relationship as a straightforward matter-of-fact statement about its long-standing commitment to the nation in its Web site. An earlier version of this online history played up the relationship of the organization to the nationalist movement, and especially to Mahatma Gandhi in a much more explicit manner. The current version however, has no reference to either Gandhi or his speech to the 4th Annual Session of FICCI on April 27, 1931. For a reference to the speech that cites the FICCI Web site as a source, see http://www.fccionline.com/. For a brief description of FICCI's history, see http://www.ficci.com/about-ficci.asp.

25. For details about the emergence of business associations in India, see Stanley A. Kochanek, *Business and Politics in India* (Berkeley: University of California Press, 1974), particularly the last four chapters.

26. As we saw earlier, some of these differences expressed in the publication of opposing documents, like the Bombay manifesto and the Bombay Plan, did play out in public.

27. As Stanley Kochanek points out, from the very beginning, FICCI was dominated by representatives from Bombay and Calcutta—the two major centers of trade and industry at that time. The friction between these two groups has indeed been well documented. However, while never necessarily completely united, the groups did manage to work within FICCI until the 1960s, when the Bombay group led by the Tatas and the Mafatlals (two of India's most prominent industrial houses) broke away from the institution. See Kochanek, *Business and Politics in India*. See also Stanley Kochanek, "The Transformation of Interest Politics in India" *Pacific Affairs* 68, no. 4 (1995–96): 529–550.

28. For a detailed overview of this factional strife, see Kochanek, "The Transformation of Interest Politics in India," particularly 532–539.

29. Ibid., 543. The thirty-seven JBCs not only acted as "forums for the discussion of trade, investment, technology transfer and other issues of concern to private sector domestic and international business" but also provided "easy access to ministers and top decision makers." As such, the attempt by FICCI and ASSOCHAM to take control of these bodies was a perfectly understandable move.

30. Ibid. In demanding reconciliation between the warring factions, the Indian government was itself responding to the angry pressure from foreign businessmen who were confused about which organization had the government's imprimatur.

31. On the rise of this new group, see Pederson, "Explaining Economic Liberalization in India"; and Kochanek, "The Transformation of Interest Politics in India."

32. Kochanek, "The Transformation of Interest Politics in India," 545.

33. Pederson, "Explaining Economic Liberalization in India," 270. On the relationship between the CII and the Indian government of the day, see Aseema Sinha, "Understanding the Rise and Transformation of Business Collective Action in India," *Business and Politics* 7, no. 2 (2005).

34. As Aseema Sinha points out, Rajiv Gandhi's patronage went a long way in helping validate the position of AIEI (and later, CII) as the top business association in the country, despite its lack of a storied past like FICCI. The invitation for AIEI members to accompany him to the Soviet Union as part of the prime minister's entourage, against the wishes of the Indian ambassador to the USSR, who protested the inclusion of private businessmen in a state delegation, is a good illustration of the continued patronage. While Sinha's carefully researched study focuses on Gandhi's own "clean" image and "reformist agenda" to explain his support for the AIEI, it is vital to not lose sight of the broader international context, which facilitated the rise of organizations favoring liberalization. See Sinha, "Understanding the Rise and Transformation of Business Collective Action in India."

35. *Economic Times* (New Delhi), February 7, 1993, cited in Kochanek, "The Transformation of Interest Politics in India," 545.

36. As the debates surrounding economic reforms unfolded within the Indian parliament, the AIEI/CII held meetings with nearly half the sitting members to persuade them of the necessity and value of neoliberal restructuring. See Kochanek, "The Transformation of Interest Politics in India," 547.

37. Pederson, "Explaining Economic Liberalization in India."

38. The relationship of various political parties to the liberalization program is, however, much more complicated than simple and clear obvious support or opposition along party lines. The extreme right (constituted by parties like the Rashtriya Swayamsevak Sangh and the Swadeshi Jagran Manch) and the extreme left (the Communist Party of India—Marxist-Leninist) have remained fervent in their opposition to liberalization. However, parties like the Bharatiya Janata Party (BJP) and the Communist Party of India-Marxist (CPI-M) have, despite initial protest on ideological grounds, themselves been involved in liberalizing measures when in power.

39. Chandrajeet Yadav, Discussion re: General Budget, *Lok Sabha Debates*, July 30, 1991.

40. Ibid.

41. The quote is from a speech made by Rao, in which he claimed that his government would accord primacy to the public sector because of its many accomplishments. Parts of this speech, along with those made by Rajiv Gandhi, were cited by CPI (M) leader Indrajit Gupta during the debate. See Indrajit Gupta, Discussions Re. General Budget, *Lok Sabha Debates*, July 31, 1991.

42. Ibid.

43. Nirmal Kanti Chatterjee, Discussions Re. General Budget, *Lok Sabha Debates*, July 30, 1991.

44. One member declaimed: "The government should take some effective steps for the upliftment of the poor and removing unemployment amongst the youth.... Steps should be taken to bridge the gap [between the urban and rural areas] and instill confidence among the people of the country. This was the Nehruvian model.... Now we have drifted from the Nehruvian model to Manmohan Singh's model. This is the beginning of a dangerous model." Chandra Jeet Yadav, Discussions Re. General Budget, *Lok Sabha Debates*, July 30, 1991. Drawing a link between the Indian prince who granted special trading rights to the East India Company in the eighteenth century and the Congress government that introduced liberalization in 1991, another member remarked during a later debate, "When Mir Jaffer allowed East India Company to carry business in India, he did not visualize the political ramifications of it. He thought it was just a trading company." See Bhogendra Jha, *Lok Sabha Debates*, September 14, 1991.

45. Anantrao Deshmukh, Discussions Re. General Budget, *Lok Sabha Debates*, July 31, 1991.

46. Geeta Mukherjee, Discussions Re. General Budget, *Lok Sabha Debates*, August 5, 1991.

47. Indrajit Gupta, Discussions Re. General Budget, *Lok Sabha Debates*, July 31, 1991.

48. Ibid.

49. While the accuracy of the figures cited is debatable, this claim resonated with the dominant public discourse surrounding NRIs in the immediate aftermath of the 1991 economic crisis. As the parliamentary debates and media discussions in that period make obvious, the withdrawal of deposits by NRIs was seen as keeping with a pattern of this group looking out for its own interests at the cost of the broader interests of the Indian nation. See K. P. Reddiah Yadav, Demands for Grants (General) 1991–92, *Lok Sabha Debates*, August 21, 1991.

50. S. B. Singh, Discussions Re. General Budget, *Lok Sabha Debates*, August 1, 1991.

51. Manoranjan Bhakta, Discussions Re. General Budget, *Lok Sabha Debates*, July 31, 1991.

52. In fact, some declared, with a rather convoluted logic, that it was not the acceptance of IMF loans per se that they had a problem with, but rather the acceptance of conditionalities that dictated the path India needed to take.

53. The reference to the 1980s was an important counter to the government's claim that the gravity of the economic crisis was in part due to the mismanagement of economic affairs by the two previous non-Congress governments. As one opposition member put it: "The Hon. Finance Minister may think over it seriously as [the] year 1980 should be taken as water-shed so far as the economic policy of this country is concerned because it was the beginning of the downfall, wrong policies, arbitrary import, country's approach to the IMF for loans. It did not begin in 1990 nor in the end of 1989 nor in the non-Congress Government period ... all this began when the

Congress was in power. All these steps taken during their rule are the main reasons for this crisis." Chandrajeet Yadav, Discussion re: General Budget, *Lok Sabha Debates*, July 30, 1991.

54. Devi Prosad Pal, Discussion re: General Budget, *Lok Sabha Debates*, July 30, 1991.

55. Ibid.

56. The budget debates of 1991 are peppered with references to the "changing global balance of power," with both opponents and supporters citing the end of the Cold War as the context that made possible the proposal of economic liberalization in India.

57. Devi Prosad Pal, Discussion re: General Budget, *Lok Sabha Debates*, July 30, 1991.

58. Ibid.

59. As expected, the government's claim of "continuity with change" was attacked by all sections of the opposition. For instance, Jaswant Singh, a stalwart of the right-wing BJP demanded to know how it was possible for "continuity" and "change" to go hand in hand, while Nirmal Kanti Chatterjee of the Communist Party of India declared that "continuity" emphasized the connections to the worst aspects of Nehruvian socialism (the alliance with the capitalists), while the "change" referred to the opening up of new markets to the profit seekers. See *Lok Sabha Debates*, July 30, 1991.

60. See, for instance, Partha Chatterjee, *Nationalist Thought and the Colonial World: A Derivative Discourse* (Minneapolis: University of Minnesota Press, 1993); Aditya Mukherjee, *Imperialism, Nationalism and the Making of the Indian Capitalist Class, 1920–1947* (New Delhi: Sage, 2002); Himadeep Muppidi, *The Politics of the Global* (Minneapolis: University of Minnesota Press, 2004).

61. Muppidi, *The Politics of the Global.*

62. See R. C. Dutt, *The Economic History of India*, 2nd ed., vols. 1 and 2 (London: Kegan Paul, Trench, Trubner, 1906). See also Nehru, *The Discovery of India* (New Delhi: Penguin, 2004), 302.

63. Two examples are illustrative of this point. In 1977, George Fernandes—the industries minister in the Janata cabinet and a staunch advocate of *swadeshi*—led a huge battle against Coca-Cola and IBM. Arguing that the two multinational corporations had violated Indian investment rules, Fernandes succeeded in "kicking them" out of India. As shown in the previous chapter, the general distrust of foreign investors was equally obvious in the controversy surrounding Swraj Paul's investments in Escorts and DCM in 1983.

64. For a more detailed discussion of this episode, see Praveen K. Chaudhry, Vijay L. Kelkar, and Vikash Yadav, "The Evolution of 'Homegrown Conditionality' in India-IMF Relations," *Journal of Development Studies* 40, no. 6 (2004): 59–81.

65. Nirmal Kanti Chatterjee, Discussions Re. General Budget, *Lok Sabha Debates*, July 30, 1991.

66. On the recommendation of Finance Minister Manmohan Singh, the AIEI/CII organized forums for parliamentary parties that were aimed at popularizing the ideas behind the reforms, emphasizing both their value and necessity. See Sinha, "Understanding the Rise and Transformation of Business Collective Action," 11.

67. M. C. Lall, *India's Missed Opportunity: India's Relationship with the Non-Resident Indians* (Aldershot, UK: Ashgate, 2001), 206.

68. E. Ahamed, Demands for Grants (General) 1991–92, *Lok Sabha Debates*, August 21, 1991.

69. Ibid.

70. The entire debate on the question of economic liberalization in the Indian parliament was peppered with references to Indians becoming "beggars," going with a begging bowl to the IMF, and needing to accept the conditionalities since beggars could not afford to be choosers. See, for instance, Discussions on the General Budget, *Lok Sabha Debates*, July 30–31, 1991.

71. Conflating the IMF and World Bank in an impassioned, albeit slightly confused, defense of the government, Congress MP Murli Deora declared: "The World Bank always advocates to reduce corporate tax. On the other hand, the Finance Minister has increased the corporate tax. Is this following the IMF advice? The IMF always wants to reduce food subsidy. The Finance Minister has increased the subsidy on food. It is said that the expenditure on the anti-poverty programmes of the Government of India must be curtailed and reduced. But the Finance Minister has increased it." Exhorting the government to defend its interactions with the IMF, he further stated, "If they have come to our rescue, there is nothing wrong in it. If some of the measures suggested by them are good for our economy, we must accept them. If they are not good for us, we must reject them." See Discussions on the General Budget, *Lok Sabha Debates*, August 1, 1991.

72. Manmohan Singh, General Budget 1991–91, *Lok Sabha Debates*, July 24, 1991.

73. P. V. Narasimha Rao, Demands for Grants (Gen.) 1991–92, *Lok Sabha Debates*, August 26. 1991.

74. Ibid.

75. Chidanand Rajghatta, *The Horse That Flew* (New Delhi: HarperCollins, 2001).

76. Ibid., 27. The Silicon Valley refers to a section of the San Francisco Bay Area, home to the largest concentration of high-tech firms in North America. However, the moniker first coined in 1971 by journalist Dan Hoefler (who used it in a series of articles he was writing on the electronic firms mushrooming in Santa Clara), despite occupying a prominent place in popular discourse, is not marked on any "map, road sign or statue." Silicon Valley, as Rajghatta argues, exists "only in the mind."

77. Ibid., 31–32.

78. Ibid. In their endeavors, they were helped by "some of the early Indians" who occupied "key positions in US academic circles." These included Amar Bose at MIT,

Tom Kailath at Stanford, C. K. N. Patel at Bell Labs, and the two Nobel laureates Hargobind Khurana (at MIT) and S. Chandrasekhar (at Chicago). The last two, Rajghatta claims, "were widely known and admired," despite being "scientists more than techies."

79. To put it differently, the NRI businessman was precisely the kind of entrepreneur the AIEI/CII claimed to represent.

80. M. C. Lall, *India's Missed Opportunity*, especially chapters 7 and 8.

81. To arrive at this contention, Lall starts with the extremely questionable claim that "a great deal of national pride rests in the fact of being an Indian from India with an intact caste." As I have shown in the two previous chapters, issues of nation and national pride had little to do with the question of "intact caste." Furthermore, while I agree with Lall's general claims that the diaspora was seen as having made the choice to dissociate from India (in the context of Nehru's stand on citizenship) and that the potential involvement of NRIs in the Indian economy was viewed with suspicion, I would argue that "ostracism" does not capture the essence of this relationship.

82. M. C. Lall, *India's Missed Opportunity*, 193.

83. It should, however, be noted that since 1991, remittances to India have increased steadily. In 1991, remittances from overseas Indians were around $2.1 billion. According to the World Bank, in 2007 India received $27 billion from its migrants, becoming the largest global recipient of remittances. By that logic—which is in many ways the extension of Lall's argument regarding economic rationality—one could argue that far from being a "missed opportunity," the Indian state has indeed succeeded in attracting at least foreign exchange from its migrant community. See Dilip Ratha and Zhimei Xu, *The Migrations and Remittances Factbook 2008*, at http://econ.worldbank.org/WBSITE/EXTERNAL/EXTDEC/EXTDECPROSPECTS/0,,contentMDK:21352016~pagePK:64165401~piPK:64165026~theSitePK:476883,00.html.

84. Manmohan Singh, Remittances of Foreign Exchange and Investment in Foreign Exchange Bonds, *Lok Sabha Debates*, September 11, 1991.

85. Ibid.

86. Following the introduction of the reforms budget in 1991, the Indian government liberalized gold imports (1992) and rolled back its currency controls (1993). Both measures were seen as exceedingly important in ensuring a steady growth of remittances. In 2000, the Indian government replaced the now highly criticized Foreign Exchange Regulation Act (FERA) with the Foreign Exchange Management Act (FEMA), which relaxed controls on foreign exchange transactions. This in turn has resulted in more NRIs being willing to place money into rupee accounts, which are also counted as part of the total remittances. See Muzaffar Chisti, "The Rise in Remittances to India," February 2007, Migration Policy Institute, at http://www.migrationinformation.org/Feature/display.cfm?id=577.

87. In that sense, the relationship between cause and effect is far more complex than a linear, teleological progression. The 1991 balance of payments crisis was

indeed a trigger that forced the adoption of a neoliberal structural adjustment program, which in turn required the diasporic reimagining of the nation. However, it is important to keep in mind that the relationship between the neoliberal restructuring of the state and the diasporic reimagining of the nation is not a simple unidirectional one of cause and effect. The successful rearticulation of the boundaries of the nation enables the continuation of neoliberal restructuring in a way that does not undermine the legitimacy of the ruling elites.

88. One important site was the blockbusters from the mainstream Hindi film industry (known in popular discourse as "Bollywood") during this period, which were not just geared toward a "global Indian" audience, but dominated by the figure of the NRI. Though framed within conventional boy-meets-girl narratives, these lavishly produced movies were self-conscious attempts to articulate what constituted India or Indianness. What makes this process interesting is that Hindi cinema has always been an important site for the production and reproduction of dominant discourses of the Indian nation-state. For instance, the Nehruvian era was dominated by movies made around themes such as the building of the "temples of modern India," the eradication of superstition, the education of villagers, and the spread of science and technology from the urban to the rural areas. In the 1970s, a growing dissatisfaction with the governing elite among the masses was reflected in movies that focused on the betrayal of the nationalist movement by corrupt politicians, a theme that was embodied in the figure of the "angry young man" who fought against the system. In the 1990s, this figure was replaced by that of the NRI—who despite being raised in a foreign land (usually, Great Britain or the United States) revealed his Indianness through his commitment to a certain set of values. See Jigna Desai, *Beyond Bollywood: The Cultural Politics of South Asian Diasporic Films* (New York: Routledge, 2003); Sumita Chakravarty, *National Identity in Indian Popular Cinema* (Austin: University of Texas Press, 1993); M. Madhava Prasad, *Ideology of the Hindi Film: A Historical Construction* (New York: Oxford University Press, 1998); Monika Mehta, "Selections: Cutting, Classifying and Certifying in Bombay Cinema" (PhD diss., University of Minnesota, 2001); and Jyotika Virdi, *The Cinematic Imagination: Indian Popular Films and Social History* (New Brunswick, NJ: Rutgers University Press, 2003).

89. The Congress government of P. V. Narasimha Rao ended its five-year term in 1996. The Congress suffered a defeat in the polls in large measure because of dissatisfaction with the liberalization program.

90. Here, I am paraphrasing a statement made by Indira Gandhi prior to the first set of nuclear tests carried out by India in 1974 (these tests were categorized as a "Peaceful Nuclear Explosion"): "India needs a demonstration." See Raja Ramanna, *Years of Pilgrimage* (Delhi: Viking, 1991), 89.

91. Press Release, Ministry of External Affairs, External Publicity Division, New Delhi, May 11, 1998.

92. In late 1995, the CIA detected signs of activity near the Pokhran range and alerted the Clinton administration to the possibility of an Indian nuclear test. The

Clinton administration responded by immediately mounting diplomatic pressure on India and spelling out in detail the implications that a nuclear test would have for the Indian economy. See World News, CNN interactive, May 12, 1998.

93. For a greater elaboration of this argument, see Latha Varadarajan, "Constructivism, Identity and Neoliberal [In]security," *Review of International Studies* 30, no. 3 (2004): 319–341.

94. In one of his early speeches to the Constituent Assembly, Nehru claimed that unlike "smaller countries," India could not be forced into alliances with "Great Powers," for "[After] all in the past, as a national movement, we opposed one of the greatest world powers. We opposed it in a particular way and in a large measure succeeded that way." See Jawaharlal Nehru, *India's Foreign Policy: Selected Speeches* (New Delhi: Publications Division, Ministry of Information and Broadcasting, 1961), 32.

95. Suo Moto statement by Prime Minister Atal Bihari Vajpayee in Parliament, May 27, 1998. See http://www.india.gov.

96. *Economist*, May 16, 1998, 38.

97. "Nobody can question our right to go ahead with this type of testing if we want to.... But, if some countries here and there talk in a way as if they are questioning our right, they have no business to do that." Indrajit Gupta (CPM); "The hands of the five nuclear weapons states are not clean. They have no business to pass judgment on us and no business to impose sanctions on us. If they do so, we will be with you to tighten our belts and march along with you to oppose those sanctions." Natwar Singh (Congress-I), *Lok Sabha Debates*, May 27, 1998.

98. Natwar Singh (Congress-I), *Lok Sabha Debates*, May 27, 1998.

99. "BJP's Search for Short-Cuts to Political Consolidation," *Economic and Political Weekly*, May 30 1998, 1299.

100. I say "in some way" because the interest rates on those bonds were an unusually high 8.5 percent. If indeed buying the bonds was an act of patriotism, it helped that the decision was economically sound. Many analysts have pointed out that a sizable portion of special bonds aimed at NRIs (such as the "Resurgent India Bonds" issued in 1998 and the "Millennium India Bonds" issued in 2000), once redeemed, have been retained in India, instead of being repatriated abroad in foreign currency. The retained amount is calculated as part of annual remittances, which in turn accounts for the sudden jump in "total remittances" for those particular years. The special bonds, however, are just part of the story. According to the Reserve Bank of India (RBI), "total remittances" are the sum of two kinds of flows: inward remittances (i.e., the direct transfer of funds from one person living abroad to another in India via a bank or wire transfer) and local withdrawals from NRI deposits (deposits set up under schemes authorized by the Government of India since the 1970s). The RBI permits the NRI deposits to be held either in foreign currency denominations or in Indian rupees. In the latter case, any funds that the NRIs withdraw from rupee-denominated deposits are counted as remittances. What makes this particular type of transaction important is that they—rather than direct, inward remittances—largely

account for the increase in total remittances in India. This, in turn, has led some analysts to argue that India's remittance boom "is largely a massive withdrawal surge." See Muzaffar Chisti, "The Rise in Remittances to India."

101. S. Gurumurthy, "India Does Not Need FDI, but China Needs it!" at http://news.indiainfo.com/2004/07/20/guru.html.

102. Press Release, Ministry of External Affairs, Government of India, August 18, 2000.

103. In 1989, the National Federation of Indian American Associations organized the first-ever convention of people of Indian origin. One of the resolutions adopted during the convention resulted in the formation of the "Global Organization of People of Indian Origin," with its declared objective of "increasing communication and cooperation between Indians living in different countries." For a detailed description of the annual meetings of this organization and its interactions with the Indian state, see http://www.gopio.net.

104. This point was reiterated by all members of the High Committee during the course of interviews conducted in New Delhi between January and April 2002. An entire section of the High Committee's final report is devoted to a study of "Other Diasporas." See chapter 23, "Other Diasporas: A Global Perspective," in *Report of the High Level Committee on the Indian Diaspora* (New Delhi: Indian Council of World Affairs, 2001).

105. The significance of this date was not lost on commentators, who quickly pointed out that it marked the anniversary of the return of the "most famous NRI"— Mahatma Gandhi—from South Africa. As government representatives claimed, in celebrating that day as Pravasi Bhratiya Diwas, the Indian nation-state was acknowledging the immense contribution of people of Indian origin in the creation of modern India.

106. The participation of FICCI in these celebrations is, of course, significant, given its position in 1991. Though the CII had taken the lead in pushing for economic reform, FICCI did not disappear from the scene. The reinvigoration of FICCI under new leadership resulted in its playing a role as important as that of the CII in sustaining and furthering the neoliberal agenda through the 1990s. While eminently capable of working in tandem, the two organizations, however, did maintain distinct identities. In 2002, the CII leadership deviated from its normal script of never publicly criticizing the government of the day to protest the communal policies of the BJP-led government in Gujarat. Though CII General Secretary Tarun Das attempted to smooth over the incident by visiting Gujarat and offering his personal apologies to Chief Minister Narendra Modi (the man widely believed to have orchestrated the communal riots), there was a distinct cooling of relations between the association and the ruling party. This perhaps was one of the reasons FICCI, and not CII, was chosen as cohost of the celebrations of Pravasi Bharatiya Divas. On the CII's relationship with the ruling party, see Sinha, "Understanding the Rise and Transformation of Business Collective Action in India," 13. For an analysis of the ways in which the

Pravasi Bharatiya Divas celebrations marked a serious attempt by the Indian state to consciously merge the categories of NRI and PIO to produce a singular historic narrative of "success" for the Indian diaspora, see Bakirathi Mani and Latha Varadarajan, "'The Largest Gathering of the Global Indian Family': Neoliberalism, Nationalism and Diaspora at Pravasi Bharatiya Divas," *Diaspora* 14, no. 1 (2005): 45–73.

107. For an argument that highlights the ways in which the emphasis on "professional success" enables the Indian state to maintain a distinction between different categories of the Indian diaspora, especially the preindependence and postindependence diaspora, even while asserting the existence of a unified "Indian" diasporic subject, see Jen Dickinson and Adrian J. Bailey, "(Re)membering Diaspora: Uneven Geographies of Indian Dual Citizenship," *Political Geography* 26 (2007): 757–774, especially 765–766.

108. Inaugural speech by Prime Minister Atal Bihari Vajpayee, Pravasi Bharatiya Diwas, January 9–11 2003, at http://www.indiandiaspora.nic.in/ch2.pdf.

109. *India Today (International)*, Special Issue, January 13, 2003.

110. The cover of the magazine featured the now-deceased U.S. astronaut of Indian origin, Kalpana Chawla.

111. *Lok Sabha Debates*, Vol. 31, May 4, 1964.

112. Quoted in Narayan Keshaven, "Swadeshi goes global," *Outlook*, April 27, 1998, 45.

113. The initial list included countries in Europe, North America, and Australasia but excluded countries in Southeast Asia, Africa, and the Middle East that had a substantial population of Indian origin. For a detailed list of the countries, see http://indiandiaspora.nic.in/DUALCITIZENSHIP.htm.

114. While the Overseas Indian Citizenship (OIC) does not automatically evolve into full citizenship, the Dual Citizenship (Amendment) Bill does provide the option to transition from OIC to Indian citizenship after a period of five years.

115. In practice, this rule has extended Overseas Indian Citizenship to PIO residing in Spain, Russia, Nigeria, and Lebanon while working to exclude those PIO who reside in Pakistan and Bangladesh, as well as those in Fiji, Malaysia, Singapore, and Trinidad and Tobago. For a detailed description of the newly amended Overseas Indian Citizenship Act, see Ministry of Home Affairs at http://www.mha.nic.in/uniquepage.asp?Id_Pk=553, especially http://www.mha.nic.in/pdfs/intro.pdf and http://www.mha.nic.in/pdfs/oci-faq.pdf.

116. See "Overseas Citizenship of India" at http://www.mha.nic.in/pdfs/intro.pdf, especially 3 (iii).

117. The word *vansh* literally means "dynasty," generally rooted in a particular territory. *Vanshi* refers to those whose roots can be traced back to that dynasty, those who are "of" that dynasty, those who hail from that land. For the full text of the speech by Prime Minister Atal Bihari Vajpayee, see *The Second Pravasi Bharatiya Divas, January 9–11 2004* (New Delhi: Ministry of External Affairs and FICCI, 2004).

118. Ibid.

119. The extent of India's foreign exchange reserves was repeatedly mentioned as indicative of a triumphant economic turnaround. This is not surprising, given that the specter of the balance of payments crisis has haunted all discussions regarding the health of the Indian economy since 1991.

120. Speech by Minister of External Affairs Shri Yashwant Sinha, *The Second Pravasi Bharatiya Divas, January 9–11 2004* (New Delhi: Ministry of External Affairs and FICCI, 2004).

121. Speech by Atal Bihari Vajpayee, *The Second Pravasi Bharatiya Divas, January 9–11 2004*.

122. Ibid.

123. The All-India Anna Dravida Munnetra Kazhagam is a political party based in the southern state of Tamil Nadu. It has played an important role in the formation of coalition governments in the center since 1996.

124. A particularly egregious illustration is the speech made by L. M. Singhvi, the chairman of the High-Level Committee on the Indian Diaspora. Singhvi began his address by claiming that the prime minister's two words to the Indian diaspora— "Welcome home"—"came from the depths of the soul of Mother India," and he could only repeat them admiringly. In addition to praising "Atalji" as "the tallest statesman and peacemaker of our times, who is committed to peace on earth and the development goals of the so-called third world," Singhvi liberally peppered his speech with poetry written by Vajpayee, as well as his own poems (in the "national language, Hindi") that praised Vajpayee.

125. As late as April 2004 (four months after the Pravasi Bharatiya Divas), the main opposition party, the Congress, was willing to concede a BJP victory. While hoping for a better result than the 112 seats they had won in the thirteenth general elections (1999), party strategists did not believe that they could stem a BJP victory. See *Economist*, April 15, 2004.

126. The Lok Sabha ("The People's Assembly"), the lower house of the Indian parliament, has 545 seats. As per the provisions of the Indian constitution, the party that gains an absolute majority in the general elections (272 seats) forms the government. In the absence of any party gaining a majority (as has generally been the case since 1989), the parliament is considered to be hung, with alliances being one way out of the impasse.

127. Initially called the Ministry of NRI Affairs, the ministry was renamed the Ministry of Overseas Indian Affairs, following criticism that emphasis on the NRIs sent out wrong signals regarding the Indian state's understanding of the diaspora.

128. As briefly mentioned in chapter 3, the colonial state had established a Department of Overseas Indian Affairs in 1936. After independence, this department was absorbed into the Ministry of Commonwealth Affairs, with most of its tasks farmed out to other ministries, such as the Ministry of External Affairs (known commonly by its acronym, MEA).

Conclusion

1. The iPods, as the recipients were to discover, were preloaded with Indian music. See Mark Landler, "'India Everywhere' in the Alps," *New York Times*, January 26, 2006, at http://www.nytimes.com/2006/01/26/business/worldbusiness/26india.html.

2. The campaign at Davos was orchestrated by the India Brand Equity Foundation (IBEF) and had been specially created by the Confederation of Indian Industries in collaboration with the Indian government's Ministry of Commerce and Industry. For more on the IBEF, see http://www.ibef.org/aboutus.aspx.

3. The delegation included P. Chidambaram (the finance minister), Kamal Nath (the minister for commerce and industry), Montek Singh Alhuwalia (deputy chairman of the Planning Commission), Tarun Das (the former secretary general and now the "senior mentor" for the Confederation of Indian Industries), Nandan Nilekani (founder and CEO of Infosys), Mukesh Ambani (chairman of Reliance Industries and cochair of the World Economic Forum meeting, 2006), and Lakshmi Mittal (the Non-Resident Indian chairman of Mittal Steel). For a list of the members who comprised Team India (including "social entrepreneurs" and a somewhat incongruous single "spiritual leader"), see http://www.indiaeverywhere.com/DreamIndia.aspx.

4. Landler, "'India everywhere' in the Alps."

5. The official Web site of the campaign makes no bones about the fact that every step of the way was plotted carefully by the steering committee of business leaders, with the full backing of the Indian government. See http://www.indiaeverywhere.com/business_delegation.aspx.

6. Ajay Khanna, chief executive of India Brand Equity Foundation. Cited in Landler, "'India Everywhere' in the Alps."

7. Nandan Nilekani, chairman of Infosys. Cited in Landler, "'India Everywhere' in the Alps."

8. The agreements include commitments by Dell to build a PC-manufacturing facility in India and by Japanese investors to look into the power sector in India. See Manjeet Kripalani, "Selling India Inc. at Davos," *BusinessWeek*, January 30, 2006, at http://www.businessweek.com/bwdaily/dnflash/jan2006/nf20060130_4381_db032.htm.

9. Rebecca Myers, "The Face of India," *Time*, June 18, 2006, at http://www.time.com/time/magazine/article/0,9171,1207151,00.html.

10. Michael Elliot, "India Awakens," *Time*, June 26, 2006, at http://www.time.com/time/magazine/article/0,9171,1205374,00.html.

11. Alex Perry, "Shaking the Foundations," *Time*, June 19, 2006, at http://www.time.com/time/magazine/article/0,9171,1205539,00.html. All quotations in the following paragraph, unless otherwise noted, are from this feature.

12. See, for instance, William Green, "India Inc.: How to Ride the Elephant," *Time*, June 18, 2006, at http://www.time.com/time/magazine/article/0,9171,1205357,00.html.

13. Ibid. This was more than three times the money invested by Foreign Institutional Investors in the preceding decade.

14. Ibid. The prevailing argument, as various respondents in Green's article make obvious, presented the plunging stock market as an opportunity that could be utilized by those who were in it for the long run, by investors with foresight who understood India's demographic advantage.

15. Madhur Singh, "Is Booming India Immune to a U.S. Downturn?" *Time*, January 24, 2008, at http://www.time.com/time/business/article/0,8599,1706475,00.html?iid=sphere-inline-sidebar.

16. Madhur Singh, "India's Biggest IPO Turns Bust," *Time*, February 13, 2008, at http://www.time.com/time/business/article/0,8599,1712822,00.html.

17. Finance Minister P. Chidambaram, quoted in Singh, "Is Booming Indian Immune to a U.S. Downturn?"

18. Industrial growth in August 2008, for instance, was 1.3 percent as against 10.9 percent the year before. Even members of the prime minister's economic council admitted that as against the past average of 8.7 percent since 2003, the GDP growth was likely to fall to 7 percent. This was in part due to the fall in exports, since the GDP forecast was predicated on exports growing by at least 20 percent per annum. For an apt analysis of the impact of the global economic crisis on the Indian economy, see K. Ratnayake, "International Financial Crisis Exposes Vulnerability of the Indian Economy," World Socialist Web site, October 13, 2008, at http://www.wsws.org/articles/2008/oct2008/indi-o13.shtml.

19. Ibid. In 2007, nearly 61 percent of India's BPO and KPO exports were to the United States, with 40 percent of Fortune 500 companies favoring India as the destination for their outsourcing services. Given the visible signs of an economy in deep crisis in the United States, it became difficult for even the Indian prime minister to pretend that the Indian economy would remain insulated from it.

20. Manjeet Kripalani, "India's Madoff? Satyam Scandal Rocks Outsourcing Industry," *BusinessWeek*, January 7, 2009, at http://www.businessweek.com/globalbiz/content/jan2009/gb2009017_807784.htm. Once the news broke, there was a virtual deluge of articles on the Satyam imbroglio; see, for instance, Elizabeth Corcoran, "The Seeds of the Satyam Scandal: How B. Ramalinga Raju's Pride and Risk-Taking Created India's Enron," *Forbes*, January 8, 2009, at http://www.forbes.com/2009/01/08/fraud-satyam-raju-biz-logistics-cx_ec_0108satyam.html; Karishma Vaswani, "Satyam Scandal Shocks India," BBC News, January 8, 2009, at http://news.bbc.co.uk/2/hi/business/7818220.stm; and "The Satyam Scandal: Offshore Inmates," *Economist*, January 15, 2009, at http://www.economist.com/businessfinance/displaystory.cfm?story_id=12943984.

21. Kripalani, "India's Madoff?"

22. Elizabeth Corcoran's article in *Forbes*, for instance, describes at length the family-oriented business model followed by Raju and how that set the stage for the debacle, despite the many apparent successes of his career. See Corcoran, "The Seeds of the Satyam Scandal."

23. Calling the move "a good diversification strategy," Raju announced on December 16, 2008, that Satyam would acquire the two companies—Maytas Infra and Maytas Properties—owned by his sons, Teja and Rama. Nine hours after the announcement, through a press release, Raju announced that "in deference to the views expressed by many investors, we have decided to call it off." See Nandini Lakshman, "Why Satyam Backpedaled So Fast," *BusinessWeek*, December 18, 2008, at http://www.businessweek.com/globalbiz/content/dec2008/gb20081218_849301.htm.

24. The chairman of Infosys, another of India's IT titans, urged investors not to "overreact" to the Satyam debacle. Apparently without a sense of irony, he declared, "I believe that India's corporate governance standards are pretty much on par with the best in the world....We have seen the debacles of Enron, WorldCom, Tyco and many Wall Street companies. That does not mean the standard of corporate governance in the United States is bad." N. R. Narayana Murthy, cited in Deepal Jayasekara and Kranti Kumara, "Gigantic Corporate Fraud at Satyam Computers Deals Body-Blow to Indian Elite's Global Ambitions," World Socialist Web site, January 27, 2008, at http://www.wsws.org/articles/2009/jan2009/indi-j27.shtml.

25. Ibid. While routinely hailed as almost a "demi-god" in his native state of Andhra Pradesh, Raju had also recently been awarded the Golden Peacock Global Award for Excellence in Corporate Governance for 2008 in a ceremony in London, by the former prime minister of Sweden.

26. Ibid. The London-based *Financial Times*, for instance, had an editorial that declared that the Satyam scandal not only cast doubts on India's outsourcing industry but also raised "disturbing questions about the risks of doing business in India—and even the sustainability of the country's much vaunted economic growth." See also "Satyam Casts a Grim Cloud on India Inc." *BusinessWeek*, January 7, 2009, at http://www.businessweek.com/globalbiz/content/jan2009/gb2009017_583675.htm.

27. For discussions about levels of agricultural per-capita output and rural poverty, in the context of increasing GDP at the turn of the century, see Jayati Ghosh, "Poverty amidst Plenty?" *Frontline* 17, no. 5 (2000), at http://www.thehindu.com/fline/fl1705/17051090.htm. For an analysis that takes into account more recent figures, see Parthapratim Pal and Jayati Ghosh, "Inequality in India: A Survey of Recent Trends," DESA Working Paper no. 45, July 2007, at http://www.un.org/esa/desa/papers/2007/wp45_2007.pdf.

28. Strangely enough, that claim was bolstered by arguments that favorably contrasted India's not so open markets (a formerly lamented remnant of the much-maligned "socialist" past) as against the unregulated markets that prevailed in countries like the United States.

29. "India's Exports Continue to Fall," BBC News, July 1, 2009, at http://news.bbc.co.uk/2/hi/business/8128449.stm; "Further Decline in Indian Exports," BBC News, September 1, 2009, at http://news.bbc.co.uk/2/hi/business/8231082.stm.

30. Reflecting the success of at least one aspect of the Indian state's production of the domestic abroad, this list included Lakshmi Mittal, the NRI tycoon based in Great Britain.

31. To be fair to the ultrarich, even they have been hit by the economic crisis. As *Forbes* noted in a follow-up a year later, at time when the stock market dropped by 44 percent in twelve months, when the Indian rupee fell by about a fifth against the dollar, only twenty-four Indians could hold on to their place in the coveted list. In fact, the situation was so dire that the combined total wealth of the four richest Indians was now a paltry $54 billion (as against the $160 billion the year before). Even mainland China now had more billionaires on the list than India. However, the Indians could take consolation in the fact that the cumulative riches of their billionaires were still more than double that of the Chinese billionaires. For an article that details these figures without any sense of irony, see Naznees Karmali, "India's Billionaire Drop-offs," March 11, 2009, Forbes.com, at http://www.forbes.com/2009/03/11/india-financial-loss-billionaires-2009-billionaires-india.html.

32. Scottish director Danny Boyle's movie, based on a novel by Vikas Swarup, was a rags-to-riches story set in the Indian city of Mumbai. With its heart-rending images of the Mumbai slums, the highly photogenic and genuinely talented young Indian actors, and most important, the easily palatable and quite conventional message of hope and love triumphing over all odds, the movie was an international sensation. In 2009, the movie swept the Oscars, winning numerous awards including the prestigious "Best Movie of the Year." The Indian media's spotlight was turned on the two native Oscar winners, Resul Pookutty (for sound mixing) and A. R. Rahman (for song and musical score), which was not surprising, given that only one other Indian (Bhanu Athaiya, costume designer for the Richard Attenborough film *Gandhi*) had won an Oscar before in a competitive category. Some reports also highlighted the fact that the Oscar winner in the short film documentary, *Smile Pinky*, was inspired by the story of an Indian girl who was ostracized by her community because of her cleft lip. All in all, it was declared to be India's year at the Oscars.

33. In addressing these question, one would, of course, take note of not only the nature of U.S.-Mexican relations (given the history of Mexico's relationship with its northern neighbor and the fact that 97 percent of Mexican immigrants reside in the United States) but also the role and influence of people like Carlos Slim Helu (the world's richest man, according to the *Forbes* list released in March 2010) in Mexican politics.

34. To relate the waxing and waning of the fervor about Russians in the near abroad to the vagaries of Russia's position within the global economy would be an essential part of any such project.

35. In many ways, the Chinese case provides interesting grounds for comparison with the Indian case. Both countries have a substantial diaspora and a bourgeoisie that have accumulated vast amounts of wealth in a short time. *Forbes* reported that this year, for the first time, China has more billionaires than India, though the cumulative wealth of the latter is much more. Both have been touted as potential economic superpowers, and in its framing of its policies toward the diaspora, the Indian state has very consciously presented China as a model to be emulated. There are, of course, numerous differences as well. Unlike the Indian case, the Chinese diaspora has

contributed substantially to FDI in the PRC. More important, claims of the strength of the Chinese economy emanate from its manufacturing sector. However, what is probably the most striking point of comparison between the two cases is the way in which the production of the domestic abroad has become an intrinsic part of the ruling elites' attempt to reinforce their power in the context of claims of stellar economic growth in societies that continue to be characterized by extreme levels of poverty and inequality.

36. It is noteworthy that Barnett's explanation of the emergence of constructivism as a theoretical tradition (which fits well within the narrative outlined here) is part of a well-regarded textbook in the field, which aims to introduce the discipline of international relations to undergraduate students. See Michael Barnett, "Constructivism," in *The Globalization of World Politics: An Introduction to International Relations*, 3rd ed., ed. John Baylis and Steve Smith (New York: Oxford University Press, 2005).

37. Latha Varadarajan, "Constructivism, Identity and Neoliberal (In)Security," *Review of International Studies* 30, no. 3 (2004): 319–341.

38. This is a criticism that could justly apply to my own earlier work on the limitations of the constructivist tradition.

39. Alexander Wendt's article on the condition of anarchy, for example, turns to Mikhail Gorbachev's "policy of New Thinking…one of the most important phenomena in contemporary global politics" to explain how self-reflection by actors can actually lead to "practice specifically designed to transform their identities and interests" and thus to change the very nature of global politics. What is striking about this argument, arguably the most cited one in the constructivist tradition, is not only the strangely uninformed accounting of Soviet history but also the optimistic and transformative glow cast around Gorbachev's policies of *glasnost* and *perestroika*. Wendt makes it clear that the importance of this "New Thinking" is that it enables the move from a "competitive security system" to a "cooperative one." See Wendt, "Anarchy Is What the States Make of It: The Social Construction of Power Politics," *International Organization* 46, no. 2 (1992): 391–425, particularly 419–420.

Bibliography

Abraham, Itty. 1998. *The Making of the Indian Atomic Bomb: Science, Secrecy and the Postcolonial State*. London: Zed.

Abraham, Itty. 2003. "State, Place, Identity: Two Stories in the Making of a Region." In *Regional Modernities: The Cultural Politics of Development in India*, edited by K. Sivaramakrishnan and Arun Agrawal, 404–425. Stanford, CA: Stanford University Press.

Abu-Lughod, Janet. 1989. *Before European Hegemony: The World System A.D. 1250–1350*. New York: Oxford University Press.

Adamson, Fiona B. and Madeline Demetriou, 2007. "Remapping the Boundaries of 'State' and 'National Identity': Incorporating Diasporas into IR Theorizing." *European Journal of International Relations* 13 (4): 489–526.

Advani, L. K., Deputy Prime Minister. Speech at Inaugural Session, First Pravasi Bharatiya Diwas Conference, http://www.indiaday.org/pbd1/pbd-LKadvani.asp.

Agnew, John. 1994. "The Territorial Trap: The Geographical Assumptions of International Relations Theory." *Review of International Political Economy* 1: 53–80.

Agnew, John. 1999. "Mapping Political Power beyond State Boundaries: Territory, Identity and Movement in World Politics." *Millennium Journal of International Studies* 28 (3): 499–521.

Agnew, John, and Stuart Corbridge. 1995. *Mastering Space: Hegemony, Territory and International Political Economy*. London: Routledge.

Ahmad, Aijaz. 1996. *Lineages of the Present*. New Delhi: Tulika.

All-India Congress Committee. 1958. Indian National Congress, Resolutions on Foreign Policy, 1947–57. New Delhi: AICC.

Althusser, Louis. 1971. *Lenin and Philosophy and Other Essays.* Translated by Ben Brewster. New York: Monthly Review Press.

Amin, Shahid. 1996. *Event, Memory, Metaphor: Chauri-Chaura, 1922–1992.* New York: Oxford University Press.

Amsden, A. H. 1990. "Third World Industrialization: 'Global Fordism' or a New Model." *New Left Review* 182 (July–August): 5–31.

Anderson, Benedict. 1991. *Imagined Communities: Reflections on the Origin and Spread of Nationalism.* Revised ed. London: Verso.

Anderson, Benedict. 1998. "Long-distance nationalism." In *The Spectre of Comparisons: Nationalism in Southeast Asia and the World,* 58–76. London: Verso.

Anderson, Benedict. 2001. "Western Nationalism and Eastern Nationalism: Is There a Difference That Matters?" *New Left Review* 9 (May–June): 31–42.

Anderson, Bridget. 2000. *Doing the Dirty Work? The Global Politics of Domestic Labour.* London: Zed.

Anderson, Perry. 1976. "The Antinomies of Antonio Gramsci." *New Left Review* Special Hundredth Issue: 5–78.

Appadurai, Arjun. 1996. *Modernity at Large: Cultural Dimensions of Globalization.* Minneapolis: University of Minnesota Press.

Apparsamy, B. 1943. *Indians of South Africa.* Bombay: Padma.

Appiah, Kwame Anthony. 1991. "Is the Post- in Postmodernism the Post- in Postcolonial?" *Critical Inquiry* 17 (2): 336–357.

Arnason, Johann P. 1990. "Nationalism, Globalization and Modernity." *Theory, Culture and Society* 7: 207–236.

Ashley, Richard K. 1988. "Untying the Sovereign State: A Double Reading of the Anarchy Problematique." *Millennium Journal of International Studies* 17: 227–262.

Athreye, Suma, and Sandeep Kapur. 2001. "Private Foreign Investment in India: Pain or Panacea?" *World Economy* 24 (3): 399–424.

Balibar, Etienne. 2002. *Politics and the Other Scene.* Translated by Christine Jones, James Swenson, and Chris Turner. London: Verso.

Balibar, Etienne. 2004. *We, the People of Europe? Reflections on Transnational Citizenship.* Translated by James Swenson. Princeton, NJ: Princeton University Press.

Basch, Linda, Nina Glick Schiller, and Cristina Szanton-Blanc, eds. 1994. *Nations Unbound: Transnational Projects, Postcolonial Predicaments and Deterritorialized Nation-States.* Longhorne, PA: Gordon and Breach.

Basch, Linda, Nina Glick Schiller, and Cristina Szanton-Blanc. 1995. "From Immigrant to Transmigrant: Theorizing Transnational Migration." *Anthropological Quarterly* 8 (1): 48–63.

Baubock, Rainier. 2003. "Towards a Political Theory of Transnationalism." *International Migration Review* 37 (3): 700–723.

Baylis, John, and Steve Smith, eds. *The Globalization of World Politics: An Introduction to International Relations.* 3rd ed. New York: Oxford University Press.

Beams, Nick. 2009. "The World Economic Crisis: A Marxist Analysis." http://wsws. org/media/nb-lecture-1208.pdf.

Beams, Nick. 2009. "The Crash of 2008 and Its Revolutionary Implications." http://wsws.org/articles/2009/feb2009/nbe4-f07.shtml.

Behal, Rana P. and Prabhu Mohapatra. 1992. "Tea and Money versus Human Life: The Rise and Fall of Indenture System in the Assam Tea Plantations, 1840–1908." *Journal of Peasant Studies* 19 (3–4): 142–172.

Berger, Mark T. 2001. "The Rise and Demise of National Development and the Origins of Post-Cold War Capitalism." *Millennium: Journal of International Studies* 30 (2): 211–234.

Bhabha, Homi K. 1985. "Signs Taken for Wonders: Questions of Ambivalence and Authority under a Tree outside Delhi, May 1817." *Critical Inquiry* 12: 144–165.

Bhabha, Homi K. 1988. "The Commitment to Theory." *New Formations* 5: 5–23.

Bhabha, Homi K. 1995. "Cultural Diversity and Cultural Difference." In *The Postcolonial Studies Reader*, edited by Bill Ashcroft, Gareth Griffiths, and Helen Tiffin. New York: Routledge.

Bhagwati, Jagdish. 1988. "Export-Promoting Trade Strategy: Issues and Evidence." *World Bank Research Observer* 3 (1): 25–57.

Bhatt, Chetan. 2000. "*Dharmo rakshati rakshitah*: Hindutva Movements in the UK." *Ethnic and Racial Studies* 23 (3): 559–593.

Bhatt, Chetan, and Parita Mukta. 2000. "Hindutva in the West: Mapping the Antinomies of Diaspora Nationalism." *Ethnic and Racial Studies* 23 (3): 407–441.

Birla, G. D., J. R. D. Tata, and Purshotamdas Thakurdas. 1945. *Memorandum Outlining a Plan of Economic Development of India*, parts 1 and 2. Harmondsworth: Penguin.

Biswas, Shampa. 2005. "Globalization and the Nation Beyond: The Indian-American Diaspora and the Rethinking of Territory, Citizenship and Democracy." *New Political Science* 27 (1): 43–68.

"BJP's Search for Short-Cuts to Political Consolidation." 1998. *Economic and Political Weekly*, May 30.

The Bombay Plan and Other Essays, A.D. Shroff Memorial Lectures. 1968. Bombay: Lalvani Publishing House.

Boughton, J. M. 2001. *Silent Revolution: The International Monetary Fund, 1979–1989.* Washington, DC: IMF.

Brand, Laurie. 2006. *Citizens Abroad: Emigrants and the State in the Middle East and North Africa.* Cambridge: Cambridge University Press.

Brenner, Neil. 1999. Beyond State-Centrism? Space, Territoriality, and Geographical Scale in Globalization Studies. *Theory and Society* 28: 39–78.

Brubaker, Rogers. 1996. *Nationalism Reframed: Nationhood and the National Question in the New Europe.* Cambridge: Cambridge University Press.

Brubaker, Rogers. 1998. "Myths and Misconceptions in the Study of Nationalism." In *The State of the Nation: Ernest Gellner and the Theory of Nationalism*, edited by John A. Hall, 272–306. Cambridge: Cambridge University Press.

Brubaker, Rogers. 2005. "The 'Diaspora' Diaspora." *Ethnic and Racial Studies* 28 (1): 1–19.

Callahan, William. 2003. "Beyond Cosmpolitanism and Nationalism: Diasporic Chinese and Neo-nationalism in Thailand and China." *International Organization* 57 (2): 481–518.

Carter, Marina. 1992. "Strategies of Labour Mobilization in Colonial India: The Recruitment of Indenture Workers for Mauritius." *Journal of Peasant Studies* 19 (3–4): 229–245.

Chakravarti, N. R. 1971. *The Indian Minority in Burma: The Rise and Decline of an Immigrant Community*. London: Oxford University Press.

Chakravarty, Sumita. 1993. *National Identity in Indian Popular Cinema*. Austin: University of Texas Press.

Chaliand, G., and J-P. Rageau. 1995. *The Penguin Atlas of Diasporas*. New York: Viking, Penguin.

Chami, Ralph, Connel Fullenkamp, and Samir Jahjah. 2005. "Are Immigrant Remittance Flows a Source of Capital for Development?" IMF Staff Papers, Vol. 52, no. 1.

Chandra, Bipan. 1979. *Nationalism and Colonialism in Modern India*. New Delhi: Orient Longman.

Chandran, Ramesh. 2000. Indian Brain Drain Being Reversed. *Times of India*, March 1.

Chang, Grace. 2000. *Disposable Domestics: Immigrant Women Workers in the Global Economy*. Cambridge, MA: South End.

Chatterjee, Partha. 1995. *Nationalist Thought and the Colonial World*. Minneapolis: University of Minnesota Press.

Chaudhry, Praveen K., Vijay L. Kelkar, and Vikash Yadav. 2004. "The Evolution of 'Homegrown Conditionality' in India-IMF Relations." *Journal of Development Studies* 40 (6): 59–81.

Chekuri, Christopher, and Himadeep Muppidi. 2003. "Diasporas Before and After the Nation." *Interventions* 5 (1): 45–57.

Chibber, Vivek. 2006. *Locked in Place: State-Building and Late Industrialization in India*. Princeton, NJ: Princeton University Press.

Chisti, Muzaffar. "The Rise in Remittances to India." Migration Policy Institute, at http://www.migrationinformation.org/Feature/display.cfm?id=577.

Clifford, James. 1994. "Diasporas." *Cultural Anthropology* 9 (3): 302–308.

Cohen, Robin. 1997. *Global Diasporas: An Introduction*. London: UCL Press.

Cook, Rebecca J., ed. 1994. *Human Rights of Women: National and International Perspectives*. Philadelphia: University of Pennsylvania Press.

Corcoran, Elizabeth. 2009. "The Seeds of the Satyam Scandal: How B. Ramalinga Raju's Pride and Risk-Taking Created India's Enron." Forbes, http://www.forbes.com/2009/01/08/fraud-satyam-raju-biz-logistics-cx_ec_0108satyam.html.

Cox, Robert. 1981. "Social Forces, States, and World Orders: Beyond International Relations Theory." *Millennium: Journal of International Studies* 10 (2): 126–155.

Cox, Robert. 1986. *Production, Power and World Order*. New York: Columbia University Press.

Das, Gurcharan. 2000. *India Unbound*. New Delhi: Viking.

Debabrata, Michael, and Munish Kapur. 2003. "India's Worker Remittances: A User's Lament about Balance of Payments Compilation." Sixteenth Meeting of the IMF Committee on Balance of Payments Statistics. BOPCOM—03/20.

Desai, Jigna. 2003. *Beyond Bollywood: The Cultural Politics of South Asian Diasporic Film*. New York: Routledge.

Desai, W. S. 1954. *India and Burma*. Bombay: Orient Longmans.

Dicken, Peter. 1997. Transnational Corporations and Nation-States. *International Social Science Journal* 151: 77–89.

Dickinson, Jen, and Adrian J. Bailey. 2007. "(Re)membering Diaspora: Uneven Geographies of Indian Dual Citizenship." *Political Geography* 26: 757–774.

Dirlik, Arif. 1994. "The Postcolonial Aura: Third World Criticism in the Age of Global Capitalism." *Critical Inquiry* 20 (2): 328–356.

Djilas, Aleksa. 1995. "Fear Thy Neighbor: The Breakup of Yugoslavia." In *Nationalism and Nationalities in the New Europe*, edited by Charles P. Kupchan, 85–106. Ithaca, NY: Cornell University Press.

Doty, Roxanne. 1996. "Immigration and National Identity: Constructing the Nation." *Review of International Studies* 22 (3): 235–255.

Duara, Prasenjit. 1995. *Rescuing History from the Nation: Questioning Narratives of Modern China*. Chicago: University of Chicago Press.

Dutt, R. C. 1906. *The Economic History of India*. 2nd ed. Vols. I and II. London: Kegan Paul, Trench, Trubner and Co.

Elliott, Michael. 2006. "India Awakens." *Time*, http://www.time.com/time/magazine/article/0,9171,1205374,00.html.

Evans, Peter, Dietrich Reuschmeyer, and Theda Skocpol, eds. 1985. *Bringing the State Back In*. Cambridge: Cambridge University Press.

Fanon, Frantz. 1990. *The Wretched of the Earth*. Translated by Constance Farrington. 3rd ed. Harmondsworth: Penguin.

Fay, Peter. 1993. *The Forgotten Army: India's Armed Struggle for Independence, 1942–45*. Ann Arbor: University of Michigan Press.

Federation of Indian Chambers of Commerce and Industry. 1934. Annual Report.

Ferguson, Niall. 2002. *Empire: The Rise and Demise of British World Order and the Lessons for Global Power*. New York: Basic Books.

Ferguson, Niall. 2004. *Colossus: The Price of America's Empire*. New York: Penguin.

Ferguson, Yale H., and Richard Mansbach. 1988. *The Elusive Quest: Theory and International Politics*. Columbia: University of South Carolina Press.

Ferguson, Yale H., and Richard W. Mansbach. 1989. *The State, Conceptual Chaos and the Future of International Relations Theory*. Boulder: Lynne Reinner.

Finnemore, Martha, and Kathryn Sikkink. 1998. "International Norm Dynamics and Poltical Change." *International Organization* 52 (4): 887–917.

Fitzgerald, Stephen. 1972. *China and the Overseas Chinese: A Study of Peking's Changing Policy, 1949–1970*. Cambridge: Cambridge University Press.

Foglerud, Oivind. 1999. *Life on the Outside: The Tamil Diaspora and Long-Distance Nationalism*. London: Pluto.

Frankel, Francine. 1978. *India's Political Economy: 1947–1977*. Princeton, NJ: Princeton University Press.

Fulcher, James. 2000. "Globalisation, the Nation-State and Global Society." *Sociological Review* 48 (4): 522–543.

"Further Decline in Indian Exports." 2009. *BBC News*, September 1, http://news.bbc.co.uk/2/hi/business/8231082.stm.

George, Jim. 1994. *Discourses of Global Politics: A Critical (Re)Introduction to International Relations*. Boulder, CO: Lynne Rienner.

Ghosh, Jayati. 2000. "Poverty amidst Plenty?" *Frontline* 17 (5), http://www.thehindu.com/fline/fl1705/17051090.htm.

Gill, Stephen. 1990. *American Hegemony and the Trilateral Commission*. Cambridge: Cambridge University Press.

Gill, Stephen, ed. 1993. *Gramsci, Historical-Materialism and International Relations* Cambridge: Cambridge University Press.

Gilroy, Paul. 1993. *The Black Atlantic: Modernity and Double Consciousness*. Cambridge, MA: Harvard University Press.

Glassman, Jim. 1999. "State Power beyond the 'Territorial Trap': The Internationalization of the State." *Political Geography* 18: 669–696.

Gopal, S. 1976. *Jawaharlal Nehru—A Biography*. Vol. I. Cambridge, MA: Harvard University Press.

Gordon, James, and Poonam Gupta. 2004. "Non-Resident Deposits in India: In Search of Return?" *Economic and Political Weekly*: 4165–4174.

Gramsci, Antonio. 1997. *Selections from the Prison Notebooks*. Translated by Quentin Hoare and Geoffrey Nowell Smith. New York: International Publishers.

Green, William. 2006. "India Inc.: How to Ride the Elephant." *Time*, http://www.time.com/time/magazine/article/0,9171,1205357,00.html.

Gumbel, Peter. 2009. "India Loses Its Davos Sparkle." *Time.com*, http://davos.blogs.time.com/2009/01/29/india-loses-its-davos-sparkle/.

Gupta, Akhil. 1998. *Postcolonial Developments: Agriculture in the Making of Modern India*. Durham: Duke University Press.

Gurumurthy S. 2004. "India Does Not Need FDI, But China Needs It!" http://news.indiainfo.com/2004/07/20/guru.html.

Gutierrerz, Carlos Gonzalez. 1999. "Fostering Identities: Mexico's Relations with Its Diaspora." *Journal of American History* 86 (2): 545–567.

Handbook for Overseas Indians. 2009. New Delhi: Ministry of Overseas Indian Affairs.

Harvey, David. 2007. *A Brief History of Neoliberalism*. New York: Oxford University Press.

Hear, Nicholas Van. 1998. *New Diasporas: The Mass Exodus, Dispersal and Regrouping of Migrant Communities*. London: University College of London Press.

Heimsath, Charles, and Surjit Mansingh. 1971. *A Diplomatic History of Modern India*. Bombay: Allied Publishers.

Held, David, ed. 1983. *States and Societies*. Oxford: Martin Robertson in association with the Open University.

Hernandez, Juan, Omar de la Torre, and Julie M. Weise. "Mexico's New Public Policies for Its Citizens." http://www.international.metropolis.net/events/rotterdam/papers/36_Torre.htm.

High-Level Committee on the Indian Diaspora. 2002. *The Report of the High Committee on the Indian Diaspora*. New Delhi: Ministry of External Affairs.

Hockenos, Paul. 2003. *Homeland Calling: Exile Patriotism and the Balkan Wars*. Ithaca, NY: Cornell University Press.

Huntington, Samuel P. 2004. *Who Are We? The Challenges to America's National Identity*. New York: Simon and Schuster.

"India's Exports Continue to Fall." 2009. *BBC News*, July 1, http://news.bbc.co.uk/2/hi/business/8128449.stm.

India Today (International). 2003. Special Issue, January 13.

James, C. L. R. 1963. *The Black Jacobins: Toussaint L'Overture and the San Domingo Revolution*. New York: Vintage.

Jayaram, N., ed. 2004. *The Indian Diaspora: Dynamics of Migration*. Vol. 4, *Themes in Indian Sociology*. New Delhi: Sage Publications.

Jayasekara, Deepal, and Kranti Kumara. 2009. "Gigantic Corporate Fraud at Satyam Computers Deals Body-Blow to Indian Elite's Global Ambitions." World Socialist Web site, http://www.wsws.org/articles/2009/jan2009/indi-j27.shtml.

Jepperson, Ronald, Alexander Wendt, and Peter Katzenstein. 1996. "Norms, Identity and Culture in National Security." In *The Culture of National Security: Norms and Identity in World Politics*, edited by P. J. Katzenstein. New York: Columbia University Press.

Jessop, Bob. 1982. *The Capitalist State: Marxist Theories and Methods*. New York: New York University Press.

Jessop, Bob. 1990. *State Theory: Putting the Capitalist State in Place*. University Park: Pennsylvania University Press.

Jessop, Bob. 2002. *The Future of the Capitalist State*. Cambridge: Polity.

Joppke, Christian. 2000. *Immigration and the Nation-State: The United States, Germany and Great Britain*. Oxford: Oxford University Press.

Karmali, Naznees. 2009. "India's Billionaire Drop-offs." *Forbes.com*, http://www. forbes.com/2009/03/11/india-financial-loss-billionaires-2009-billionaires-india.html.

Katzenstein, Peter J., ed. 1996. *The Culture of National Security: Norms and Identity in World Politics.* New York: Columbia University Press.

Keck, Margeret E., and Kathryn Sikkink. 1998. *Activists beyond Borders: Advocacy Networks in International Politics.* Ithaca, NY: Cornell University Press.

Keshaven, Narayan. 1998. "Swadeshi Goes Global." *Outlook*, April 27.

Khagram, Sanjeev, James V. Riker, and Kathryn Sikkink, eds. 2002. *Restructuring World Politics: Transnational Social Movements, Networks and Norms.* Minneapolis: University of Minneosta Press.

Kidder, Thalia, and Mary McGinn. 1995. "In the Wake of NAFTA: Transnational Workers Networks." *Social Policy* 25 (4): 14–22.

King, Charles, and Neil Melvin. 2000. "Diaspora Politics: Ethnic Linkages, Foreign Policy, and Security in Eurasia." *International Security* 24 (3): 108–138.

Klotz, Audie. 1995. *Norms in International Relations: The Struggle against Apartheid.* Ithaca, NY: Cornell University Press.

Kochanek, Stanley A. 1974. *Business and Politics in India.* Berkeley: University of California Press.

Kochanek, Stanley A. 1995–96. "The Transformation of Interest Politics in India." *Pacific Affairs* 68 (4): 529–550.

Kofman, Eleanor, and Gillian Young, eds. 1996. *Globalization: Theory and Practice.* London: Pinter.

Kolstø, Pål. 1999. "Territorializing Diasporas: The Case of Russians in the Former Soviet Republics." *Millennium Journal of International Studies* 28 (3): 607–631.

Kondapi, C. 1951. *Indians Overseas: 1838–1949.* New Delhi: Oxford University Press.

Koslowski, Ray. 2000. *Migrants and Citizens: Demographic Change in the European States System.* Ithaca: Cornell University Press.

Kripalani, Manjeet. 2006. "Selling India Inc. at Davos." *BusinessWeek*, January 30, http://www.businessweek.com/bwdaily/dnflash/jan2006/nf20060130_4381_db032.htm.

Kripalani, Manjeet. 2009. "India's Madoff? Satyam Scandal Rocks Outsourcing Industry." *BusinessWeek*, http://www.businessweek.com/globalbiz/content/jan2009/gb2009017_807784.htm.

Krishna, Sankaran. 1996. "Cartographic Anxiety: Mapping the Body Politic in India." In *Challenging Boundaries: Global Flows, Territorial Identities*, edited by M. Shapiro. Minneapolis: University of Minnesota Press.

Kumar, Arun. 2007. "West Bengal Left Front's Pro-Investor Land Grab Results in Deadly Clashes." http://wsws.org/articles/2007/jan2007/beng-j26.shtml.

Kumar, Sudarshan, ed. 2000. *Pioneers of Prosperity.* New Delhi: Antar Rashtriya Sahyog Parishad.

Kumara, Kranti. 2007. "Leading Indian Intellectuals Condemn West Bengal's Stalinist-Led Government." http://wsws.org/articles/2007/mar2007/beng-m19.shtml.

Kupchan, Charles P., ed. 1995. *Nationalism and Nationalities in the New Europe*. Ithaca, NY: Cornell University Press.

Kurien, Prema. 2001. "Religion, Ethnicity and Politics: Hindu and Muslim Indian Immigrants in the United States." *Ethnic and Racial Studies* 24 (2): 263–293.

Laguerre, Michel S. 1999. "State, Diaspora and Transnational Politics: Haiti Reconceptualized." *Millennium Journal of International Studies* 28 (3): 633–651.

Laitin, David. 1998. *Identity in Formation: The Russian-Speaking Populations in the Near Abroad*. Ithaca: Cornell University Press.

Lakshman, Nandini. 2008. "Why Satyam Backpedaled So Fast." *BusinessWeek*, http://www.businessweek.com/globalbiz/content/dec2008/gb20081218_849301.htm.

Lall, M. C. 2001. *India's Missed Opportunity: India's Relationship with Non-Resident Indians*. Ashgate: Aldershot.

Landler, Mark. 2006. "'India Everywhere' in the Alps." *New York Times*, http://www.nytimes.com/2006/01/26/business/worldbusiness/26india.html.

Lapid, Yosef. 1994. "Theorizing the 'National' in International Relations Theory." In *International Organization: A Reader*, edited by Friedrich V. Kratochwil and Edward Mansfield. New York: Harper Collins College.

Lever-Tracy, Constance, David Fu-Keung Ip, and Noel Tracy. 1996. *The Chinese Diaspora and Mainland China: An Emerging Economic Synergy*. New York: Macmillan.

Lewis, Michael. 2000. *The New New Thing: A Silicon Valley Story*. New York: Norton.

Little, I. M. D. 1982. *Economic Development: Theory, Policy and International Relations*. New York: Basic Books.

Liu, Hong. 1998. "Old Linkages, New Networks: The Globalization of Overseas Chinese Voluntary Associations and Its Implications." *China Quarterly* 155: 582–609.

Lok Sabha Debates, 1952–2001.

Lowe, Lisa. 1996. *Immigrant Acts*. Durham: Duke University Press.

Ludowyk, E. F. C. 1966. *The Modern History of Ceylon*. London: Weidenfeld and Nicholson.

Mamdani, Mahmood. 1996. *Citizen and Subject: Contemporary Africa and the Legacy of Late Colonialism*. Princeton, NJ: Princeton University Press.

Mani, Bakirathi, and Latha Varadarajan. 2005. "'The Largest Gathering of the Global Indian Family': Neoliberalism, Nationalism and Diaspora at Pravasi Bharatiya Divas." *Diaspora* 14 (1): 45–73.

Marden, Peter. 1997. "Geographies of Dissent: Globalization, Identity and the Nation." *Political Geography* 16 (1): 37–64.

Matthew, Biju, and Vijay Prashad. 2000. "The Protean Forms of Yankee Hindutva." *Ethnic and Racial Studies* 23 (3): 516–534.

Mearns, David James. 1995. *Shiva's Other Children: Religion and Social Identity amongst Overseas Indians.* New Delhi: Sage.

Mehta, Monika. 2001. "Selections: Cutting, Classifying and Certifying in Bombay Cinema." PhD Dissertation, University of Minnesota.

Melvin, Neil. 1995. *Russians beyond Russia: The Politics of National Identity.* London: Pinter.

Ministry of External Affairs, External Publicity Division. 1998. Press Release. New Delhi, May 11.

Ministry of External Affairs, Government of India. 2000. Press Release. August 18.

Mishra, Vijay. 1996. "The Diasporic Imaginary: Theorizing the Indian Diaspora." *Textual Practice* 10 (3): 421–447.

Mishra, Vijay. 1992–93. "Introduction" *SPAN* 34–35: 1–2.

Mitchell, Katharyne. 1997. "Different Diasporas and the Hype of Hybridity." *Environment and Planning D: Society and Space* 15 (5): 533–553.

Mitchell, Katharyne. 2004. *Crossing the Neoliberal Line: Pacific Rim Migration and the Metropolis.* Philadelphia: Temple University Press.

Mitchell, Timothy. 1991. *Colonizing Egypt.* Berkeley: University of California Press.

Mittleman, James, ed. 1997. *Globalization: Critical Reflections.* Boulder: Lynne Reiner.

Mohan, R. 1982. "Industrial Policy and Control." In *The Indian Economy: Prospects and Problems,* edited by Bimal Jalan, 85–115. New Delhi: Penguin.

Mukherjee, Aditya. 2002. *Imperialism, Nationalism and the Making of the Indian Capitalist Class, 1920–1947.* New Delhi: Sage.

Muppidi, Himadeep. 2004. *The Politics of the Global.* Minneapolis: University of Minnesota Press.

Muppidi, Himadeep R. 1998. "Competitive Economic Restructuring in the Global Economy: A Critical Constructivist Approach." Department of Political Science, University of Minnesota, Minneapolis.

Myers, Rebecca. 2006. "The Face of India." *Time,* http://www.time.com/time/magazine/article/0,9171,1207151,00.html.

Nanda, H. P. 1992. *The Days of My Years.* New Delhi: Viking.

Nayyar, Deepak. 1994. *Migration, Remittances and Capital Flows.* Delhi: Oxford University Press.

Nehru, Jawaharlal. 1961. *India's Foreign Policy: Selected Speeches.* New Delhi: Publications Division, Ministry of Information and Broadcasting.

Nehru, Jawaharlal. 2004. *The Discovery of India.* New Delhi: Penguin.

Ong, Aihwa. 1999. *Flexible Citizenship: The Cultural Logics of Transnationalism.* Durham: Duke University Press.

Ong, Aihwa, and David Nonini, eds. 1997. *Ungrounded Empires: The Cultural Politics of Modern Chinese Nationalism.* London: Routledge.

An On-looker. 1944. *The Status of Indians in the Empire.* Allahabad: Kitabistan.

Oren, Ido. 1995. "The Subjectivity of 'Democratic' Peace: Changing US Perceptions of Imperial Germany." *International Security* 20: 147–184.

Oren, Ido. 2003. *Our Enemies and US: America's Rivalries and the Making of Political Science*. Ithaca, NY: Cornell University Press.

Ottaway, Marina. 2001. "Corporatism Goes Global: International Organizations, Nongovernmental Organization Networks, and Transnational Business." *Global Governance* 7 (3): 265–285.

Pal, Parthapratim, and Jayati Ghosh. 2007. "Inequality in India: A Survey of Recent Trends." DESA Working Paper no. 45, http://www.un.org/esa/desa/papers/2007/wp45_2007.pdf.

Palumbo-Liu, David. 1999. *Asian/American: Historical Crossings of a Racial Frontier*. Stanford: Stanford University Press.

Panitch, Leo. 1994. "Globalization and the State." In *Socialist Register*, edited by R. Milliband and Leo Panitch. London: Merlin.

Paranjape, Makarand, ed. 2001. *In Diaspora: Theories, Histories, Texts*. New Delhi: Indialog.

Pasha, Mustapha Kamal, and David L. Blaney. 1998. "Elusive Paradise: The Promise and Perils of Global Civil Society." *Alternatives* 23 (4): 417–450.

Patel, I. G. 2002. *Glimpses of Indian Economic Policy: An Insider's View*. London: Oxford University Press.

Pederson, Jørgen D. 2000. "Explaining Economic Liberalization in India: State and Society Perspectives." *World Development* 28 (2): 265–282.

Perry, Alex. 2006. "Shaking the Foundations." *Time*, http://www.time.com/time/magazine/article/0,9171,1205539,00.html.

Pinney, Christopher. 2004. *Photos of the Gods: The Printed Image and Political Struggle in India*. London: Reaktion.

Portes, Alejandro. 1999. "Conclusion: Towards a New World—The Origins and Effects of Transnational Activities." *Ethnic and Racial Studies* 22 (2): 463–477.

Portes, Alejandro, Luis E. Guarnizo, and Patricia Landolt. 1999. "The Study of Transnationalism: Pitfalls and Promise of an Emergent Research Field." *Ethnic and Racial Studies* 22 (2): 217–237.

Poulantzas, Nicos. 1974. "The Internationalization of Capitalist Relations and the National State." *Economy and Society* 3 (2): 145–179.

Poulantzas, Nicos. 2000. *State, Power, Socialism*. Translated by Patrick Camiller. London: Verso.

Prakash, Gyan. 1999. *Another Reason: Science and the Imagination of Modern India*. Princeton, NJ: Princeton University Press.

Prasad, M. Madhava. 1998. *Ideology and the Hindi Film: A Historical Construction*. Delhi: Oxford University Press.

Price, Richard. 1998. "Reversing the Gun Sights: Transnational Civil Society Targets Landmines." *International Organization* 52 (3): 613–644.

Price, Richard, and Christian Reus-Smit. 1998. "Dangerous Liaisons? Critical International Theory and Constructivism." *European Journal of International Relations* 4 (3): 259–294.

Ragazzi, Francesco. 2009. "Governing Diasporas." *International Political Sociology* 3 (4): 378–397.

Rajagopal, A. 2000. "Hindu Nationalism in the US: Changing Configurations of Political Practice." *Ethnic and Racial Studies* 23 (2): 467–496.

Rajghatta, Chidanand. 2001. *The Horse That Flew: How India's Silicon Gurus Spread Their Wings*. New Delhi: HarperCollins.

Rajkumar, N.V. 1951. *Indians outside India*. New Delhi: All India Congress Committee.

Ramanna, Raja. 1991. *Years of Pilgrimage*. Delhi: Viking.

Ramaswamy, P. 1992. "Labour Control and Labour Resistance in Plantations of Colonial Malaya." *Journal of Peasant Studies* 19 (3–4): 87–105.

Rao, P. V. N. 1995. *P.V. Narasimha Rao: Selected Speeches*. New Delhi: Ministry of Information and Broadcasting.

Ratha, Dilip, and Zhimei Xu. 2008. *The Migrations and Remittances Factbook 2008*. http://econ.worldbank.org/WBSITE/EXTERNAL/EXTDEC/EXTDECPROSP ECTS/0,,contentMDK:21352016~pagePK:64165401~piPK:64165026~theSite PK:476883,00.html.

Ratnayake, K. 2008. "International Financial Crisis Exposes Vulnerability of the Indian Economy." World Socialist Web site, http://www.wsws.org/articles/2008/ oct2008/indi-o13.shtml.

Resch, Robert Paul. 1992. *Althusser and the Renewal of Marxist Social Theory*. Los Angeles: University of California Press.

"Reserve Bank against Nationalization." 1948. *Times of India*, March 23.

Reserve Bank of India. 1988. *Exchange Control Facilities for Investment by Non-Resident Indians*. New Delhi.

Reserve Bank of India. *RBI History*, vol. 1. http://www.rbi.org.in/scripts/RHvol-1. aspx.

Risse, Thomas, Stephen C. Ropp, and Kathryn Sikkink, eds. 1999. *The Power of Human Rights: International Norms and Domestic Change*. Cambridge: Cambridge University Press.

Risse-Kappen, Thomas, ed. 1995. *Bringing Transnational Relations Back In: Non-State Actors, Domestic Structures and International Institutions*. Cambridge: Cambridge University Press.

Robinson, William. 2002. "Capitalist globalization and the Transnationalization of the State." In *Historical Materialism and Globalization*, edited by Mark Rupert and Hazel Smith. London: Routledge.

Rodriguez, Gregory. 2003. "Vicente Fox Blesses the Americanization of Mexico." *Los Angeles Times*, December 10.

Ruggie, John Gerard. 1993. "Territoriality and Beyond: Problematizing Modernity in International Relations." *International Organization* 47 (1): 139–174.

Rupert, Mark. 1995. *Producing Hegemony: The Politics of Mass Production and American Global Power*. Cambridge: Cambridge University Press.

Saccarelli, Emanuele. 2008. *Gramsci and Trotsky in the Shadow of Stalinism*. New York: Routledge.

Safran, William. 1991. "Diasporas in Modern Societies: Myths of Homeland and Return." *Diasporas* 1 (1): 83–99.

Sahadevan, P. 1995. *India and Overseas Indians: The Case of Sri Lanka*. New Delhi: Kalinga.

Said, Edward. 1978. *Orientalism*. London: Routledge and Kegan Paul.

Sandhu, K. S. 1969. *Indians in Malaya*. Cambridge: Cambridge University Press.

Sarkar, Sumit, and Tanika Sarkar. 2008. "A Place Called Nandigram." In *Nandigram and Beyond*, edited by Gautam Ray. Kolkata: Sangehil.

Sastry, Chandrashekhar. 1991. *The Non-Resident Indian: From Non-Being to Being*. Bangalore: Panther Publishers.

"Satyam Casts a Grim Cloud on India Inc." 2009. *BusinessWeek*, http://www.businessweek.com/globalbiz/content/jan2009/gb2009017_583675.htm.

"The Satyam Scandal: Offshore Inmates." 2009. *Economist*, http://www.economist.com/businessfinance/displaystory.cfm?story_id=12943984.

Saxenian, Annalee. 1996. *Regional Advantage: Culture and Competition in Silicon Valley and Route 128*. Cambridge, MA: Harvard University Press.

The Second Pravasi Bharatiya Divas, January 9–11 2004. 2004. New Delhi: Ministry of External Affairs and FICCI.

Shain, Yossi. 1989. *The Frontier of Loyalty: Political Exiles in the Age of the Nation-State*. Middletown, CT: Wesleyan University Press.

Shain, Yossi. 1993. "Democrats and Secessionists: U.S. Diasporas as Regime De-stabilizers." In *International Migration and Security*, edited by M. Weiner. Boulder, CO: Westview Press.

Shain, Yossi. 1994/1995. "Ethnic Diasporas and U.S. Foreign Policy". *Political Science Quarterly* 109 (5): 811–841.

Shain, Yossi. 1999. *Marketing the American Creed Abroad: Diasporas in the US and Their Homelands*. Cambridge: Cambridge University Press.

Shain, Yossi. 1999–2000. "The Mexican-American Diaspora's Impact on Mexico." *Political Science Quarterly* 114 (4): 661–691.

Shain, Yossi. 2000. "American Jews and the Construction of Israel's Jewish Identity." *Diaspora* 9 (2): 163–201.

Shain, Yossi. 2002. "The Role of Diasporas in Conflict Perpetuation or Resolution." *SAIS Review* 22 (2): 115–144.

Shain, Yossi, and Aharon Barth. 2003. "Diasporas in International Relations Theory." *International Organization* 57 (2): 449–479.

Sharma, Kavita. 1998. *On-Going Journey: Indian Migration to Canada*. New Delhi: SAB.

Sheffer, Gabriel. 1986. *Modern Diasporas in International Politics*. New York: St. Martin's.

Shukla, Sandhya. 1999–2000. "New Immigrants, New Forms of Transnational Community: Post-1965 Indian Migrations." *Amerasia Journal* 25 (3): 19–36.

Sikkink, Kathryn. 1993. "Human Rights, Principled Issues Networks and Sovereignty in Latin America." *International Organization* 47 (3): 411–441.

Singh, I. J. Bahadur, ed. 1979. *The Other India: The Overseas Indians and Their Relationship with India*. New Delhi: Arnold Heinemann.

Singh, K. Natwar. 1988. Speech at the 42nd Session (16th Plenary meeting) of the United Nations, 29th September, http://www.meadev.nic.in/un/vol2/s42a.htm.

Singh, Madhur. 2008. "Is Booming India Immune to a U.S. Downturn?" *Time*, http://www.time.com/time/business/article/0,8599,1706475,00.html?iid=sphere-inline-sidebar.

Singh, Madhur. 2008. "India's Biggest IPO Turns Bust." *Time*, http://www.time.com/time/business/article/0,8599,1712822,00.html.

Sinha, Aseema. 2005. "Understanding the Rise and Transformation of Business Collective Action in India." *Business and Politics* 7 (2).

Smith, Anthony. 1991. "The Nation: Invented, Imagined, Reconstructed?" *Millennium: Journal of International Studies* 20 (3): 353–368.

Smith, Craig S. 2001. "Reaching Overseas, China Tries to Tether Its Own." *New York Times*, August 3, A3.

Smith, Robert. 1998. "Transnational Public Spheres and Changing Practices of Citizenship, Membership and Nation: Comparative Insights from the Mexican and Italian Cases." Paper read at ICCCR Conference on Transnationalism.

Smith, Robert. 2000. "How Durable and New Is Transnational Life? Historical Retrieval through Local Comparison." *Diaspora* 9 (2): 203–234.

Smith, Robert. 2003. "Diasporic Memberships in Historical Perspective: Comparative Insights from the Mexican, Italian and Polish Cases." *International Migration Review* 37 (3): 724–759.

Smith, Tony. 2000. *Foreign Attachments: The Power of Ethnic Groups in the Making of American Foreign Policy*. Cambridge, MA: Harvard University Press.

Stenson, M. R. 1980. *Class, Race and Colonialism in West Malaysia: The Indian Case*. St. Lucia: University of Queensland Press.

Stevens, Jaqueline. 1999. *Reproducing the State*. Princeton, NJ: Princeton University Press.

Sundaram, Lanka. 1933. *Indians Overseas: A Study in Economic Sociology*. Madras: G. A. Natesan and Co.

Taylor, Peter. 1994. "The State as Container: Territoriality in the Modern World-System." *Progress in Human Geography* 18: 151–162.

Taylor, Peter. 1995. "Beyond Containers: Internationality, Interstateness, Interterritoriality." *Progress in Human Geography* 19: 1–15.

Thakurdas, Purshotamdas, J. R. D. Tata, G. D. Birla, Ardeshir Dalal, Shri Ram, Kasturbhai Lalbhai, A.D. Shroff, and John Matthai. 1945. *Memorandum Outlining a Plan of Economic Development for India*, parts 1 and 2. Harmondsworth: Penguin.

Thelen, David. 1999. "Re-thinking History and the Nation-State: Mexico and the United States." *Journal of American History* 86 (2): 439–455.

Thomas, Paul. 1994. *Alien Politics: Marxist State Theory Revisited*. New York: Routledge.

Times of India, May–June 1936.

Tinker, Hugh. 1974. *A New System of Slavery: The Export of Indian Labour Overseas, 1830–1920*. London: Oxford University Press.

Tinker, Hugh. 1976. *Separate and Unequal*. Vancouver: University of British Columbia Press.

Tinker, Hugh. 1977. *The Banyan Tree: Overseas Emigrants from India, Pakistan, and Bangladesh*. London: Oxford University Press.

Tölöyan, Khachig. 1991. "The Nation-State and Its Others: In Lieu of a Preface." *Diaspora: A Journal of Transnational Studies* 1 (1): 3–7.

Twaddle, Michael. 1990. "East African Asians through a Hundred Years." In *South Asians Overseas: Migration and Ethnicity*, edited by C. Clake, C. Peach, and S. Vertovec, 149–163. Cambridge: Cambridge University Press.

Vajpayee, Atal Bihari, Prime Minister. Inaugural address, First Pravasi Bharatiya Diwas Conference, http://www.indiaday.org/pbd1/pbd_PM.asp.

Vajpayee, Atal Bihari, Prime Minister. 1998. Suo Moto statement in Parliament. May 27, http://www.india.gov.

Varadarajan, Latha. 2004. "Constructivism, Identity and Neoliberal (In)security." *Review of International Studies* 30: 319–341.

Varadarajan, Latha. 2008. "Out of Place: Re-Thinking Diaspora and Empire." *Millennium: Journal of International Studies* 36 (2): 267–293.

Vaswani, Karishma. 2009. "Satyam Scandal Shocks India." *BBC News*, http://news.bbc.co.uk/2/hi/business/7818220.stm.

Vertovec, Steven, and Robin Cohen, eds. 1999. *Migration, Diasporas and Transnationalism*. Cheltenham, UK: Edward Elgar.

Virdi, Jyotika. 2003. *The Cinematic Imagination: Indian Popular Films and Social History*. New Brunswick: Rutgers University Press.

Wade, R. 1996. "Globalization and Its Limits: Reports of the Death of the National Economy Are Greatly Exaggerated." In *National Diversity and Global Capitalism*, edited by S. Berger and R. Dore. Ithaca, NY: Cornell University Press.

Wainwright, Joel. 2008. *Decolonizing Development: Colonial Power and the Maya*. Hoboken, NJ: Wiley-Blackwell.

Walker, R. B. J. 1993. *Inside/Outside: International Relations as Political Theory*. Cambridge: Cambridge University Press.

Wapner, Paul. 1995. "Politics beyond the State: Environmental Activism and World Civic Politics." *World Politics* 47 (3): 311–340.

Wapner, Paul. 1996. *Environmental Activism and World Civic Politics*. Albany: State University of New York Press.

Waterbury, Myra. 2006. "The State as Ethnic Activist: Explaining Continuity and Change in Hungarian Diaspora Policies." PhD diss., New School for Social Research.

Waters, Malcolm. 1995. *Globalization*. New York: Routledge.

Wayland, Sarah. 2004. "Ethnonationalist Networks and Transnational Opportunities: The Sri Lankan Diaspora." *Review of International Studies* 30: 405–426.

Weiss, Linda. 1998. *The Myth of the Powerless State: Governing the Economy in a Global Era*. Ithaca: Cornell University Press.

Weldes, Jutta, Mark Laffey, Hugh Gusterson, and Raymond Duvall, eds. 1999. *Cultures of Insecurity: States, Communities, and the Production of Danger*. Minneapolis: University of Minnesota Press.

Wendt, Alexander. 1992. "Anarchy Is What the States Make of It: The Social Construction of Power Politics." *International Organization* 46: 391–425.

Wendt, Alexander. 1999. *Social Theory of International Politics*. Cambridge: Cambridge University Press.

"What Price NRI Deposits?" 2004. *Business Line*, July 31, http://www.thehindubusinessline.com/2004/07/31/stories/2004073100071000.htm.

Willems-Braun, Bruce. 1997. "Buried Epistemologies: The Politics of Nature in (Post) colonial British Columbia." *Annals of American Geographers* 87 (1): 3–31.

Winichakul, Thongchai. 1994. *Siam Mapped: A History of the Geo-Body of a Nation*. Honolulu: University of Hawaii Press.

Wood, Ellen Meiskins. 2002. "Global Capital, National States." In *Historical Materialism and Globalization*, edited by Mark Rupert and Hazel Smith. London: Routledge.

World News. 1998. *CNN interactive*, May 12.

"A World of Exiles." 2003. *Economist*, January 2.

Zamindar, Vazira Fazila-Yacoobali. 2007. *The Long Partition and the Making of Modern South Asia: Refugees, Boundaries, Histories*. New York: Columbia University Press.

Zehfuss, Maja. 2001. "Constructivism and Identity: A Dangerous Liaison." *European Journal of International Relations* 7: 315–348.

Zevelev, Igor. 2001. *Russia and Its New Diaspora*. Washington, DC: USIP Press.

Web Sites

Global Organization of People of Indian Origin. http://www.gopio.net.

India Brand Equity Foundation. http://www.ibef.org/aboutus.aspx.

Indiaday.org. http://www.indiaday.org/government_policy/dual_citizenship.asp.

India Everywhere at Davos, 2006. http://www.indiaeverywhere.com/DreamIndia.aspx.

Index